SOCIAL CASEWORK:
Theories in Action

edited by
HERBERT S. STREAN

The Scarecrow Press, Inc.
Metuchen, N.J.   1971

"The Library of Congress Cataloged the Original Printing of
This Title as:".

Strean, Herbert S   comp.
    Social casework: theories in action, edited by Herbert S.
Strean. Metuchen, N. J., Scarecrow Press, 1971.
    344 p.   22 cm.
    CONTENTS: Introduction, by H. S. Strean.—The contribution of
psychoanalysis and ego psychology to social casework, by K. Wood.—
The systems model and social systems theory: their application to
social work, by I. L. Stein.—The application of role theory to social
casework, by H. S. Strean.—The application of organization theory
to social casework, by S. Merle.—Communication theory and social
casework, by W. N. Brown.—The behavior modification model and
social casework, by E. J. Thomas.—Application of small groups to
casework.

    1. Social case work—Addresses, essays, lectures.   I. Title.

HV43.S863   361.3   76-160282
ISBN 0-8108-0408-5   MARC

Library of Congress   71 ₍60-2₎

Contents

Chapter 1: Introduction

by Herbert S. Strean

This book examines social and behavioral science
orientations applicable to the theory and practice of social
casework. Several preliminary tasks confront us in this
chapter as we set the stage for this examination. One is to
investigate what is casework. The definitions advanced by
scholars and practitioners will be reviewed so that casework's mission in society can be clarified, its goals explicated, and its methods defined. We shall review casework's
origins and its present status, including developments and
innovations.

Another aim of this chapter is to clarify the relevance
of theory to the caseworker. To intervene appropriately in
the person-situation configuration that daily confronts him,
the caseworker must be guided by theoretical understanding.
We shall therefore study the meaning of theory and review
some of the terms which are helpful in the conceptualization
of casework.

Our final objective here is to discuss how we may
select hypotheses, concepts, and constructs that can enhance
the theory and practice of social casework and to review
briefly those concepts, constructs, and hypotheses borrowed
from other fields which have been considered helpful to both
the casework practitioner and casework scholar.

The Meaning of Theory

The term theory has been variously defined. In science, a theory is a more or less verified explanation of observed facts or phenomena. A scientific theory is expressed
formally as a series of related statements which together explain a class of phenomena. Especially outside science,
however, theory has had a more casual usage as a tentative
proposal or conjecture put forth in explanation of certain
phenomena, a proposal which serves as a basis of argument

or experimentation and is not expressed in the rigorous form required of scientific theory. In science such a tentative proposal would be called a hypothesis, rather than a theory. The essence of the looser popular usage is revealed in the oft-heard statement, "This idea is offered only as a theory." In social work writing both usages appear and the distinctions between them often are not acknowledged.

Even scientific theories vary in rigor, i.e., some are not expressed formally or are not strictly confirmed by evidence and are commensurately speculative. In general, social science theories are less rigorous than theories in physical science. For example, certain psychoanalytic theories have been little confirmed in experimental investigation. Yet such theories have nevertheless been found useful as a basis for clinical work and as a source of new perspectives on human behavior (81). In fact, all theories of science are held with some tentativeness, no matter how great is the accumulation of findings consistent with them. A respected theory in science is considered the most probable or efficient way of accounting for certain phenomena in the light of present knowledge, but it is always open to revision. It is never considered an utterly final formulation (14).

In general, the utility of a theory in modern science is to summarize existing knowledge, to provide an explanation for observed events and relationships, and to predict the occurrence of as yet unobserved events and relationships on the basis of the explanatory principles embodied in the theory (81).

"Theory" in Social Casework

In addition to being largely dominated by theoretical approaches based on implicit conceptions of the nature of man (19), discussions of casework theory frequently suffer from confusion about what is theory as a whole and also about its component elements. This is demonstrated in casework's failure either to develop a consistent set of terms for thinking about theory or to adopt the more consistent terms developed and used in analysis of theory by other disciplines. Among philosophers of science and social science theorists, one does find a reasonably consistent set of terms and ideas which facilitate communication about theory and the further development of it.

Relating to casework's lack of a consistent set of terms for thinking about theory, Boehm (10) has called attention to two terms that frequently appear in the social casework literature which are used interchangeably, namely, "principle" and "concept." He notes an important difference between these terms: a principle is a rule for action or a guide for behavior, whereas a concept is an identification in abstract terms of a series of observed situations, activities or events which are considered to be related to each other. For instance, self-determination, respect for the human personality, the caseworker-client relationship as the primary medium of help, confidentiality, are among the principles of social casework. These principles call forth certain types of behavior on the part of the worker toward the client. Diagnosis, treatment, adjustment, insight are concepts--they are abstractions which convey ideas about certain activities but do not prescribe a given behavior or action.

A clear terminology is not only important in avoiding ambiguous communication but is also of importance for the student of casework phenomena. For example, the term "adjustment" is used by caseworkers to mean a process of social interaction such that societal norms with which a client is in disagreement are nevertheless acceded to by the client other than by force. This view of the concept of "adjustment" involves the application of the principles of self-determination and participation of the client in the casework process.

Other social work and casework scholars have called attention to casework's failure to develop a consistent set of terms for the theory and practice of casework (21, 30, 37, 54, 5). To fill the lacunae, they have attempted to provide terms which would facilitate communication about theory, develop it further and stimulate research. One of the first writers to suggest a set of terms for the building of a casework theory was Kahn (45). Like Boehm, he noted the difference between "principles" and "concepts" but he also identified "facts," which are stated and verified relationships between concepts. As a science seeks to systematize itself and advance its research, it orders its facts into "theories," which state the relationship between facts. The "knowledge" in a given field is the sum total of available theory that is considered to be highly confirmed (45).

"Construct," another term pertinent to casework, is cited by Greenwood (30). Constructs are a special set of concepts in that they have no observable referents to which

they may be directly related. The unconscious, the id, or
the ego are examples. A construct, as the term implies,
is constructed in our minds in order to explain, integrate,
and impart order to phenomena of which we have no direct
sensory experience. The prime utility of a construct lies
in its potential for interrelating several concepts, and thereby organizing under one rule the classes of relationship to
which these concepts refer. The psychological construct,
the "unconscious", integrates such phenomena as anxiety,
defensiveness, phobias and rationalizations. The construct
possesses the utility of helping to comprehend these varied
behaviors with a clarity much greater than would be possible
without it (30).

"Reification, " or the fallacy of taking constructs literally,
stems from the common tendency to consider as objective
what is essentially subjective and to impute reality to useful
mental fictions. For example, the unconscious is frequently
portrayed as though it were the submerged portion of an ice-
berg; the marginal man is sometimes pictured as teetering
precariously between two cultures (30).

Edwin Thomas, a writer who has contributed extensively
to the growth of casework theory (85), proposes that social
work theorists adopt a systematic conception of theory, the
one we characterized at the opening of this chapter as the
definition of scientific theory. According to this conception,
a theory is a series of related hypotheses (hunches, expressed as verbal statements) in which claims are made
about certain concepts. Establishment of the worth of hypotheses, of the asserted relations among them, and the
appropriateness of the concepts appearing in them depends
upon evidence collected to test these aspects. Thomas has
suggested that we locate the important concepts in our work
(such as ego, self, internalized norm, alienation, affect)
and define them appropriately. Concepts, according to
Thomas, are "the building blocks of the substantive knowledge in behavioral science, and those pertaining to the
same subject matter constitute the analytic vocabulary by
which the phenomena thus designated are categorized and
thereby made amenable to symbolic manipulation" (85, p. 7).
He has pointed out that concepts alone are not enough. In
order to predict and explain behavior, we must at least have
an "hypothesis. " An hypothesis is a statement that relates
concepts to one another so as to imply causation or con-
comitant variation of the phenomena expressed. "Behavior
that is punished tends to be suppressed" is an example of

an hypothesis from psychology. Hypotheses range from the
plausible speculation, which lacks empirical support, to the
fully supported claim which is often called a law in the
physical sciences. When hypotheses are meant to account
for future events, we speak of them as predictions; when
they are devised to account for past events, they are referred to as explanations. "Without hypotheses, the prog-
noses and diagnoses of casework practice would be impossible" (85, p. 8), and knowledge in social casework would be
desperately impoverished.

A theory, according to Thomas, consists of hypotheses
that are logically related. This accords, of course, with the
customary conception of scientific theory. Using this
definition we can recognize that many theories utilized in
casework are relatively weak, because their logical interrelationships have not been well developed and the component
hypotheses have not been corroborated. Such sets of hypotheses, however, may be useful when they are relevant to
problems commonly encountered in casework and they seem
superior to wholly non-scientific language. Parts of those
fields which we shall consider in this text, such as role
theory, small-group theory, organizational theory, communication theory, psychoanalytic theory, and social system
theory, offer examples. Some theories, it should be noted,
are better developed logically, and those with proper empirical support are the preferred form of behavioral science
knowledge (85).

The inconsistencies and general untidiness of writing
about theory of casework and social science theory as applied
in casework cannot be overcome in a book that attempts to
give a reasonably comprehensive introduction to the subject
today. In time we can hope for a better consensus to
emerge among writings on theory in casework and social
work. Meanwhile, a book like this one will reflect these
problems and, unfortunately, the reader must face them.
The current alternatives seem to offer greater disadvantages.

One could report only such work as employs the terms
he considers appropriate. This, we think, would produce an
extremely limited picture of theory in casework, one which
excluded as spurious a high proportion of writings on the
subject. Or one could attempt translating into terminology
he considers best all work done that employed different
terms. Many would say the result was a meaningless parody
of the "translated" works, since their original terms carry

a freight of meaning that cannot be borne by different ones.

Theory of social casework and of social work in general is becoming extensive, but is not yet well developed.

Changing Ideas of the Goal of Casework

A number of reasons have been offered as to why casework has not developed its own consistent set of theoretical terms, its own body of knowledge, and its own theory. In contrast to older professions which have focused upon single areas of human functioning--such as law, medicine, and religion--casework and social work have been concerned with a wide array of human problems and life situations. Social work and casework values and concepts have stressed helping as a service in such a way that doing and feeling, rather than analyzing, have been emphasized. The urgent needs of a society involved in wars and a depression have focused interest on direct services. Casework's preoccupation with direct services, and with constantly modifying them in accordance with the social and psychological needs of the populace, has caused its interest in research, until recently, to be minimal. Furthermore, research has tended to remain separated from practice; whereas in a profession like medicine individuals are employed in practice and research concurrently, in casework these activities have usually not been combined in the same person (15).

Perhaps one of the more cogent reasons for the lack of coherent theory in casework is that casework, with its ever changing emphases and goals, has appeared almost to defy a stable definition. If casework is difficult to define and locate, it would follow that its major concepts, constructs, and hypotheses would also be difficult to define and locate. As Perlman has advised, "To attempt to define social casework takes courage or foolhardiness or perhaps a bit of both. So many knowledgeable caseworkers have attempted it, so many definitions have been produced, and yet at some point in every caseworker's professional life he faces and struggles to answer with some greater clarity and precision than existing definitions have provided the question of what casework is" (63, p. 3). Professional schools, social agencies, casework practitioners and casework scholars have been exceedingly troubled and confused when they have attempted to define, describe, or classify casework.

Bowers culled thirty-four definitions of social casework from
the literature, beginning with Mary Richmond in 1915 and
ending with Charlotte Towle in 1947. His integrated conclusion was as follows: "Social casework is an art in which
knowledge of the science of human relations and skill in
relationship are used to mobilize capacities in the individual
and resources in the community appropriate for better adjustment between the client and all or any part of his total
environment" (13, p. 127). Yet, Bowers' definition was
criticized as being so general that it would not be helpful
for those actively engaged in the practice of casework.
Grinker, for example, stated that a more operational definition of casework, which would emphasize as a system the
changing aspects of transactions between client and worker,
seemed imperative (31). Although Grinker and his colleagues emphasized the importance of viewing casework in
terms of concepts borrowed from field theory, communication
theory, information theory, role theory, transactional theory,
and systems theory, they did not make an attempt to define
casework.

Because social casework has been considered to be so
complex, dynamic, and always in a state of modification and
evolution, many caseworkers have wondered whether or not
casework will always continue to defy definition. The sundry
definitions of casework in many ways parallel casework's
historical development. When one examines casework from
an historical perspective, its ever modifying functions appear
to correspond to the specific definitions of particular eras.

Economic Problems Become Psychological Conflicts

Although casework has for some time been interested
in helping individuals to meet and cope with their economic,
social, psychological, and health problems, casework had its
origins in the alleviation of poverty (26). Casework saw as
its first mission to supply economic assistance to individuals
who were in severe economic need, and Mary Richmond in
1915 defined casework as "the art of doing different things
for different people by cooperating with them to achieve at
one and the same time their own and society's betterment"
(73, p. 374). As the caseworkers or "friendly visitors" (as
they were termed) supplied their client's material needs and
offered advice on how to elevate themselves from poverty,
the workers were often frustrated by the fact that their
services did not result in the desired improvement in their

clients--some responded positively to their interventions and
some did not. Caseworkers began to recognize the existence
of internal factors in their clients' character and sought to
modify them (6). The personality of the client, his wishes,
desires, and character traits assumed importance.

In 1922, Richmond wrote that casework's theories, its
aims and its best intensive practice all seem to be converg-
ing toward one central idea, namely, toward the development of personality. In the same year, in her book, What
is Social Casework? she defined casework as "those processes which develop personality through adjustments consciously effected, individual by individual between men and
their social environment" (72, p. 98). Contemporaries of
Richmond began to emphasize the saliency of the human
personality in their definitions of casework. Also in 1922,
Watson defined casework as "the art of untangling and re-
constructing the twisted personality in such a manner that
the individual can adjust himself to his environment" (88,
p. 415). Queen, in the same year, defined casework as "the
art of adjusting personal relationships" (68, p. 18) and Lee,
in 1923, viewed casework as "the art of changing human
attitudes" (49, p. 119). In 1924, Bowers quotes Wright, who
saw casework as "a search for the truth for creative purposes in the personality of the client and in all his relationships" (13).

From the definitions of casework that appeared in the
1920's, it can be seen that the primary focus of the caseworker was on the internal problems of the individual. Casework was responsive to the mood of the larger culture of
which it was a part, a culture which placed almost exclusive
responsibility on the individual to cope with virtually any
stressful social problem with which he was confronted. The
1920's was a period in American culture characterized by
relative indifference to social reform and social problems.
Consequently, casework saw as its main function to "untangle
and reconstruct the twisted personality, " and "change human
attitudes" so that the client could "adjust" to his environment. Definitions of casework reflected its compatibility
with psychoanalytic psychology and its emphasis on the
internal forces in the human personality (44).

Interdependency of Man and His Social Environment

While the emphasis on the human personality, particularly the conflicting forces within it, has never escaped
casework's focus nor its definitions, the evolving and modifying tasks confronting casework have caused it to alter its
definitions at different periods. During the 1930's the
Depression brought into prominence the interdependency of
the human personality and man's social environment. Despite
the inevitability of human problems activated by the Depression, caseworkers noted that different personalities
coped differently with their social and economic problems.
Despite the strength of certain personalities and personality
traits, unemployment induced an array of tangible problems
which, to a large extent, seemed unrelated to individuals'
capabilities and personality. Consequently, the 1930's saw
definitions of casework emphasizing the social as well as the
emotional difficulties that produced maladjustment. Bertha
Reynolds, who, in the late 1920's, was defining casework as
"a process of counselling the client on a problem which is
essentially his own ...," by 1935 viewed casework as "that
form of social work which assists the individual while he
struggles to relate himself to his family, his natural groups,
and his community" (70, p. 235). Rich, in 1936, defined
casework as "the remedial and preventive treatment of social
and emotional difficulties that produce maladjustment in the
family" (71, p. 3). Lowry defined casework in 1937 as "a way
of assisting people to meet their personal and social needs"
(51, p. 264) and in 1939, DeSchweinitz referred to casework
as "those processes involved in giving service, financial
assistance or personal counsel to individuals by repre-
sentatives of social agencies" (18, p. 39).

In the 1930's, American thought moved towards acceptance
of the notion that social and economic variables influenced
man's behavior, and definitions of casework during this
period seem to express this theme. Just as the wider
culture was tending to concede that man's functioning was
dependent, to some extent, on social and economic institutions external to himself, casework was attempting to
assist the individual while "he struggled to relate himself
to his family and his community" (70). Casework saw one
of its necessary functions, during this period, as intervening in the client's environment; in contrast to the 1920's
when the individual was helped to modify his psychic
apparatus so that he could function in society, caseworkers

in the 1930's were attempting to modify and manipulate the
client's environment so that their clients' adaptations could
be enriched.

The Utility of the Social Sciences

The experience of World War II again altered casework's
view of man and society, and definitions of casework were
again modified. Problems in morale, leadership, propaganda,
separation, and communication induced many professionals
in social work and in allied disciplines to consider the
utility of the social sciences. A greater emphasis on the
client's ego, particularly that part of the ego concerned with
object relations, prompted greater interest in the social
environment of the client, particularly as a factor contributing to difficulties in social functions (44). Definitions of
casework began to include the intricate network of socio-
psychological forces operative in understanding and helping
the individual. In a book published in 1940, Strode defined
casework as a process of assisting the individual to the best
possible social adjustment through the use of the social case
study, social resources, and knowledge from related fields
of learning (13, p. 79). In 1946, Wilsnak pointed out that as
casework fused pertinent social science data with the findings
of psychology, it would emerge into a "therapeutic discipline
for encouraging ego-development" (90, p. 303).

As man and his relationship to his social environment
has been viewed as more complex, as knowledge has increased, as the needs of man--psychological, social,
economic, and physical--have come to appear both more
profound and subtle, and therefore more difficult to understand, attempts by casework scholars to define casework
have diminished. Definitions of casework since the 1950's
have been somewhat elusively broad. In 1951, Gordon
Hamilton stated that in the many attempts to define the casework process, the concept repeatedly elaborated is the inter-
connection of personal adaptation of the individual and
society's betterment (32). She went on to conclude that of
the many phrasings on casework the ones that seemed best
were Mary Richmond's definitions of 1915 and 1922. Perlman, in 1957, defined casework as "a process used by certain human welfare agencies to help individuals cope more
effectively with their problems in social functioning" (63,
p. 4). Other casework scholars during the 1950's defined
casework's goal as the "enhancement of social competence" (41).

New Frontiers

The third discovery of poverty in the United States in the 1960's induced casework to re-examine its functions as well as its definitions. The antipoverty efforts, tied as they were to the determination to end discrimation and to facilitate racial integration, brought education to the forefront as a pivotal social welfare measure and caseworkers became involved in the planning and development of new types of basic educational measures. Of particular interest to caseworkers were the measures which helped disadvantaged children overcome environmental and interpersonal deprivation so that they could enter into normal activities in school and in work. This development enriched the rather exclusive clinical concern of the modal caseworker. In the 1960's many caseworkers were attempting to legitimize educational, advice-giving, and socializing procedures which traditionally had been assigned a low status (46).

With poverty and discrimination attracting general concern in the 1960's, new roles and definitions were prescribed for the caseworker. For the many clients who had limited verbal and cognitive skills and who experienced much anxiety in relating to their environment, caseworkers have been functioning as their "advocate" or "social broker." De-emphasized by many during this decade are the traditional psychotherapeutic functions of the caseworker; emphasized instead is the necessity for the caseworker actively to manipulate the client's environment and to bring to him those necessary social utilities and resources that healthy social functioning requires (75).

Like the culture which rediscovered poverty, casework has begun to rediscover some of its ignored roles and functions. As casework has been extending its interest into the lives of a total community, rich and poor, black and white, other new functions are being considered. The caseworker is being defined by some as one "whose function is to intervene in a crisis" (62) such as school entry, death, and hospitalization; he is regarded, too, as the "middle man" who negotiates the disputes between welfare clients and their landlords and city officials, and, he is lately considered by some as the "convener" and "stimulator" who attempts to help individuals in a community recognize that they have social problems and then organizes them into groups to discuss and resolve some of their social problems (75).

16   Social Casework

It can be safely concluded from this historical review
that casework's definition and objectives have always been
undergoing modification. Stimulated by the current societal
concerns and stresses at a particular epoch, casework has
attempted to define its task. However, as Bowers stated in
concluding his review of thirty-four definitions of casework,
virtually all of the definitions "are defective, since each
could be applied to endeavors admittedly beyond the scope
of casework" (13, p. 105). As early as 1931, MacIver
commented that all the processes of life are, in varying
degree, processes which develop personality and that individual adjustments between men and their social environment
are being effected in many places (55). One is inclined to
concur with MacIver; while all the definitions alluded to
above imply that casework attempts to assist individuals by
studying internal and external aspects of their lives and endeavors to arrange change in the person or the environment
or both, many professionals such as vocational counselors,
psychologists, and psychiatrists would define their tasks
quite similarly. It would appear that we have not yet
established the essential aspects in casework firmly enough
so that it may be defined.

CASEWORK--A METHOD AND A FUNCTION

The historical development of social casework and the
definitions of social casework that have evolved at particular
times make it apparent that casework has carved out its
tasks in response to society's concerns. Casework changes
its function and hence its definition as society presents it
with certain social mandates pertaining to human concern
and human distress. The human problems confronting
workers in any casework agency reflect the community's,
the state's, or the nation's social ills. For example, caseworkers have responded to psychosocial problems activated
by a tornado in a local town; they have attempted to insure
the civil rights of individuals whose rights were disallowed,
and they modified their caseloads, techniques and policies
when the national government expressed concern over poverty
in the 1960's.

Caseworkers may, therefore, be viewed as agents of
society who are sensitive to social difficulties of a particular social unit and who help ameliorate them. However,
this is an area that the political leader, policy maker, or
community organizer might call his, as well. It is the case-

worker's method in relating to social problems that sets him
off from these others and his major concern is the individual, i. e., the case.

Casework, at this point, has no unique function and thus
can have no unique operational definition, but casework has
to be separated from other fields and occupations, if for no
other reason, by its discrete reality. Although not completely distinctive, the caseworker has a perspective on man and
the social environment as a field of interacting forces, and
he sees as the focus of his professional activities, intervention in that aspect of man's functioning which lies primarily in social relationships or social role performance.
This is a perspective that casework shares with other professions, particularly psychotherapeutic ones, but the focus
on social functioning and social relationships may be considered a characteristic which distinguishes and differentiates it from other helping disciplines (12).

The Casework Method

As the caseworker strives to effect an enriched personal
adaptation for the individual client and is concomitantly concerned with society's betterment, he utilizes an orderly and
logical method which has enjoyed popular acceptance by those
who have practiced casework for the past fifty years:

a) Social study--The purpose of a social study is to
understand the person who has a problem as well as the
problem itself. Significant people and events in the client's
life experience, present and past, and his feeling toward
them, are explored. The client's subjective and objective
psychosocial reality are both carefully investigated. As the
worker listens to the client's request to see where it will
lead, he strives also to grasp its social context. He
attempts to correlate socio-economic, cultural, and psychological data (32).

The worker especially notes what areas of living the
client discusses reluctantly or resists discussing.

Aspects considered in a social study include the following: precipitating factors; how the client has managed in the
past and what he has already done about the problem that
has brought him to the caseworker's attention; significant
persons involved in the problem; how the individual is

18   Social Casework

affected and affects his cultural milieu; and facts that relate
socio-economic, psychological, and cultural factors for the
individual and his family.

In addition to the client's own account, collateral sources
such as relatives and employers are used. However, as
many authors have noted, the best way to obtain a clear
picture of the client and his situation is to induce in the
client sufficient confidence toward the worker so that he
speaks fully and frankly.

In the social study phase, techniques are utilized to
induce the person to move from readiness to ask for help
to a readiness to use it (32).

b) Psychosocial diagnosis--A customary element of
a psychosocial diagnosis in casework is identification of a
problem causing or being caused by some breakdown or failure
in adaptation to society. Diagnosis in casework is the meaning derived from relevant facts; it is concerned with purposive inferences drawn from these facts. Always utilizing
a person-situation formulation, the psychosocial diagnosis is
a systematic attempt to understand the client's present need.
A good diagnosis helps to explain phenomena and in a
limited way to predict. It is a design for action, not just
a classification. In diagnosing a client and his situation the
worker offers a professional opinion as to the nature of the
client's need and the problem he presents. The problem
bringing him to the caseworker may be basic or only
symptomatic (32).

Diagnosis, according to Hollis, is always treatment
oriented; it is undertaken to answer the question, "How can
this person be helped?" Its objective is the formulation of
treatment plans (42). Hollis' three steps in diagnosis have
been utilized by many caseworkers. They are:

1) Assessment--The worker weighs the facts to see
    where the trouble lies. In organizing the facts,
    the worker asks, "What is the reality by which
    this person is confronted, and is his reaction
    distorted or realistic?" In assessment the worker
    studies the interaction between the client's
    "presses" (housing, neighborhood, income, employ-
    ment, family relationships) and the client's
    "stresses" (Libidinal-aggression balance, ego
    qualities, superego pressures, symptomology).

2) Dynamic-Etiological--Emphasis here is on transaction and interaction between the client and
others. It represents the worker's effort to
understand causative factors. Why has the
current situation arisen? The dynamic-etiological
diagnosis attempts to establish relationships
among factors responsible for poor social
functioning.

3) Categorization--This is a part of the diagnosis in
which the client is assigned a psychiatric label,
e. g. , neurotic, psychotic. Although "categorization" is utilized by most caseworkers,
some contend that because many individuals are
suffering from exclusively social problems, e. g. ,
poor housing, a psychiatric diagnosis is not
usually necessary for appropriate casework
intervention.

More recently, caseworkers have been attempting to
arrive at diagnostic classification schemes. For example,
Voiland (86) characterized four types of disordered families:
perfectionistic, inadequate, egocentric, and unsocial.

Regensberg (69) has devised categories of disturbed
marital relationships: those in which tensions are gratifying,
those in which tensions are ungratifying, those in which
mutual gratification is disturbed by crisis and those dis-
solved by separation although the partners are still involved
with each other.

Ripple (77) in another classification scheme has listed
the types of individual problems confronting a caseworker:
1) Economic dislocation; 2) Social dislocation; 3) Economic
maladjustment; 4) Social maladjustment; 5) Interpersonal
conflict; 6) Intrafamilial conflict; 7) Maladaptive interpersonal
relationships; 8) Maladaptive intrafamilial relationship; 9)
Personality disturbance, client; 10) Personality disturbance,
other than client.

In the above categorization, the scheme divides all
situations into: those in which the problem to be solved is
defined at least in part by external factors (dislocation--the
client is the victim of circumstances); those in which the
client contributed substantially to the problem (maladjustment); and finally, those in which the problem is one of
interpersonal relationships or personality disturbance.

    c) <u>Treatment</u>--Since the early 1920's, social case-
work scholars have advanced close to twenty treatment
typologies.   Essentially, these typologies describe technical
procedures used by caseworkers which are designed to enable individuals to cope with internal and external problems.
Mary Richmond's four procedures written in 1922 comprised
the first casework treatment typology:

    1. The client is provided insight into his individual
        personal characteristics.

    2. The client is offered insight into the resources,
        changes and influences of the social environment.

    3. "Direct action of mind upon mind"--The worker
        attempts to influence and reorganize the client's
        thinking.

    4. Indirect action--The client's "significant others"
        are enlisted to help the client in his social
        functioning (72).

    Richmond's procedures have been repeated by other
scholars, although different terms have appeared.   Thus,
Porter Lee, in 1923, viewed casework treatment as involving two procedures: 1) <u>executive</u>, which involves the discovery by the worker of a particular resource and he ar-
ranges for its use by the client; and 2) <u>leadership</u>, which
involves the personal influence of the worker, such as in
modifying the client's attitudes in a parent-child relationship (49).   Hamilton, in the 40's, devised three treatment
categories: 1) <u>Administration of a Practical Service</u>--in
which the worker assists the client to choose and to use a
social resource afforded by the community; 2) <u>Environmental
Manipulation</u>--the emphasis here is on situational modification; the worker attempts to correct or improve the
social situation so that there is a reduction of strain and
pressure; and 3) <u>Direct Treatment</u>--which involves a series
of interviews for the purpose of inducing or reinforcing
attitudes favorable to the maintenance of emotional equilibrium.   Techniques such as clarification, mobilizing affect,
and interpretation leading to insight are utilized (32).
Austin, in 1947, referred to <u>social treatment</u> (modification
of the social environment without modification of attitudes
and behavior), <u>ego supportive therapy</u>, <u>experiential therapy</u>,
and <u>insight therapy</u> (3).

Most recently, Florence Hollis in her text, Casework:
A Psychosocial Therapy, has outlined a series of six treatment procedures in effecting treatment: 1) sustaining (supportive remarks); 2) direct influence (suggestion and advice);
3) helping the client to ventilate (catharsis); 4) reflective-
consideration of the current person-situation configuration;
5) encouraging the client to think about the dynamics of his
response patterns or tendencies; and 6) encouraging the
client to think about the development of his response patterns
or tendencies.   In environmental work, Hollis contends, the
above procedures, with the exception of number 6, can be
utilized with significant others in the client's social orbit
such as making sustaining remarks to a client's employer,
helping a landlord ventilate, or influencing a teacher (42).

The above components of the casework process: Study,
diagnosis, and treatment, frequently operate concomitantly.
The worker cannot study his client and the latter's situation
without simultaneously making some diagnostic inferences.
By the same token, he cannot always diagnose problems of
the client without making sustaining remarks.   The latter is
particularly true with more action-oriented, non-verbal
clients who frequently resist talking and being talked with (75).

Inasmuch as the client is both subject and object of the
casework process, the caseworker shifts his activity depending on the unfolding of the case situation.

Most recently, casework scholars have suggested
modifications in, or have attempted to enrich, the traditional
casework method.   Meier (53), recognizing that the person-
situation configuration is virtually always in the forefront in
casework, has suggested a diagnostic-treatment classification
in which treatment attempts to modify either the situation,
the person or both.   All situations that clients bring to the
caseworker may be classified, according to Meier, into six
groupings.   The situation may: 1) be deficient in providing
opportunities for the client to find satisfactions in his
essential strivings; 2) prevent the client from expressing
his strivings; 3) make unrealistic demands; 4) reactivate
unresolved conflicts; 5) stimulate unacceptable impulses;
and 6) make contrary demands to values.   Treatment in
this classification consists of two categories: 1) providing
opportunities to increase the client's satisfactions; and 2)
modifying the manner in which he expresses his wishes.

Krill (48) has also proposed a diagnostic-treatment
framework for determining client modifiability; it is based
on the premise that there are five types of modifiability.
The client: 1) wishes to endure an unchangeable situation
and have available a helping person who cares and understands his circumstances; 2) is interested in changing a
specific behavior or an isolated symptom; 3) seeks general
improvement in meaningful relations and/or in an environmental activity; 4) wishes to establish direction (meaning)
in his life; and 5) seeks extensive and thorough rational-
emotional self-understanding.   The associated treatment
goals, which are numbered in accordance with the basic
categories, are: 1) Sustaining relationship; 2) Specific
behavior (symptom) change; 3) Relationship and/or environmental change; 4) Directional change (personalizing values);
and 5) Insightful psychoanalysis.

Boehm (9) has divided the casework process into two
parts: purposes and activities.   The purposes are: 1)
improvement or restoration of a person's impaired capacity;
and 2) preservation and enhancement of threatened social
functioning.   The activities of the worker are: 1) assessment; 2) planning for solution; 3) implementing the plan; and
4) evaluating the outcome.   While Boehm's contribution
parallels the traditional study, diagnosis and treatment
trinity, it has two advantages which surpass the traditional
abstraction.   First, it induces the worker consciously to
make a treatment plan, i. e. "planning for solution," and
secondly, it adds the step of "evaluating the outcome," which
is missing in most prescribed typologies.   The fourth step
suggests that the caseworker be a researcher, at least of
his own work.

Meyer and others (60) have criticized the study, diagnosis, and treatment abstraction because it gives only
secondary attention to the crucial activity of social influence.
They believe that a more comprehensive framework of behavioral tasks is required to include all the major activities
and the related decisions involved in the helping process.
Their scheme classifies these activities into three categories:
1) obtaining information, which includes getting facts, feelings,
and evaluations relating to the client's problem; 2) processing
information, which involves understanding the client's difficulty and planning what to do about it; and 3) exerting social
influence, which involves setting the conditions of change,
maintaining the interpersonal helping relationship, achieving
and stabilizing change objectives, and terminating the relation-

ship.

Although there have been differing points of view and
emphases among casework scholars who have contributed to
the development of a casework method, there is a high degree of concurrence in the application of some aspects of
the method. All writers, for example, appear to consider
the person-situation configuration central to casework; they
all conceive of the individual as a bio-psychological unit in
constant interaction with its environment. Each individual
piece of behavior is viewed within a large gestalt of component parts which are in constant interaction. To understand individual behavior, the caseworker needs to comprehend not only the client's situation--family, friends,
employer--but his biological equipment, the significant
experiences of the individual during the course of his life,
and how he has experienced them.

Implicit in the application of the casework method is a
belief in the worth of the individual, i. e. the right of each
person to live his life in his own unique way, provided, of
course, that he does not infringe upon the rights of others
(41). Deriving from casework's belief in the worth of the
individual are two principles which appear to be also
implicit in the writings of those scholars who have explicated on the casework method: acceptance of the client,
and his right to self-determination. As Gordon Hamilton
advised: caseworkers shall not impose upon the client their
own goals or standards of behavior, but shall concede the
person's right to be himself and make his own decisions
and plans (32).

Virtually all of the casework methodologists are explicit
that the client-caseworker relationship is the primary medium
of giving help. According to Hamilton, the handling of this
relationship is what characteristically gives the professional
quality to casework. She has described it as an association
in which the caseworker "gives of his understanding, of his
own ego strength, and even of his own superego, " and in
which he uses "his whole self as consciously as possible"
in the interests of another person (33).

The final theme that appears to pervade the casework
literature on method is the assumption that the human personality is capable of change and that casework attempts to
foster change. The aim of casework help, according to
most casework theorists and practitioners, is to enable the

client to achieve improvement in some aspect of his social living and to do so by reinforcing his ability to find suitable solutions to his problems and to operate on a more satisfactory level (57).

THEORY IN CASEWORK

Although the study, diagnosis and treatment trinity may be considered a high level abstraction of the casework process, the call has been issued many times by leading casework scholars to fill in the details of the abstraction with verifiable concepts, constructs, and hypotheses (4, 16, 9, 30, 45).   From the days of Richmond to the present, casework has criticized itself and has been censured by others for having insufficient theoretical underpinning to relate to the person-situation configuration with precision and predictability.   Although the profession has consistently stressed that successful professional practice is more directly the result of purposefulness and internal consistency in applying theoretical propositions, it has also been recognized that casework has frequently accepted propositions on faith or personal preference alone.   It has been alleged that choices of concepts, constructs, etc. , have not been made from a scientific perspective and that casework has neglected to give sufficient attention to the scientific status of the perspective that it chooses.   Kadushin, for example, who has written extensively on the inadequate knowledge base of social work and casework, has suggested that perhaps the theoretical knowledge which would permit us to succeed most often with the client is not available.   He further states that there may be some truth in "the old quip that social work is an art based on a science which has not been invented yet" (44).

Casework--Science or Art?

One of the factors that has probably prevented casework from molding an extensive body of theory is its helping function.   In their paper, "The Growing Science of Casework," Ross and Johnson pointed out: "There are some who maintain that social casework cannot become a science by virtue of its helping function.   They have voiced the attitude that interest in scientific observation (and theory) must be sacrificed when the purpose of the work is to help someone" (78, p. 49).

A scientific attitude with sound theoretical underpinning has often been linked to aloofness and impersonality toward the client and these latter qualities have been viewed as an antithesis to a sound casework posture. The orderly, step-by-step, logical scheme associated with a scientific stance based on theoretical proposition has been referred to as "mechanical" and, therefore, devoid of the human touch (78).

Although the assertion that casework is an art does not, ipso facto, imply that it becomes or should become divorced from scientific theory, some caseworkers have viewed the two as having no relationship with eath other. Bowers, who does not see science and art as incompatible, has said: "Art applies knowledge by the method of science, but an art is more than mere application; it is an adaptation, skill in the adaptation of knowledge to the unique, creative purposes of life" (13, p. 106).

In The Contribution of Sociology to Social Work, Robert MacIver discussed social work as an art. He observed that while an art presupposes a science, it steps beyond science. Science stands apart from the world, surveying it as it is; casework, an art, is universed in the world, seeking to change something in it, to add something to it, even to re-make it (55). The notion of casework as an art with an emphasis on the primacy of experience in practice, has often conflicted with the notion that scientific knowledge and theory is the foundation for professional competence. According to Eaton (20), "how science and experience are to be used is the unsettled question in social work." Eaton has further pointed out that this unsettled question invades the graduate schools of social work which have not yet quite decided how much emphasis should be placed on personal qualities and how much on intellectual. The bases for the appeal of case-work to college students have tended to stress altruism and personality characteristics rather than interest in knowledge. If the student merely "likes to work with people," the schools of social work have perpetuated a system whereby the majority of its members may be inclined towards an anti-theoretical orientation.

It is important to recognize, however, that in recent years the schools of social work have been taking a more favorable position toward the study of theory by their students, and the caseworker's need for theory has been receiving much stronger affirmation in many quarters (44).

The Need for Theory in Casework

Dr. Ralph Tyler, an eminent educator and consultant to
social work educators, identified two essential characteristics
of a valid profession: 1) the existence of a recognized code
of ethics which commits the members of the profession to
certain social values; and 2) the basing of its techniques
upon principles rather than simple routine skills. "As a
profession becomes more mature it recognizes that the
principles used in the profession must be viewed in an increasingly larger context and that, correspondingly, the
science needed by the profession must be continually extended
to more basic context rather than restricted only to the
obvious applied science" (84, p. 56).

A social work educator and former dean of the Columbia
University School of Social Work, Edward Lindeman (50),
stated that among the many criteria for measuring the
maturity of a profession are the capacity to absorb relevant
data and devices from ever-widening and varied sources so
long as these assimilations do not lead to confusion, and
the ability to merge the content which derives from empirical
sources (experience) with that which comes from science
(theoretical) into a unifying stream of applicable knowledge.

The social casework literature dealing with the problem
of establishing a scientific theoretical base is by now considerable. Theoretical concepts, constructs, and hypotheses
yield a meaning to the kinds of human conditions and events
that caseworkers need to understand and utilize in professional action (56). While the special circumstances of
the individual client are always in the forefront, it is now
generally agreed that unless social casework draws on a
sound theoretical base, its work will be a "hit or miss"
and "trial and error" affair (21). Stated Cockerill: "It is
important to note that... there has been increasing emphasis
upon the necessity for establishing a theoretical base [for
casework] since it is recognized that all professional practice proceeds from a set of clear principles and concepts
about human beings and their needs which are consciously
held, teachable as such, and which constitute the logical
justification for the practice" (16, p. 60).

Pollak has noted that lack of necessary conceptual equipment may lead to the failure of the caseworker to take
important facts into account in the consideration of a pro-

fessional problem, since phenomena for which technological terminology is not available to the practitioner tend to remain unconsidered (65).

Casework, at its present stage of professional development, is just beginning to define and test the concepts of psychosocial behavior with which it works. Frequently, the caseworker has to proceed without generally experimental verification. As Finestone has stated, "At the very least, however, we ought to know what concepts we are utilizing, where the concepts come from, and the state of their verification" (21, p. 320).

Theories Used by Casework

Although casework is essentially derivative as a field of study, the processes of casework that deserve analysis in their own right and investigation of casework concepts may ultimately produce a significant body of systematic professional knowledge. Most casework scholars and practitioners, however, would agree that this professional knowledge would inevitably be in debt to the behavioral and social sciences. The caseworker ought therefore to acquaint himself with the salient materials in sociology, psychology, psychoanalysis and other cognate disciplines (56). Although casework recognizes what Merton has reiterated, that "a comprehensive theory of social problems does not yet exist, " and that useful work will succeed only with the utilization of a variety of working models (59), the question remains how does casework or the caseworker select those models which are relevant and can be economically and systematically employed in the casework process?

Difficulties inherent in choosing relevant material have been noted by several social work writers. Maas has called attention to the fact that no single theory can provide an adequate basis for the development of policy, program, or practice (53). Morton Deutsch has contended that there is no one sovereign explanation, no single ruling motive, no dominant psychological process that can adequately characterize the doings of men. Appreciation of human complexity negates the out-dated and grandiose notion that there can be one general theory which will embrace all social psychological phenomena. Deutsch has reminded us that physics has a muddle of theories and that there is need for a variety of conceptual frames and theories to embrace the richness of human behavior (19).

Borrowing from a variety of conceptual frames and theories has not been neglected by casework. Kadushin, assessing some of the difficulties that confront social work and casework in the borrowing of knowledge, called attention to several problems:

> One hazard lies in the fact that interdisciplinary movement of knowledge is likely to involve a greater time lag than intra-disciplinary movement of the same knowledge. We are more likely to borrow yesterday's knowledge rather than today's. Secondly, we are likely to endow borrowed knowledge with a greater degree of certainty than is granted it by the discipline which originally developed this knowledge. We are often not aware of the intense disagreement among different sectors of the 'lending' discipline regarding the validity of the knowledge we borrow. A third hazard lies in the fact that we are likely to borrow a simplified version of the truth and one falsified to the degree that it is simplified. A further hazard lies in the danger that the borrowed material will remain an undigested lump in the body politic of social work, interesting but unintegrated and unused (44).

Dr. Florence Hollis (41), in cautioning the caseworker to scrutinize knowledge from other disciplines before taking it as a guide, called attention to common errors in the acquisition of theory. One is "the peril of suggestibility. " Once a phenomenon is appreciated, one tends to look for it and, perhaps, to use it indiscriminately. One can surround the casework process by a respectable flock of theoretical perspectives relevant to total professional pursuits, but not particularly relevant to the casework process. Hollis warns that we must always ask, "Does it make a major contribution or a minor one? How important is it? How useful is it?"

CRITERIA FOR THE UTILIZATION OF
THEORETICAL MATERIALS FROM OTHER DISCIPLINES

In a publication of the National Association of Social Workers, Bartlett (5) identified some of the gaps and deficiencies characteristic of social work, including casework. They are: 1) lack of orderly systems of thinking (frames of reference) to identify and relate the essentials of social

work and to bring together in logical relationship, with suitable distinctions, the characteristics that place social work
in the social scene, in relation to those it serves, other
professions and society; 2) imbalance in use of theory from
biopsychosocial sources; 3) selection and use of knowledge
from other disciplines without effective integration in a social
work frame of reference; 4) low level of curiosity about
social phenomena; 5) lack of recognition of social work's own
knowledge and relatively little interest in formulating social
work generalizations; 6) low level of responsibility in analyzing practice and testing assumptions; and 7) use of value and
knowledge together, often quite effectively but without awareness and conscious control.

Bartlett's criticisms suggest guides in determining whether
a particular theoretical model is relevant to casework.
These criteria have been used in choosing the theoretical
models treated in this text.

Orderly definition of its own characteristics and needs
is required if casework is to choose theoretical material
directly relevant to its own needs.   In gleaning concepts
and constructs from the social and behavioral sciences, and
aware of the problems faced by casework, workers can more
consistently adopt concepts in social science that address
problems paralleling those faced by casework.

If he is equipped with a scientific orientation, the caseworker will attempt to ascertain how much evidence is available, either through research or general experience, that
a theory is valid, verified, or verifiable.   In considering
the theory, one can ask, "How well established is it?   Does
it offer a clearer explanation than we now have?"

If caseworkers can better conceptualize their method,
they will be in a better position to recognize whether a theory
being considered can be directly linked to the casework
process, e.g., study, diagnosis, and treatment.   When his
method is appraised scientifically and better understood
conceptually, a caseworker will recognize which aspects of
the casework processes can be altered by the assimilation
of a theory and which facet of the trilogy is least likely to
be affected by use of the theory.   As Hollis has suggested,
the caseworker must ask, "Does the theory adapt itself to
our own casework framework?" (41).   Furthermore, perhaps
some, but not all, of the theory's abstractions are applicable
to the casework process.

In borrowing a particular theory for casework, the profession must decide whether it is borrowing today's precepts
or yesterday's outdated knowledge. Sometimes the discipline
from which we are borrowing has begun to question the
theory (44).

PROMINENTLY PROPOSED THEORIES FOR
THE PRACTICE OF SOCIAL CASEWORK

The brief review of theories that follows does not ex-
haust the perspectives that may be productive for casework.
It is limited to proposals already made in social casework
scholarship and, further, to theories which appear fundamental to casework as a procedure for modifying the person-
situation configuration.

Inasmuch as the remaining chapters of this text will
present the major theoretical concepts of the theories and
demonstrate their relevance to the casework process, here
we need merely to identify the theories that will be presented and offer one or two major reasons why the theory
is considered relevant.

Psychoanalytic Theory

As noted in our historical review of casework, when the
friendly visitors of the 1920's were frustrated by the client
who did not respond to advice and material help, they began
to examine his personality in psychoanalytic terms, i. e. ,
in terms of their needs and failures, their maladjustments
and conflicts. Beyond the social problems involved, the
caseworker faced complications and difficulties not obviously
related to outer circumstances, but presented instead by the
personality of the client. The social diagnosis required a
personality diagnosis and the casework concept, "psychosocial diagnosis" came into use. Casework gradually moved
toward an affiliation with psychoanalysis. So many of the
human problems confronting caseworkers of the 1920's could
be explained by psychoanalytic theory.

The client who did not cooperate with the caseworker
could be understood better through use of the psychoanalytic
construct, "resistance. " His positive or negative relationship with the caseworker could be partially interpreted by

examining his "transference" reactions (the ascribing to the caseworker of feelings and thoughts that the client has toward significant people in his past) (26).   Psychosocial development, another construct from psychoanalysis, gave the caseworker a perspective from which to view normal and pathological behavior.   Treatment procedures such as interpretation, clarification, suggestion, all were borrowed from psychoanalysis.   Consequently, in studying, diagnosing, and treating, psychoanalysis seemed to afford many contributions to the casework process.

Role Theory

As caseworkers began to focus on the communication, interaction, and transactions between family members, a useful way of describing these was found in the concept, "social role." By "role" is meant behavior prescribed by the social situation--the role being governed jointly by the actor's motivation and his society's values.   The stability of a transactional field such as a marriage or family depends upon a certain complementarity of roles.   By focusing on the complementarity or lack of complementarity in a reciprocal role relationship, caseworkers began to realize that a "good" marriage did not necessarily have to consist of two neurosis-free individuals.   Hence, role theory provided casework with means of more precisely diagnosing marital, family, and other forms of interaction in which the client was involved.

The concept of social role provided caseworkers a vehicle for defining more precisely what is meant by social functioning.   Social functioning could be analyzed by dissecting it into clusters of tasks accompanying certain roles, such as the roles of husband, wife, parent or child.   A more accurate picture of family interaction could be achieved by understanding not only how the role of each member is actually performed but also by considering the expectations each member has of his own role and the roles of others.   Each role implies a number of activities, some of which seem so essential for the role that impaired performance or failure to perform them can be called social dysfunctioning.

As Boehm has cautioned, "... the concept of social role is only one of a large array of concepts needed for effective casework....   All the role concept can do is specify what

is meant by social functioning, to help the caseworker
identify crucial roles in social functioning and the essential
activities within these crucial roles" (9).

System Theory

As the role concept became part of casework thinking
and activity, inevitably caseworkers began to assimilate
other facets of system theory and utilized many of the
latter's concepts, particularly in study and diagnosis.   To
appreciate role interaction and transaction, the analyst again
followed sociologists who view role interactions and transactions as part of a larger system of group behavior which
strives for equilibrium.

System theorists view the human personality as an open
system in constant interplay with its surroundings, receiving
stimuli from the environment and modifying its internal
mechanisms to maintain its equilibrium while adjusting to
changes without.   As Hollis has brought out, since system
theory sees each system as composed of certain structural
parts which interact to keep the system both functioning and
changing, the familiar id, ego, and superego of Freudian
personality theory can be viewed as such structural components of the personality (41).

System theory contends that a change in part of the
system always induces changes in other parts of the system;
thus the person-situation configuration may be viewed in these
terms, i. e. , a change in the client's situation induces change
in his personality and vice versa.   Similarly, this notion of
system theory is valuable in looking at casework treatment,
particularly in family interaction.   As one part of the family
system is modified, one looks to see what happens to other
parts.

System theory was introduced to caseworkers in 1956 by
Werner Lutz (52) and many caseworkers agree that it seems
to provide a framework into which casework concepts fit
extremely well (41).

Small Group Theory

As caseworkers rediscovered "the family" and began to
call on theoretical concepts from role theory and system

theory to appreciate its functioning, they became acquainted
with a related literature in social psychology: writings on
the small group. Some components of theories on small
groups--leadership, the "follower," group membership, group
morale, "the scapegoat"--seemed to adapt very well to the
study and treatment of family interaction. Instrumental and
expressive leadership, for example, which small group
theorists contend are customarily discernible in a well-run-
ning group, could be utilized in helping mothers and fathers
adopt more complementary roles as leaders in their family
groups.

Caseworkers have employed small group theory largely
in the treatment arena. Since the group theorist sees any
two individuals in interaction as a small group, some of the
data on how a group is stabilized could be employed in the
stabilization and preservation of a caseworker-client "group."
More important, perhaps, has been the incorporation by caseworkers of the data from studies of small groups about the
socialization process. In small groups the individual learns
a range of roles and how to enact them. Consequently,
many casework agencies have applied theories about the
small group to help children learn how to relate better inter-
personally. Parents interacting in small groups set up by
casework agencies have been able to reenact roles familiar
in their family life and, with the aid of their new role partners, to modify parts of their role set as parents so that
their own family system can be brought into more harmonious
equilibrium.

Communication Theory

Psychotherapists who utilized several of the theoretical
facets of role, system, and small group theories as part of
their orientation to the treatment process began to regard
psychotherapy as a process of communication (24, 31, 61).
Casework also has begun to incorporate communication
theory. Ruesch and Bateson (79) regarded communication
as the social matrix of psychiatry as a whole. Ruesch has
indicated that human problems may be viewed in terms of
quantitative alterations of communications or as forms of
exchange not fitting the social situation. The communication
theorist takes the position that there is no need to regard
the personality in action as a conglomerate of several
instinctual forces and defenses, since all are contained in
communicated messages which express the total person with

his memories of the past and anticipations of the future.

Caseworkers are taking particular note of one of the theory's main principles, namely, that to understand communications of the client, the worker must be a subjective participant in the communication process as well as an objective observer. Particularly because the caseworker deals in verbal and nonverbal communication, he needs to be an expert in understanding language as it is related to thinking and behavior.

Learning Theory

As caseworkers found limitations in the psychoanalytic treatment model for the person-situation configuration of casework, they began to consider other guides to intervention. One of the better conceptualized treatment models that has been enjoying considerable popularity is operant conditioning. Caseworkers have long regarded the treatment process as involving learning and relearning and, therefore, the concepts of positive and negative reinforcement, conditioning, reward, and punishment have great applicability in considering how to effect and account for change in the person-situation configuration.

Although many caseworkers have contended that the theoretical components of operant conditioning help us become more aware of the learning process and have reported success by the use of this method where other methods have failed, some have objected that it does not bring the whole man into the treatment process and offers no place for the principle of the client's self-determination (41).

Organization Theory

Otto Pollak, the well-known sociologist, recently stated that if he were asked to propose a further development of the theoretical underpinning of casework practice, he would emphasize an integration of organization theory and psychoanalytic theories of personality development (65). The organizational model reflects a significant trend of social change--the increase of large organizations of men whose members' significance is in their contribution to an organization's goals, rather than in their personal qualities. Since most of the clients of caseworkers work in large-scale

organizations, an appreciation by caseworkers of the impact
of bureaucratic organizations is crucial in the study and
diagnosis of the person-in-his-situation.

Caseworkers who have adapted the organizational model
to their practice note that their interviews have become
richer and more comprehensively oriented because the
emotional impact of bureaucratic existence has received
more recognition as a source of the client's emotional mal-
functioning and social maladjustment.

Almost all casework is performed in an organization,
i. e. , the social agency is typically a large organization.
The organization of the agency greatly affects the quality
and quantity of services provided.   Consequently, it behooves
caseworkers to examine organizations in which they work,
the effects of organizational variables upon staff and client
relations, the structural features of organizations and the
issues and dilemmas pertaining to them (85).

In the following chapters on theoretical models, each
contributor has been presented with the same outline so
that a similar systematic approach will emerge as the reader
goes from chapter to chapter:

1.   A definition of the theoretical model--e. g. , what
do we mean by "role, " "system, " "organization. "

2.   Major concepts, constructs and hypotheses of the
particular theoretical model.

3.   The application of the particular theoretical model
to the psychosocial problems that confront a caseworker in
daily practice, with a particular emphasis on how the theory
can be applied to casework's familiar trilogy--social study,
psychosocial diagnosis, and treatment.

4.   The limitations of the theory's applicabilty to the
theory and practice of social casework.

References

1.   Ackerman, Nathan.   "The Diagnosis of Marital Inter-
        action, " in Cora Kasius, ed. , Social Casework in the
        Fifties (New York: Family Service Association of Ameri-
        ca, 1962), pp. 148-162.

2. *American College Dictionary* (New York: Random House,
        1959), p. 1256.

3. Austin, Lucille N.   "Trends in Differential Treatment
        in Social Casework, " *Social Casework*, Vol. 29, June,
        1948, pp. 203-11.

4. Bartlett, Harriet M.   "The Generic Specific Concept in
        Social Work Education and Practice, " in Alfred J.
        Kahn, ed. , *Issues in American Social Work* (New
        York: Columbia University Press, 1959), p. 178.

5. _____. "Characteristics of Social Work, " in *Build-
        ing Social Work Knowledge* (New York: National
        Association of Social Workers, 1964), pp. 1-16.

6. Beatman, Frances L.   "Family Interaction: Its Signi-
        ficance for Diagnosis and Treatment, " in Cora Kasius,
        ed. , *Social Casework in the Fifties* (New York:
        Family Service Association of America, 1962),
        pp. 212-225.

7. Bernstein, Saul.   "Self-determination--King or Citizen
        in the Realm of Values?" *Social Work*, Vol. 5,
        January, 1960, pp. 3-8.

8. Bibring, Grete L.   "Psychiatry and Social Work, " in
        Cora Kasius, ed. , *Principles and Techniques in Social
        Casework* (New York: Family Service Association of
        America, 1950), pp. 300-313.

9. Boehm, Werner W.   *Objectives of the Social Work
        Curriculum of the Future*, Vol. I (New York: Council
        on Social Work Education, 1959).

10. _____. "The Terminology of Social Casework, "
        paper read at 81st National Conference of Social Work,
        Atlantic City, N. J. , May, 1954.

11. _____. "The Social Work Curriculum Study and Its
        Implications for Family Casework, " in Cora Kasius,
        ed. *Social Casework in the Fifties* (New York: Family
        Service Association of America, 1962), pp. 345-358.

12. _____. "The Nature of Social Work, " *Social Work*,
        Vol. 3, April, 1958, pp. 10-18.

13. Bowers, Swithun. "The Nature and Definition of Social
    Casework," Social Casework, Vol. 30, Nos. 8, 9, 10
    (October, November and December, 1949); reprinted
    in Principles and Techniques of Social Casework
    (New York: Family Service Association of America,
    1950), pp. 97-126.

14. Braithwaite, Robert B. Scientific Explanation: A Study
    of the Function of Theory, Probability, and Law in
    Science (Cambridge, England: Cambridge University
    Press, 1955).

15. Building Social Work Knowledge (New York: National
    Association of Social Workers, 1964).

16. Cockerill, Eleanor. "The Interdependence of the Pro-
    fessions in Helping People," in Cora Kasius, ed.,
    Social Casework in the Fifties (New York: Family
    Service Association of America, 1962), pp. 55-67.

17. _____ . A Conceptual Framework for Social Case-
    work (Pittsburgh, Pa.: University of Pittsburgh
    Press, 1951).

18. DeSchweinitz, Karl. Survey Monthly, Vol. 75, 1939.

19. Deutsch, Morton and Robert K. Krauss. Theories in
    Social Psychology (New York: Basic Books, 1965),
    p. 215.

20. Eaton, Joseph W. "A Scientific Basis for Helping,"
    in Alfred J. Kahn, ed., Issues in American Social
    Work (New York: Columbia University Press, 1959),
    pp. 270-292.

21. Finestone, Samuel. "The Scientific Component in the
    Casework Field Curriculum," in Cora Kasius, ed.,
    Social Casework in the Fifties (New York: Family
    Service Association of America), pp. 311-325.

22. Freud, Sigmund. An Outline of Psychoanalysis (New
    York: W. W. Norton Company, 1947).

23. _____ . "Lines of Advancement in Psychoanalytic
    Therapy," Vol. 17 of Standard Edition of the Complete
    Psychological Work of S. Freud (London: Hogarth
    Press, 1955).

38   Social Casework

24. Fromm-Reichmann, Freda. Principles of Intensive Psychotherapy (Chicago: University of Chicago Press, 1950).

25. Garrett, Annette. "Transference in Casework," in Cora Kasius, ed., Principles and Techniques of Casework (New York: Family Service Association of America, 1950), pp. 277-284.

26. _____. "Historical Survey of the Evolution of Casework," in Cora Kasius, ed., Principles and Techniques of Casework (New York: Family Service Association of America, 1950), pp. 393-411.

27. _____. "The Worker-Client Relationship," in Howard J. Parad, ed., Ego Psychology and Dynamic Casework (New York: Family Service Association of America, 1958), pp. 53-72.

28. _____. "The Professional Base of Social Casework," in Cora Kasius, ed., Principles and Techniques of Social Casework (New York: Family Service Association of America, 1950), pp. 34-47.

29. Gomberg, Robert. "Family Oriented Treatment of Marital Problems," in Cora Kasius, ed., Principles and Techniques of Social Casework (New York: Family Service Association of America, 1950, pp. 212-225.

30. Greenwood, Ernest. Lectures in Research Methodology for Social Welfare Students, Chapter III (Berkeley, Calif.: University of California, 1962), pp. 1-18.

31. Grinker, Roy R., Sr. Psychiatric Social Work: A Transactional Case Book (New York: Basic Books, 1961).

32. Hamilton, Gordon. The Theory and Practice of Social Casework (New York: Columbia University Press, 1951).

33. _____. "The Underlying Philosophy of Social Casework," in Cora Kasius, ed., Principles and Techniques of Social Casework (New York: Family Service Association of America, 1950), pp. 7-22.

34. _____ . "Helping People--The Growth of a Pro-
     fession, " in Cora Kasius, ed. , Principles and Techni-
     ques in Social Casework (New York: Family Service
     Association of America, 1950), pp. 82-96.

35. _____ . Psychotherapy in Child Guidance (New
     York: Columbia University Press, 1947), pp. 126-128.

36. Hartman, Heinz. "Comments on the Psychoanalytic
     Theory of the Ego, " in The Psychoanalytic Study of
     the Child (New York: International University Press,
     Vol. 5, 1950), pp. 74-96.

37. Hearn, Gordon. Theory Building in Social Work
     (Toronto: University of Toronto Press, 1958).

38. Hellenbrand, Shirley. "Client Value Orientations:
     Implications for Diagnosis and Treatment, " Social
     Casework, Vol. 42, April 1961, pp. 163-169.

39. Hollingshead, August B. and Fred Redlich. "Social
     Stratifications and Psychiatric Disorders, " American
     Sociological Review, Vol. 18, 1953, p. 163.

40. Hollis, Florence. "The Techniques of Casework, "
     in Cora Kasius, ed. , Principles and Techniques in
     Social Casework (New York: Family Service
     Association of America, 1950), pp. 412-426.

41. _____ . "...And What Shall We Teach? The
     Social Work Educator and Knowledge, " The Social
     Service Reveiw, Vol. 42, No. 2, June, 1968,
     pp. 184-196.

42. _____ . Casework: A Psychosocial Therapy
     (New York: Random House, 1964).

43. Hunt, J. and Leonard S. Kogan. Measuring Results
     in Social Casework (New York: Family Service
     Association of America, 1950).

44. Kadushin, Alfred. "The Knowledge Base of Social
     Work, " in Alfred J. Kahn, ed. , Issues in American
     Social Work (New York: Columbia University Press,
     1959), pp. 39-79.

45. Kahn, Alfred J. "The Nation of Social Work Know-
     ledge, " in Cora Kasius, ed. , New Directions in Social
     Work (New York: Harper, 1954), pp. 194-214.

46. _____ . "New Policies and Service Models, "
     American Journal of Orthopsychiatry, Vol. 35, No. 4,
     pp. 652-662.

47. _____ . "The Function of Social Work in the
     Modern World, " in Alfred J. Kahn, ed. , Issues in
     American Social Work (New York: Columbia Universi-
     ty Press, 1959), pp. 3-38.

48. Krill, Donald F. "A Framework for Determining
     Client Modifiability, " Social Casework, Vol. 49,
     No. 10, December, 1968, pp. 602-611.

49. Lee, Porter. "Social Work: Cause and Function, " in
     Fern Lowry, ed. , Readings in Social Casework, 1920-
     1938 (New York: Columbia University Press, 1939).

50. Lindeman, Edward C. "Social Casework Matures in a
     Confused World, " The Compass, Vol. 27, No. 2,
     1947, pp. 3-9.

51. Lowry, Fern. "Objectives in Social Casework, " The
     Family, Vol. 18, December, 1937.

52. Lutz, Werner A. Concepts and Principles Underlying
     Social Casework Practice (New York: National
     Association of Social Workers, 1956).

53. Maas, Henry S. "Social Work Knowledge and Social
     Responsibility, " Journal of Education for Social Work,
     Vol. 4, No. 1, Spring, 1968, pp. 37-48.

54. _____ . "Developing Theories in Social Work
     Practice, " in Building Social Work Knowledge (New
     York: National Association of Social Work, 1964),
     pp. 48-59.

55. MacIver, Robert M. The Contribution of Sociology to
     Social Work (New York: Columbia University Press,
     1931).

56. McConnel, T. R. "The Professional School and the
     University, " Social Work Reporter, Vol. 16, No. 1,

March, 1968, pp. 24-25.

57. McCormick, Mary J. "The Old and the New in Case-work," in Cora Kasius, ed., Social Casework in the 1950's (New York: Family Service Association of America, 1962), pp. 16-27.

58. Meier, Elizabeth. "Interactions between the Person and His Operational Situations: A Basis for Classification in Casework," Social Casework, Vol. 46, No. 9, November, 1965, pp. 542-549.

59. Merton, Robert K. and Robert A. Nisbet. Contemporary Social Problems (New York: Harcourt, Brace and World, 1966), p. v.

60. Meyer, Henry, Eugene Litvak and Edwin Thomas. "Social Work and Social Welfare," in Paul Lazersfeld, The Use of Sociology (New York: Basic Books, 1967), pp. 156-192.

61. Mullahy, Patric. The Contributions of Harry Stack Sullivan (New York: Hermitage House, 1952).

62. Parad, Howard. Crisis Intervention (New York: Family Service Association of America, 1965).

63. Perlman, Helen H. Social Casework: A Problem Solving Process (Chicago: The University of Chicago Press, 1957).

64. Pollak, Otto. "Relationship between Social Science and Child Guidance," American Sociological Review, Vol. 16, No. 1, 1951, pp. 61-67.

65. _____. "Contributions of Sociological and Psychological Theory to Casework Practice," Journal of Education for Social Work, Vol. 4, No. 1, Spring, 1968, pp. 49-54.

66. _____. Social Science and Psychotherapy for Children (New York: Russell Sage Foundation, 1952).

67. _____. Integrating Sociological and Psychoanalytic Concepts (New York: Russell Sage Foundation, 1956).

68. Queen, Stuart. Social Work in the Light of History (New York: Russell Sage Foundation, 1922).

69. Regensburg, Jeannette. "Application of Psychoanalytic Concepts to Casework Treatment of Marital Problems," Social Casework, Vol. 35, December, 1954, pp. 424-432.

70. Reynolds, Bertha. "Rethinking Social Casework," The Family, Vol. 16, 1935.

71. Rich, M. Current Trends in Social Adjustment through Individualized Treatment, International Univ. Press, N.Y. 1936.

72. Richmond, Mary E. What is Social Casework? (New York: Russell Sage Foundation, 1922).

73. _____. The Long View (New York: Russell Sage Foundation, 1930).

74. _____. Social Diagnosis (New York: Russell Sage Foundation, 1917).

75. Riessman, Frank, J. Cohen, and A. Pearl. Mental Health of the Poor (New York: Free Press, 1964).

76. Ripple, Lillian. "Problem Identification and Formulation," in Norman A. Polansky, ed., Social Work Research (Chicago: University of Chicago Press, 1960), pp. 41-43.

77. _____. "Motivation, Capacity, and Opportunity as Related to the Use of Casework Service: Theoretical Base and Plan of Study," The Social Service Review, Vol. 29, No. 2, June, 1955, pp. 172-193.

78. Ross, Helen and Adelaide M. Johnson. "The Growing Science of Casework," in Cora Kasius, ed., Principles and Techniques in Social Casework (New York: Family Service Association of America, 1950), pp. 48-56.

79. Ruesch, J. and Gregory Bateson. Communication, The Social Matrix of Psychiatry (New York: W.W. Norton, 1951).

80. Ruesch, J. "The Observer and the Observed: Human
     Communications Theory," in Roy Grinker, ed.,
     Toward a Unified Theory of Human Behavior (New
     York: Basic Books, 1951).

81. Selltiz, Claire, Maria Jahoda, Morton Deutsch, and
     Stuart W. Cook. Research Methods in Social Relations
     (New York: Holt, Rinehart and Winston, 1965).

82. Stamm, Isabel L. "Ego Psychology in the Emerging
     Theoretical Base of Casework," in Alfred J. Kahn,
     ed., Issues in American Social Work (New York:
     Columbia University Press, 1959), pp. 80-109.

83. Stark, Frances B. "Barriers to Client-Worker
     Communication at Intake," Social Casework, Vol. 36,
     April, 1955, pp. 147-155.

84. Tyler, Ralph W. "Distinctive Attributes of Education
     for the Professions," Social Work Journal, Vol. 33,
     No. 2, 1952.

85. Thomas, Edwin J. Behavioral Science for Social Work-
     ers (New York: The Free Press, 1967).

86. Voiland, Alice L. Family Casework Diagnosis (New
     York: Columbia University Press, 1962).

87. Waelder, Robert. "The Scientific Approach to Casework
     with Special Emphasis on Psychoanalysis," in Cora
     Kasius, ed., Principles and Techniques in Social Case-
     work (New York: Family Service Association of
     America, 1950), pp. 23-33.

88. Watson, J. The Charity Organization Movement in the
     United States (New York: Lippincott Company, 1922).

89. Weiss, Viola W. and Russel R. Monroe. "A Frame-
     work for Understanding Family Dynamics," in Cora
     Kasius, ed., Social Casework in the Fifties (New York:
     Family Service Association of America, 1962),
     pp. 175-197.

90. Wilsnack, William H. "Handling Resistance in Social
     Casework," American Journal of Orthopsychiatry,
     Vol. 16, April, 1946.

91.   Young, Pauline.   Social Treatment in Probation and
        Delinquency (New York: International University Press,
        1937).

Chapter 2

The Contribution of Psychoanalysis and Ego Psychology
to Social Casework

by Katherine M. Wood

If indeed social casework is "an art based on a science
which has not been invented yet" (74), certainly the history
of casework as a derivative theory and art has reflected a
talent for wholesale borrowing--a concept here, a theor-
tical construct there, from a smorgasbord of the psychological and social sciences. As yet casework is still "becoming," and has not yet really integrated a cohesive
theory of its own.

Historically, the metapsychology of Freud has been one
of the theories that has had major impact upon the development of casework theory and practice. It is asserted on
the one hand, that it was the assimilation of the psychoanalytic view of the person--his needs, wishes, motivations,
conflicts--that transformed casework from a trial-and-error
art, provided an understanding of the why of some of its
early failures and successes, and served as an impetus for
development of a framework for intervention with people.
On the other hand, it is also asserted that this microcosmic
concentration on the person has diverted our attention from
social work's historic concern with social ills, and has re-
defined the practitioner's role from the broad one of
intervener in the total person-situation gestalt to that of
narrow clinician.

It is now roughly half a century since the impact of
Freudian ideas began to be felt in social casework. The
marking of that milestone may therefore be an appropriate
point at which to summarize the main tenets of its contribution, and to assess in what ways it has been useful and
in what ways less useful, where and how it has catalyzed
casework toward more professional maturity, and where and
how it may have distorted our focus and our social mission.

DEFINITION OF THE THEORETICAL MODEL

It is necessary to begin a discussion of the relevance
and utility of psychoanalysis for casework by drawing a
distinction between psychoanalysis as a theory of psychic
development and functioning, and psychoanalysis as a system
of treatment techniques utilized by the particular school of
psychotherapy that also bears this title. It is also necessary
to recognize that psychoanalysis--both as personality theory
and as treatment method--has traveled beyond its originator;
the contributions, revisions, and modifications of some of
the major "neo"-Freudians and "post"-Freudians must additionally be taken into account.

Psychoanalysis as a Theory of Personality

The psychoanalytic theory of the psychosexual development and psychic functioning of human beings was developed
by a Viennese neurophysiologist, Sigmund Freud, over a
period of some forty-odd years until the time of his death
in 1939.   Freud's metapsychology is but one of a myriad of
psychobiological theories that have been advanced in the past
several generations, but it has been by far the most influ-
ential.   His ideas have set the direction of much of twentieth-
century psychological and social science--psychology, anthropology, sociology.   His concepts and terminology have infil-
trated the thinking even of those who most vigorously repu-
diate his views.   The Freudian conception of man has influenced not only social casework but also, to a greater or
lesser degree, art, literature, law, education, even re-
ligion--almost every arena of modern life.   To this extent
it has permeated not only the casework method, but also
the social reality within which social casework is embedded.

Not all of Freud's theory of personality was or is
accepted, even by his most orthodox followers. A good
many of his essential ideas have been modified by later
theorizers, and some--for example, his notion of "Thanatos,"
or the death instinct--have been rejected almost totally (93).
This in itself, however, does not necessarily render them
less actively or potentially useful.   Freud was in essence
less a scientist than a philosopher--perhaps the last of the
great philosophers, those concerned with universal meanings;
perhaps even less a healer than the maker of a system of
thought.   He said of his own ideas that they "... are part of

a speculative superstructure ... any portion of which can be abandoned or changed without loss or regret the moment its inadequacy has been proved" (92).

It probably is more accurate to speak of Freud's theories as operational concepts that have been of use in understanding the needs and behavior of people. Other, more empirically verifiable and more tightly-woven concepts may indeed replace them, and we may, some day, have the comprehensive and ultimate theory of personality that at present does not exist. Yet, psychoanalytic ideas about personality formation, structure, and functioning have been more operationally useful for casework than any other personality theory to date. This means that they have been of immediate, pragmatic value to the casework practitioner in understanding and seeking to help his client. It has been a two-sided coin, however; in some ways, the particular frame of reference represented by psychoanalytic theory has served to narrow as much as it has deepened and enriched the casework method of human service.

Let us review some of the major concepts that casework has appropriated from psychoanalysis, many of them so tightly woven by now into our theory and practice that they are part of casework's own fabric. The following is of course not an exhaustive explication of either psychoanalytic or casework theory, which has elsewhere required volumes. Further, our examination of some of the positive and negative influences of psychoanalysis on the casework processes of study-diagnosis-treatment can be no more than arbitrarily selective and illustrative.

Fundamental Assumptions

Some of the operational concepts of psychoanalytic personality theory have received so much empirical confirmation that they are generally used as if they were indeed established "laws of the mind. " Brenner (10) considers two such fundamental hypotheses: the principle of psychic determinism, or causality; and the proposition that consciousness is an exceptional rather than a regular attribute of psychic processes. The first principle holds that in mental functioning, nothing happens randomly or by chance; each psychic "event" is determined by the ones which preceded it. There are always causal connections and continuities. The second hypothesis holds that unconscious mental

processes are of great significance and frequency in normal
as well as in abnormal functioning. "It is precisely the
fact that so much of what goes on in our minds is unconscious, that is, unknown to ourselves, that accounts for
the apparent discontinuities in our mental lives" (114).   To
these might be added two other hypotheses, closely related
to the foregoing but distinctive and as substantively basic.
The "gestalt hypothesis" holds that concepts constructed for
the explanation of behavior pertain to its various components
and not to different behaviors.   All behavior is indivisible;
but is multi-faceted and multiply-determined (or, in Freud's
term, over-determined).   The "organismic hypothesis" holds
that no behavior can be seen in isolation from the total
personality; that "all behavior is integral to, and characteristic of, the behaving personality" (112).

These fundamental hypotheses undergird the whole
structure of psychoanalytic personality theory.   The theory
is not comprehensible without reference to these basic ideas.

To date, the mainstream of casework thinking has
accepted these hypotheses: students are taught, and workers
function in their practice, in accordance with the notions
that behavior is purposeful, is part of a holistic gestalt--
"the whole person"--and that the action cannot be artificially
separated from the actor, is not simplistic or mechanistic
but expresses and is related to a variety of motivations and
determinations. Virtually all caseworkers now contend that
there exists a part of the mind that cannot be reached
directly, but can only be viewed as it is expressed through
its "derivatives" in overt behavior.

The "sociobehavioral approach, " the latest theoretical
contribution to casework, in large measure appears to deny
these fundamental assumptions--see, for example, Eysenck
and Rachman (20), Eysenck (19), Wolpe (157), and Thomas
(140, 141).   One may only note Bruck's (12) suggestion that
since "man is a sufficiently complicated being that no one
theory of personality and treatment is adequately comprehensive, " and that "behavioral, cognitive, and psychodynamic
theory may be focusing only on different facets of human
development and behavior that are dynamically interlocked
in the person, " casework cannot afford to be closed-minded
concerning any theory, be it by now "traditional" or with
the freshness of novelty, and that upon closer examination different theories may not be as diverse as initially appears.

Freud saw the human personality from four distinct but intermeshing and cogwheeling points of view: the dynamic; the topographic; the structural; and the economic. To these later was added the genetic. These vantage points or dimensions are merely different ways of viewing the same mental phenomena through different "prisms"; none takes priority over the others and they are not mutually exclusive, but rather mutually interdependent. One cannot be understood without reference to the others, and the personality as a totality must be viewed through all prisms concurrently and in terms of the dynamic interplay among them.

1) The dynamic dimension, or Freud's instinct theory, is "concerned with the ultimate underlying dynamics of personality functioning" (40).

Freud held that all behavior is ultimately drive-determined. He repeatedly modified over the years his ideas concerning instincts; and his final dichotomous theory of "Eros" and "Thanatos" has not been widely accepted (93). His thinking, however, represented a decided advance over the psychologies of his day which postulated a "multitude of small occasional instincts" (94), such as an instinct for play, for self-assertion, and the like. Freud, the physiologist, insisted on the physiological, genetic derivation of the instincts or "drives" (a better translation of the original German "Trieb, " as it distinguishes human drives from what are called instincts in the lower animals). His concept was that of a psycho-physiological phenomenon--a psychic energy derived from a state of excitation of the body, this excitation having been created either by internal bodily processes or by external events which have acquired stimulus value. "Instinct appears to us, " he wrote, "as a borderline concept between the mental and the physical" (30).

The tension thus created by the drive, or energy, Freud called "libido. " The operational sequence of a drive is: tension or need, motor activity, and cessation of tension or gratification. The direction implicit in this sequence was conceptualized as the "pleasure principle. " Wish fulfillment is the cognitive equivalent of the pleasure principle; this concept made it possible to include phenomena like dreams, hallucinations, daydreams and reveries in the theory of motivational behavior, and provided the theoretical matrix for the understanding of free associations and projective techniques (115).

Hendrick states, "The most fundamental of Freud's laws of instinctual activity is that the psychological (and social) activities are determined by a constant need to reduce emotional tension. These tensions are the locomotor factor in human life; and the production of the tensions is the function of the instincts. They are consciously perceived as painful or disagreeable feelings" (e. g. , sexual tension, hunger, anger); "activity is initiated by the need to perform some specific function which will reduce this tension; and the fulfillment of this tension-reducing function thereby evokes the experience of pleasure. Freud therefore termed this fundamental law of instinct the 'pleasure principle'. " Hendrick compares this formulation of psychoanalytic theory to the notion of "homeostasis, " first propounded by Cannon (13) and further explored since by several other disciplines and fields (most recently, as a cardinal concept of General Systems Theory): "their investigations have been in separate realms yet their final conclusions in regard to the fundamental processes of life are the same: the psychoanalyst, that psychological processes are initiated by the need to restore an emotional equilibrium, which is experienced as pleasure; the physiologist, that all organic processes are initiated by the need to restore a physiochemical equilibrium which is experienced as health" (58).

The dynamic theory therefore implies that behavior may be triggered internally as well as by external stimulation; and that behavior, which is causally determined, evinces a goal-directedness, a purposive, teleological character.

Rapaport (113) notes that "psychoanalysis was one of the first theories to recognize the interaction of nature and nurture in the development of behavior. Drives represent the 'nature' factor; and their vicissitudes, in the course of experience, the interweaving of nature and nurture. Moreover, the coordination of drive and drive object ... is a psychological representation of the biological adaptedness of the species to its environmental niche. "

Freud's emphasis in the dynamic point of view was on the variety of mental forces, the conflicts among them, and the compromises that are worked out. The conditions of modern civilized life require that only relatively infrequently can we express our primitive biologically-determined needs directly; their control and channeling is the essential function of civilization, of society. He made a cogent case, however, against the two extremes of the misuse of this reality: the

Victorian sexual repressiveness that obtained in his era and
culture in turn-of-the century Vienna, on the one hand, and
the unbridled explosion of man's aggressive drives represented
by war, on the other (28).

Two other basic concepts are involved in the dynamic
viewpoint, that of "fixation" and "cathexis." Freud's concept
of libido was that of a psychic energic quantum which may
become bound up or "fixated" upon specific objects. We
speak, therefore, of a person being fixated at an immature
level of development (e. g. , the "oral character"), or upon
a specific object as in sexual fixations such as fetishism or
homosexuality. The amount of psychic energy or libido
which is directed toward a particularized object is known as
"cathexis. " The greater the degree of psychological importance we attach to a person or a thing, the greater is the
degree to which it is cathected.

An instinct has four characteristics: a source, an aim,
an object, and an impetus. The source is a bodily condition
or need, e. g. , hunger, sexual arousal, aggression. The aim
is the removal of this somatic excitation. The object includes not only the object in reality upon which the need is
focused, e. g. , food, but also all the activities necessary to
secure it, such as walking to the refrigerator, eating, etc.
The impetus of an instinct is its strength, which is determined by the force or intensity of the underlying need, e. g. ,
hunger or sexual need or aggression may vary quantitatively
in different individuals or in the same individual at different
times.

Freud modified and remodified his instinct theory, but
in general assumed that all instincts could be classified
either as libidinal or aggressive drives. The libidinal drive
includes not only the sexual drives, but all survival needs,
such as hunger. Freud's conceptualization of the "sexual"
instincts was therefore much broader than that of adult
genital activity. He viewed these drives as not one but
many: a multiplicity of bodily needs, and related them to
different bodily erogenous zones which are relatively separate
in childhood but in normal adulthood tend to fuse to serve
jointly the purpose of renewal of life or reproduction--the
oral, the anal, the genital zones.

Freud's treatment of sexuality per se was, for his time,
novel to the point of scandal. He was driven to stating that
he was "for once ... in agreement with the opponents of

psychoanalysis" that sexuality is not everything (95); and
attempted to explain that he had never said it was. His
critics tended, and some still tend, to equate sex, psycho-
sexuality, libido, and drive or instinct--an equation Freud
did not make. Most shocking to his audience of the day was
his recognition of the sexuality of the small child. He ex-
ploded the Victorian myth that sexual capacity develops
suddenly and full-blown at puberty, and argued that our
sexual nature is from birth an integral part of our human
nature--an observation corroborated by those who have
opportunity for close observation of young children. As the
physical sexual organs exist from the beginnings of life, so
does the drive for sexual satisfaction and activities, although
the latter are defined by the child somewhat differently than
by the adult. Sexuality, as any function, has beginnings
which are not identical with the ultimate maturational results;
but without these beginnings, the results could not come
about. The classic example of infantile stimulation of an
erotogenic zone is thumb-sucking--Freud used this to ex-
emplify childhood sexual activity at its most primitive and
simple. The auto-gratification of masturbation is discovered
by most children early in life. "The libidinal drive proceeds
from its early narcissistic stage, forming first oral dependent relationships, then moving to adult object relationships"
(Hollis, 72). When Freud spoke of infantile sexuality, he
did not mean adult sexuality; he referred to the steps in
psychosexual development which, if unimpeded, eventually
evolve into adult sexuality. This is as true for sexual
functioning as for the slow maturational development of
intellectual functioning, motor functioning, social functioning,
etc. But one of the basic postulates of Freud's genetic
dimension, to be discussed later, is that each stage of
human development is an outgrowth of and in certain ways
recapitulates all the stages that went before. In effect,
none is completely "grown out of. " What we call foreplay
in adult sexual behavior includes the phases of sexual
development throughout the first years of life. The individual
who is unable to enjoy sexual play, who is made anxious or
guilt-ridden because such activities were prohibited during
childhood, will have difficulty in achieving full adult sexuality.

    Freud's notion of the available quantity of original libidi-
nal energy being limited, and of its fixation at various
levels of development short of maturity in some individuals,
was to provide the basis of his theory of the neuroses. The
advances of ego psychology have since outmoded the libido
theory, narrowly construed as the distribution of energies

proceeding from the anatomical erogenous zones.   Freud did
not give as much weight as did the later ego psychologists--
Hartmam (52), Kris (80), Loewenstein (57), Rapaport (110)--
to the intervention of the ego, the "self," in the management
of instinctual drives; and in light of their later formulations,
his original instinctual theory is incomplete and simplistic.
But man's history illustrates that although he may be "more
than the animals, but less than the angels," he denies at his
peril the existence within himself of the primitive libidinal
and aggressive drives that he shares with other creatures.
As Hartmann notes, "... the psychoanalytic theory of instinctual drives is broad enough to show also many impressive
parallels with the findings of a modern school of zoologists
(ethnologists)" (53).

      The aggressive instincts were not theoretically as well
developed by Freud as were the libidinal drives.   He did
not give a name comparable to "libido" to the energy through
which they are expressed, nor did he attempt to identify their
specific bodily sources, other than speculation that they a-
rise from the catabolic or breaking-down processes of the
body: "the goal of all life is death" (26).   Freud saw
aggressiveness as self-destruction (the "death instinct")
turned outward against substitute objects.   He initially gave
less emphasis to the aggressive instincts than to the libidinal; it took World War I to convince him that man's need
to destroy was as sovereign as his need to survive and re-
produce.   In our later examination of ego psychology, we
shall refer to the neo-Freudian concept that the libidinal and
aggressive instincts can fuse together and "neutralize" each
other.   Satisfying one's hunger, for example, involves a
fusion of both instincts: a certain amount of aggression is
necessary for the act of reaching out for food, of biting and
ingestion, etc.   "Aggression" is not therefore exclusively
concerned with violence and destructiveness.   Freud's notion
of aggression was that of a drive inherent in human nature,
of energy--a powerful force that may be used for constructive
or destructive purpose.   He likened aggression to a peaceful
river, its potential usable for the construction of electrical
power, or wildly destructive when torrentially swollen by
floods or blocked in its course.   The young human, the
child too small to have yet become "civilized" is--by adult
standards--a savage: violent, destructive, interested only in
the immediate satisfaction of his own needs, remorselessly
egocentric.   Any experienced mother knows that she leaves
an 18-month or 2-year-old alone with the newborn sibling at

the latter's risk.

Melanie Klein (78) built her neo-Freudian theory of
psychoanalytic understanding of childhood in large part around
this recognition of the capacity of the uncivilized human young
for aggression and sadism.   It is the task of society, through
its social institutions and primarily the family, to "socialize"
and civilize this little savage.   Freud held that "a progressive renunciation of ... instincts ... appears to us to
be one of the foundations of the development of human
civilization" (29).   Years earlier, he had argued for the
positive role of cultural and societal restrictions in controlling the explosiveness of sexual drives (when such restrictions
were used humanly and sensibly, not as in Victorian Vienna);
later, he argued that society can exist only to the extent
that aggressive forces are also controlled, and sometimes
renounced.   This is a more difficult task for society than
the control of its members' sexual needs, since aggression,
unlike libido, is usually incapable of being fully discharged.
But men, Freud felt, need the protection and security of
civilized society so deeply that they are willing to exchange
for it the renunciation of instinctual gratification.   Human
passions are sufficiently powerful, and so potentially dangerous, that they require an equally powerful system of re-
straints: "as a rule this cruel aggressiveness waits for
some provocation or puts itself at the service of some other
purpose, whose goal might also have been reached by milder
measures.   In circumstances that are favourable to it, when
the mental counterforces which ordinarily inhibit it are out
of action, it also manifests itself spontaneously and reveals
man as a savage beast..." (36).

Freud wrote two essays on war, in which he held that
"our unconscious will murder even for trifles" (33), and that
man can vicariously fulfill his aggressive impulses via the
state: "the state has forbidden to the individual the practice
of wrong-doing, not because it desires to abolish it, but
because it wishes to monopolize it ..." (34).   War sanctions
naked aggression and murder; those impulses which society
and the culture have sought to hold under control are freed
and legitimized.   Aggression is therefore both an inborn
given and environmentally stimulated, according to Freud.
He posited that childhood is a learning, a socializing period;
and that the fusion and thereby the control of both libidinal
and aggressive needs is its major task: "by the admixture
of erotic components the egoistic instincts are transformed
into social ones" (35).   Here he was referring to the reso-

lution of his famous "oedipal situation" in which the child
learns to repress his murderous wishes, not only through
fear, but also through love.

In the early heyday of casework's marriage with psychoanalysis, the instinctual dimension of looking at human beings
and their needs and behavior was over-emphasized. This
was also true for psychoanalysis until the later revisions,
particularly the development of ego psychology. Caseworkers talked and wrote--we are not convinced that many
practiced this way--as if the client had no ego, no environment, was but a mass of confused instinctual needs which
would somehow sort themselves out if we only were "passive"
enough and encouraged sufficient "abreaction." The pendulum
swung back as we developed more practice experience; and
is now perhaps moving to the opposite extreme. Because
of what seems to us from our present vantage point of a
generation later as the narrowness and simplistic quality
of Freud's assigning inordinate weight to his instinctual
theory, there is a tendency to discard the seminal truths it
may still contain for our practice. Garrett (38) points out
that the term ego psychology "is sometimes used in contrast
to libido psychology, but mistakenly as if it were supplanting
libido psychology." Man is more than his instincts, he is a
synthesizing, thinking being also, but he is not only ego.
Alexander (1) notes that "in the deep unconscious all men
are akin; individuality is formed nearer the surface. Ego-
psychology permits us to recognize and estimate those
features of personality which are molded by the cultural
environment and are superimposed upon a more or less
biological and emotional substratum".

Hollis argues for the need for the caseworker to understand the "balance of forces" in the client and his situation:
"on the one side ... the immature or unusual needs and
drives, the view of the world distorted by early childhood
experiences, and the infantile modes of thought ... on the
other side, we have the healthy or potentially healthy part
of the personality" (62). To this we might add "and the
healthy or potentially healthy parts of the social situation
itself--family, other groups, community response, etc. --
that might be tapped and utilized." Hollis, however, assigns
major importance to the evaluation of the client's "libidinal
and aggressive characteristics" as part of casework study
and diagnosis; under these she subsumes "narcissism,
dependence, residuals of oral, anal, and phallic developmental stages, capacity for mature love relationships, am-

bivalence, hostility, aggressiveness, sexual immaturities or
deviance, and unresolved attachments or hostilities toward
parents" (63).

The caseworker, throughout the casework process of
study-diagnosis-treatment, takes into account the quality and
degree of the client's or client group's libidinal and aggressive drives. Are we seeing this client at a maturational
life stage when, as in adolescence, there is an upsurge in
libidinal and aggressive needs with which he must struggle
to cope and channel? Or is this a character disorder, still
oriented toward immediate discharge and gratification of
tensions and impulses, with inadequate ego and superego
development to enable him to handle them more constructively? Or is he an "uptight" neurotic, so plagued
still by the burden of a repressive childhood's superego
that he cannot allow himself to feel his own needs? Or is
he Perlman's "diminished man" (103), bureaucratized and
machined by our culture to the extent that he has lost sight
of the instinctual roots that relate him to all other nature,
and thereby to his sense of his self? Does this family
foster or forbid expression of its members' tenderness and
anger--either or both? What is the attitude of the client's
cultural and religious group referents, the other social
institutions with which he interacts, regarding allowable
expression of libidinal and aggressive needs? And, of
course, how can the caseworker help this person or this
family, through the casework experience itself, through this
slice of his life experience that is happening now, to come
to terms with his own needs? What is the need of this
client to be provided with different learning experiences than
he has had in the past? What is the necessity for his
social milieu to adjust to his basic human needs as well as
he to adjust to it?

Freud's attempt to unify body and mind in his theory of
the instincts is narrow and incomplete. Certainly his theory
of psychic illness being related as totally as he posited to
the repression or distortion of instinctual forces only, today
seems naive (in many of the patients he diagnosed as neurotic, a modern psychiatrist or caseworker would see borderline or psychotic disturbance behind the neurotic facade).
Wheelis (150) argues that this represents a change in the
culture rather than in the nature of instinctual drives, "that
a Carthaginian general was instinctually no different from an
American businessman. " He points out that while no society
could long endure which thwarted human needs, "instinctual drives

do not determine the patterns of culture; it is culture that
determines the patterns of instinctual drives. " In our present American society, instinctual drives that were culturally
forbidden in Freud's era are encouraged, and vice versa;
but the constant of biologically given needs remains.

2) The genetic dimension of Freudian personality theory
was not formulated by Freud himself, but it is so implicit
in his other dimensions and so important a part of his overall theory that it has since been conceptualized on a plane
with the other dimensions of his metapsychology. In this
dimension are explored the developmental experiences of an
individual from birth. It is posited that personality patterns
at any given time are "functions of constitutional predis-
positions as shaped by previous experiences and present
situational pressures" (116). This thesis implies that all
behavior is part of a complementary, sequential, genetic
series; part of an historical sequence which has been shaped
both constitutionally and by the individual's life experiences,
each experience building on and being molded by the experiences that went before it. It does not ignore the importance of here-and-now forces and conditions (although
these are more implied than explicitly stated, and are not
given the weight assigned by later theorizers), but asserts
that any understanding of present behavior is incomplete
without some understanding of its genetic roots and antecedents.

The genetic viewpoint implies that the past lives in the
present: that part of our childhood lives on in each of us,
that entire cultures live on by the incorporation of the
traditions and learnings of the past in the egos and superegos of each member. It assumes that with each man
"maturity is a tenuous achievement. A defusion of instincts,
and a return to earlier developmental stages, are always
possible. For Freud the passions of men lie just below the
surface of life" (Roazen, 118).

Freud posited that during the first five or so years of
life, the child experiences a series of dynamically differentiated stages, so important that he held that these
early years are decisive for the formation of personality.
At about the time of school entrance, the instinctual dynamics
become "latent" and more or less stabilized, only to erupt
again with the onset of puberty, until maturity.

Each of the early stages of development is defined in terms of the particular capacities and reactions of a zone of the body. During the oral stage, the mouth is the principle somatic focus of dynamic activity. After the infant loses his physical connection with his mother's body by the process of birth, the mouth is not only the principle bodily organ that makes possible nourishment and survival; it is the principle somatic modality by which he interacts with his human and physical environment. Feeding is the infant's first experience in relationship with another human. The importance of this earliest phase for psychological as well as physical development of the child seems to be attested by later research, particularly on the devastating physical and emotional effects of inadequate relationship--"mothering" --even in circumstances when the child's physical needs are well met. (See, for example, Spitz (126, 127, 128), Leitch and Escalona (81), Mittelman (86), Ribble (117), and Bowlby (9).)

Following the preoccupation with oral activities and pleasures, Freud hypothesized that the infant's emotional interests and instinctual cathexes turn to the organs and functions of elimination. It is suggested that the anal phase is for the child his first experience that now he has the capacity to give and to withhold, to please and to say "no"; and that how he resolves this intriguing choice may have far-reaching implications for his adult personality. This phase is represented also as the first collision of the young human, until now oriented only to his own needs and wishes, with the demands and prohibitions of the culture; in response, the child learns either to acquiesce, to rebel, or to bargain.

In the phallic stage the instinctual scene shifts to the last of the primary erogenous zones, the genital. The stage is set by virtue of the child's increased physical maturation; his growing sense of a sexual identity--that he is a male "like daddy" or female "like mother"; his probable (in most children) experience by now with masturbatory activity and the fantasies that accompany it; and the conflicts posed by the residuals of the previous two stages around the child's previous insistence on his omnipotence and the primacy of his own needs on the one hand, and his growing perception of the reality of his smallness and need for his parents, on the other. According to Freud, the little boy's omnipotence, his wish to be just like father, and the growing pressure of libidinal needs, by now localized genitally, lead him to cathect sexually his mother and to seek to displace his father.

The unique conflict of this "oedipal situation" is not only that, normally, neither parent will permit this state of affairs, but that the child comes to recognize that he cannot afford to win the contest--for fear not only of father's retaliation (via castration), but also because of fear of loss of reciprocation of the love the child also feels for his admired and respected father. The "resolution," according to Freud, is conversion by the child of his feelings for his mother into more neutral tender affection, and identification with the father. In effect, the child's libidinal and aggressive drives are fused and "neutralized," a concept later developed by the ego psychologists, in the resolution of this early conflict of the "family drama." The child learns that he has two parents, that he is like and unlike both, that they and the culture will not permit the uncontrolled expression of his primordial nature. The effect of this resolution, normally, is a dawning recognition of the "must-nots" of the culture, i.e., the beginning of an in-built system of self-imposed prohibitions and restrictions--the superego. The child solves his problem by identifying with, literally taking into himself ("introjecting") the personalities and the values, standards, prohibitions, and other rewards and sanctions of society as personified by his parents, his major culture-bearers and culture-communicators.

The development and fate of the oedipal situation differ somewhat in the girl and are more involved, according to Freud. She is placed in the position of having to shift from her original love object, mother, to father. According to Freud, the motivation for this is her traumatic discovery that she lacks the interesting sexual appendage of the male, that she has been castrated--and she holds mother responsible for the damage (mother is the one upon whom she has previously relied for everything), and transfers her love to father. Freud suggested that the little girl's attachment to her father, her relationship with her brothers in the family, and later her attitude toward all men, are mixed with this early-established "penis envy."

The notion of the oedipal situation has been both attacked and defended. Kennedy (76) notes that "ethnologists believe that some form of 'nuclear family' exists in every human culture, and many would agree that an oedipus complex, or some complex which would be an equivalent for that type of social organization, occurs as a result of the prolonged dependence of the human child upon the care of parents or parent surrogates." Still, it may be argued that the idea

of an oedipal situation as above described may well be a
cultural derivative, idiosyncratic to Western culture with its
unique family structure as contrasted to those of other
cultures, and not--as Freud held--a biologically determined
universality.   His concept of "penis envy" may indeed be so
culturally, rather than biologically derived, based on the
culturally-supported superiority and dominance of the male
in our society, and the ways in which young females and
males both are early acculturated to this expectation.   Some
of the recent research on human sexual activity, beginning
with Kinsey (77) but most particularly Masters and Johnson
(85), gives evidence that Freud's "penis envy" may be
culturally rather than instinctually determined--their finding,
for example, that women are physiologically capable of more
intensive, more repetitive, and more sustained orgasmic
activity than are males.   (Near the end of his life, Freud
admitted that he really did not understand the psychology of
women very well: "The great question that has never been
answered, and which I have not yet been able to answer
despite my thirty years of research into the feminine soul,
is: what does a woman want?"   Most women might reply
that the task is not really that difficult; Freud just didn't
ask the right questions.)

    After the stage of instinctual quiescence represented by
the latency period, Freud posited that puberty brings a re-
crudescence in force and quantity of the biological drives.
The adolescent is faced with the crucial life task of establishing social channels through which his instinctual needs can
be both expressed and controlled.   The essential narcissism
of the young child, directed by what Freud termed the
"pleasure principle, " becomes transformed--ideally--into a
capacity for true object relationships, for altruism, for
socialization, for cognizance of the world of reality as well
as the world of self--the "reality principle. "   The individual establishes the characteristic personality patterns and
adaptations that, although like those of all other men, uniquely
mark him as his own person.

    One of the basic ideas of the Freudian genetic theory
is that pregenital interests and needs are never left behind
completely; they fuse and synthesize into maturity.   The
major task of adolescence, which to some extent continues
throughout adult life as the world of reality changes, is the
synthesis and fusion of the genetic stages that went before.
"The final organization of personality represents contributions
from all four stages" (43).

Freud's reply, when asked what he considered the criteria of "mental health" or of "maturity," was simple but classic: the capacity "to love and to work."

An important concept connected with the genetic theory is that of regression. Whereas the concept of "fixation," referred to earlier, means arrest at some early stage of development, so that in some areas of functioning at least there is an interruption and "freezing" of normal development toward maturity, regression means that although progress to a higher level of functioning may have occurred, under stress the person reverts to an earlier behavior pattern. The regression of a previously weaned and housebroken three-year-old to babyish ways after the arrival of a new baby is the most common illustration of this phenomenon, or the regression to less mature patterns of behavior of the previously well-functioning adult under the stress of illness or other severe emotional pressure. Regression is a reaction to some kind of stress that the person cannot handle with his current adaptive capacities; he is driven back, literally, to earlier patterns of adaptive behavior, and to a more pleasantly-remembered time of gratifications than the present stressful challenge. Fixation, on the other hand, is thought to be caused either by severe deprivation at an earlier developmental level, rendering the individual unable to cope with the specific life-tasks and materials required at the stage, and thus unable to move on to the next stage of emotional growth; or to the obverse of extreme overindulgence which offers no incentives, no impetus of normal frustration, to develop further.

In his genetic theory, Freud was attempting to relate the psychic realm to the physical in quite unilateral fashion. He saw the emotional and psychic development of the child at each stage of development as the direct outgrowth of emerging sensitivities of the major erogenous zones of the body. Today, we are much less concrete and literal-minded, and recognize that it is not the particular mechanics and specific timing of weaning and toilet-training experiences, for example, that are important, but rather the total emotional climate in the relationship between the child and his parents that surrounds these experiences. Freud criticized his own theory as "too narrowly oriented around the libidinal drives, pleading lack of sufficient time and insight for more careful investigation of the aggressive instinct and of the development and function of the ego" (Munroe, 93).

It is interesting to note, however, how even later rival
theorists of development in effect embody much of Freud's
theory of epigenesis.   For Piaget, for example, "much of
a child's role confusion and conflict is parallel to the emotional conflicting loyalties in the Oedipal situation" (Maier, 83).
And even Sears, the behaviorist, "stresses that during the
same age span the parent of the same sex as the child is
apt to be the instigator as well as the recipient of greatest
aggression, while the opposite parent tends to be more lenient
and consequently more approachable" (Maier, 83).   Odier's
(98) comment that "the strongest aspect of the Freudian
psychoanalytic doctrine is the weakest of Piaget's doctrine,
and vice versa"; and Wolff's (156) that "despite their
methodological differences and divergent goals, the two
methods (Piagetian analysis and Freudian psychoanalysis)
may complement each other in providing a comprehensive
picture of the developmental process, each supplying the data
in those areas where the other is deficient, " reminds us that
different theorists may be the proverbial blind men with the
elephant--each describing a different aspect of the same
animal.

Erikson (15, 16), a neo-Freudian psychoanalyst, accepted
Freud's theory of genetic stages of instinctual development,
but generalized beyond it, placing development within its
social and cultural matrix and emphasizing the tasks of ego
mastery presented by each stage of maturation.   His eight
"nuclear conflicts" or maturational stages of the growing
personality--trust vs. mistrust, autonomy vs. shame and
doubt, initiative vs. guilt, industry vs. inferiority, identity
vs. role diffusion, intimacy vs. isolation, generativity vs.
stagnation, and integrity vs. despair--roughly correspond to
Freud's stages of orality, anality, genitality, latency, adolescence, etc.   Freud's theory is by implication a social as
well as a bio-instinctual one--the outcome of each stage
depends as much on the response and interaction of the
social and human environment as on the force of the instinctual drives--but Erikson's more focused emphasis on social
components and his stress on ego mastery provided a bridge
from Freud's too-exclusive emphasis on the instinctual.

As Freud has been criticized for being "too biological, "
so have the later genetic theorists for over-emphasizing the
social and in effect denigrating what is also the biological,
innate, unchanging and unchangeable nature of man.   Danger
exists of dichotomizing the two; of failing to see that the
description of man as a social animal means that he is both

a social being and a creature of nature.

All of the genetic theorists, beginning with Freud, have
at least implied that the process of development of human
personality is a process of learning. Although both Erikson
(see especially 15) in his discussion of maturational life
tasks with which the individual must learn to cope, and
Hartmann (56, 52) and the other "ego psychologists" in
their exploration beyond Freud of the adaptational capacities
of the personality, implied a view of development as learning, this has only begun to be explicated (see Piaget, 104,
105, 106; and Sears, 121, 122).

As seems to have been true generally of the history of
the integration of other aspects of Freudian-based theory into casework, in the beginning of the dynamic psychiatry-case-
work union, the genetic theory was applied naively and
shallowly, leading to an ineffectual bastardization of casework's own practice and focus. Hamilton, for example,
describes amusingly some of the Freudian-influenced caseworkers of the 30's and 40's waiting with bated breath to
"get a peek at the (client's) infantile neurosis" (50). Freud's
concentration in his own therapeutic work on the experiences,
memories, fixations of earliest life as he discovered their
residuals in his adult patients, led to the misperception that
inclusion of a genetic dimension in casework diagnosis and
treatment applied only to the relationship to current behavior
of the person's long-distant experiences and influences of
earliest childhood. Today, the insights of ego psychology
and of the social sciences renders such a view narrow and
simplistic. It remained for Hartmann and Kris, for example,
to explicate that the genetic series anteceding a given behavior
do not necessarily constitute an "infantile regress"; they
lead back to an historical situation in which a particular
solution of a drive demand was first achieved, or a particular
apparatus was first put to a certain kind of use" (56).

As casework practitioners and scholars developed more
sophisticated understanding about the usefulness and applicability of Freudian theory for their own profession and
practice, the application of genetic understanding of the
client-in-situation became more focused. Hollis (64) points
out that in study and diagnosis the caseworker is "looking for
coherent patterns. " Hamilton (45) criticizes the routinized,
sterile history taken for history's sake or to fill up the case
record, but notes that "today there is reemphasis upon appropriate psychogenetic history as there is support for a well-

directed psychosocial study.   The chief improvement derives
from greater skill in the method of inquiry, as well as in
clearer focus and aim for the exploration required by the
problem.   That one may not always need to obtain a thorough
history or a complete social study in no wise changes this
fundamental realization of life patterns. "   In terms of casework treatment, however, Hamilton (45) refers only to the
usefulness of psychogenetic material for purpose of the client's
"reliving or abreaction"; and Hollis (65) to its use by the
client for "development of understanding" of the influence of
genetic and historical experiences on his modes of reaction
now.   It is Perlman (101) who addresses most directly and
relevantly the use of genetic material by the caseworker in
relation to his shaping of the casework experience itself:
"the history of the adverse experiences (that the client) has
encountered, but particularly the history of his successful
or unsuccessful adaptations to them--his 'solution' of his
difficulties... by retreat, by intrenchment, by blind fighting,
or by compromise, detour, and constructive substitutions--
this history of his development as a problem-encountering,
problem-solving human being may provide the caseworker
with an understanding of what his client suffers from and
what the extent of his coping ability is likely to be" (italics
Perlman's).

    The caseworker needs to learn something about the
broad patterning of the client's previous experiences, life
successes and failures, interactions with significant others
in the past, areas of fixation and regression and whether
these seem to be reactive to an immediate stressful situation
or longer-standing and characterological in nature: in short,
psychogenetic understanding of this person as a person, how
he came to be who he is, something of "his story"--
"history. "

    Throughout casework literature, diagnosis and treatment
are viewed as two sides of the same coin: Perlman (102),
for example, emphasizes that diagnosis is a "design for
action, " not an intellectual exercise but a ground plan for
what the worker is going to do.   The genetic dimension of
psychosocial diagnosis, when so used, enriches and focuses
casework treatment.   Alexander's (2) concept of the treatment experience as a "corrective emotional experience" is
familiar to most caseworkers.   If the worker's understanding
of the kinds of life and developmental experiences this person
has had in the past leads to a psychogenetic diagnosis that
some of his present difficulties are due to an immature, de-

manding, voracious "oral" personality structure, then what
does this imply for the kind of treatment experience he needs?
What kind of transactional experiences--what kind of learning
within the context of the casework relationship--can the
worker make available to him now, directly or indirectly,
to free him somewhat from his fixated level of emotional
development and help him grow and mature? Was the
emotional fixation caused by deprivation of the emotional
security and supplies needed for normal growth earlier, so
that the client is left still "hungry" and must turn to wife
or husband or children or other current significant others
for the kind of childhood emotional nourishment that should
have been available years earlier? If so, how does this
shape the worker's focus and activity in the treatment interaction with him now? Or is this a client who was so over-
indulged at an earlier level of development that he was
never able to grow beyond it; and what does he need from
the therapeutic relationship now in terms of learning to cope
with frustration? Is this a character-disordered client with
"lacunae" in superego development, failures to introject
standards and values; in what ways must the worker represent for him now the parent, the caring but firm authority,
he genetically missed earlier? The parent who functions
well in most life areas, but feels the same antipathy to one
scapegoated child in the family as did he to a resented
sibling in his own childhood--what connection between the
then and the now? What developmental level is this total
family at, as a group? Are they what has been called a
"playpen family, " with the parents as well as the youngsters
still children emotionally, all relating to each other as
siblings: can they be worked with as a family therapy group;
are there enough indices of current or potential capacity for
more mature functioning, for the family to become a problem-
solving group; or are these parents so infantile and needy,
so competitive with each other and the children, that they
need to be helped individually to grow a little, first? What
kinds of exacerbations of old feelings and needs, reawakening
of old conflicts from previous life stages, is the adolescent
client experiencing; what does he need now from the worker,
this new adult in his life who is like and yet unlike a parent?
Is this an ordinarily well-functioning adult who is regressing
under the stress of crisis? Or is this a chronologically
adult but still emotionally adolescent client who has been
searching for years but has never found his self, his identity;
what kind of experience does he need to be provided with by
the caseworker? What other life experiences, situations, resources, systems, does the worker need to help the client

to locate and utilize as further learning and growth experi-
ences--as "social therapy" as well as psychological therapy
(Siporin, 125)? Is the situation of this person-in-situation,
be he child or adult, one so inimical to his developmental
needs that the situation itself is what needs to be changed:
should the worker's response be directed toward situational
intervention such as advocacy?

     3) The topographic is a qualitative dissection of the
personality: it examines the anatomy of the personality in
terms of its various "layers" and processes--the
"conscious, " the "preconscious, " and the "unconscious. "

     The conscious is that portion of our mental activities
that we are fully aware of at any given time.

     The preconscious refers to the host of thoughts, feelings,
memories, and perceptions which are not immediately available but can fairly easily be brought into consciousness when
required.   They can easily become conscious because they
do not have to overcome powerful counterforces.

     The concept of the unconscious has been termed the
foundation of psychoanalytic theory.   This concept holds that
man is more than he appears on the surface, more than a
mere reacting machine: he carries within him his own rich
microcosmic world of buried motivations, desires, drives,
memories, attitudes, of which he is not aware.   Psychoanalytic theory holds that without our realizing it, such unconscious needs and memories and attitudes are responsible
for many of our conscious actions, feelings, and thoughts,
and they influence our relationships with others.

     Unconscious processes abide by rules different from
those that obtain for conscious processes. The unconscious
includes mental processes of which we are usually totally
ignorant (such as the "primary process" mental functioning
normally known to us only in dreams), as well as those we
have been aware of at one time but which have been pushed
out of consciousness for any of a variety of reasons.   This
keeping out, or, later, pushing out of consciousness of ideas,
memories, or emotions that are experienced as painful, unacceptable or dangerous, Freud termed repression.   The unconscious, and the concept of repression, are two of the
cardinal tenets of psychoanalytic theory.

Primary process thinking is the most primitive form of mental activity, and is a process of the unconscious. It is found in normal dreams, in hypnogogic states, under the influence of some drugs such as LSD, and in the thought processes of some forms of psychosis. Indeed, dreams have been called "normal psychoses," a kind of safety valve in which unconscious pressures and conflicts can be relived and relieved. In addition, there seems to be some evidence that ego processes continue in the unconscious dream state, that "tag-ends" of unsettled problems and worries of the day previous can be worked out, and that even some kinds of learning, such as materials to be memorized, can continue in the sleep state. Some of the evidence of recent psycho-physiologic research on sleep and dreaming seems to indicate that dreams are necessary for emotional and mental stability, and that deprivation of the opportunity to dream (not only to sleep) can cause temporary psychotic states.

In primary process thinking, there is no sense of time; symbols are interpreted literally; one thing is substituted for another, or is condensed and telescoped; contradictions exist side by side; displacement and distortion occur liber-ally--in short, primitive, alogical processes of thought obtain. Primary mental process is the maximal level of the newborn, what William James described as the infant's perception of the world as a "booming, buzzing confusion."

Secondary process thinking, in contrast, is what is usually meant by the term "thinking": logical, orderly, conscious processes of perception, cognition, evaluation, and reasoning. The psychic energies are more bound and focused than in primary process, there is the sense of time and of spatial relationships that is lacking in the more primitive mode, and capacity for delayed discharge--the "reality principle"--dominates. The primary process obeys the pleasure principle; the secondary process the reality principle. Primary process deals in mental images divorced from or only loosely and symbolically connected to reality; the mental images of secondary process of reasoning, weigh-ing, judging are related to reality.

An analysis of any of our thinking gives evidence that our thought processes are usually a mixture of conscious and unconscious, of primary and secondary process. Com-paratively rarely and for short periods of time are we cap-able of completely "logical, orderly, conscious processes of perception, cognition, evaluation, and reasoning" without contamination by unconscious feeling and motivation in the form of mind-wandering, daydreaming, emotionally-distorted perceptions and judgment, etc. People are not only "logical"; they are "psycho-logical."

Freud's notion of the existence of an unconscious part of the mind began with his studies of hypnosis, and was refined in his work on dreams. He concluded that dreams are not merely haphazard nonsense, but have a purpose and function for the personality (an observation that was empirically validated only many years later, in the recent research on sleep and dreaming referred to earlier). Rapaport (110) notes that "the observation that in hypnosis and in the course of free associating, patients became aware of past experiences or of relations between them, or of relations between past and present experiences, led to the assumption of the 'nonconscious' survival of such experiences and the 'nonconscious' existence of such relationships. But only the discovery that such nonconscious experiences and relationships are subject to rules (e. g., the pleasure principle and the mechanisms of the primary process) different from those of our conscious behavior and thinking made the abovementioned memory phenomena... into evidence for the assumption of unconscious psychological processes." Hartmann (54) states that "there is rather wide agreement that conscious data are insufficient for the explanation of a considerable part of behavior."

There has been a good deal of debate over the years concerning the existence of unconscious processes. The psychological formulations underpinning behavior modification theories give little emphasis to the role of the unconscious, highlighting rather the conscious, stimulus-and-response processes involved in learned behavior; and it has been proposed that it is for this reason that these theories are so limited. At present, most personality theorists have tended to accept the role of unconscious motives; the question today "seems to be less a matter of whether such factors exist than a matter of under what conditions and how strongly they operate" (Hall and Lindzey, 41). There seems reason to believe that the content of the unconscious has changed since Freud's day (see, for example, Wheelis, 149, and Seeley, 124). In the nineteenth century the unconscious consisted of ideas, emotions and motivations that had been rejected by the superego as unacceptable; and much of this was sexual. But such material is comparatively rarely repressed today, as evidenced in the decline of cases of classic hysteria. Hysteria depends upon repression of needs and drives unacceptable to the superego; if sufficiently strong, these drives achieve a distorted symptomatic discharge which constitutes the illness. Today, we see more and more character and personality disorders, characterized not so much by superego-directed repression and consequent symptom-formation as by deficiencies in superego development and warped ego functioning. Wheelis (151) posits that the unconscious of Freud's patients, being made up of superego rejects, was therefore more homogeneous and more subject to inference. Today the unconscious is comprised largely of ego rejects and is heterogeneous, due to the "contraction of the unconscious."

Be this as it may, that the unconscious has "shrunken" in terms of the size of the reservoir it represents and the pressure of its contents, most caseworkers today accept the notion that unconscious motivations, needs, drives, pressures, memories, feelings, thought processes--all at some times and to greater or lesser degree direct not only their clients' but their own behavior. The working treatment concepts of transference and countertransference are largely based on the idea of the unconscious.

Hollis opines (66) that "the caseworker certainly needs to know a great deal about the unconscious: its nature and the generally recognized ways in which it plays a part in the mental life and behavior of the individual. Such knowledge is essential both for diagnostic understanding and for treatment of problems of interpersonal adjustment, for the unconscious as well as the conscious is always involved in such problems."

Controversy swirled for years, however, concerning whether and to what extent caseworkers "should" become involved with the client's unconscious. In retrospect, the major obstacle for casework in this area was our earlier blanket assumption of the techniques of psychoanalytic therapy for dealing with unconscious material, i.e., a deliberate bringing of such material into consciousness so that it could be "interpreted." The first counter-reaction to the recogntion that this technique was not only inappropriate but dangerous for use by caseworkers untrained and unskilled in its application, but also that it was not appropriate to the kinds of clients and client problems we saw in practice, was a fearfulness among caseworkers to approach anything that smacked of the unconscious. Students were taught that "casework does not deal with the uncon-

scious. " Workers became edgy and insecure about their
"right" to discuss with a client her upset over her dream of
the night before that she had killed her child, or her mother,
--or the caseworker. For some time, it was difficult for
casework to see that it not only should not, but could not
avoid dealing with the client's unconscious, as its derivatives
were displayed in behavior. Strean (138) has noted that
"the social worker, if he is to function scientifically, accepts,
understands, and attempts to influence the unconscious of
his client. To assert that the difference between casework
and psychotherapy is that the caseworker works only with
the conscious, as many have alleged, is to reject a good
part of man and therefore to limit our diagnostic and therapeutic effectiveness with him. "

Perhaps the major difference between the psychoanalytic
and casework response to the client's unconsciously derived
needs, feelings, and motivations is that psychoanalysis'
major tool in response is verbal interpretation, whereas
casework deals with the same material experientially--in
terms of the kind of total response and experience the worker
provides to the client. The client whose unconscious need
is to be cared for, and for whom this is his unconscious
motivation in engaging in the relationship with the worker,
may need to be either gratified or frustrated depending on
total psychosocial diagnosis; but the worker must first
recognize and understand the unconscious dynamics of what
is transpiring between himself and the client. The worker
cannot understand the client and what he needs of the transaction unless he understands at least the patterning of the
unconscious sources or "dynamics" of the client's expectations
of significant others, of his interaction with other people,
of his perceptions and expectations of the caseworker (the
transference), and of the areas of fixation or "freezing" of
aspects of his personality in immature adaptational modes.

The borrowed insights of ego psychology have con-
centrated casework's attention in recent years on the conscious ego processes as well as unconscious processes,
on the ego strengths and adaptational capacities of the client,
and on the strengths and resources, the deprivations and
pathologies of his real-life social situation. Casework seems
to have come to a more rounded and sophisticated recognition
that the client--and all of us--live on different levels at the
same time. With more skill and ability to involve the
client's conscious ego, the caseworker is aware that both
levels do exist. The client who, for example, says on one

level, "I want help with my problem with money, or my
relationship with my child--help me learn to use the abilities
and capacities I have to handle my life better," on another
level may be saying, "love me and take care of me--that's
why I'm really here"; or, "don't get too close to me, because that will demand of me a reciprocation, an ability to
relate, that I just don't have or that seems very frightening
to me." The worker must be aware that both coexist in the
client, and in every one of the "pieces" of interaction and
transaction that transpire between them.   The worker's responses to the client--verbal or nonverbal--are often on the
same multi-layered levels as are the client's: in the context of conscious, reality-oriented response to the client's
conscious, reality-oriented communication, the worker is
also communicating a response in terms of his recognition
("diagnosis") of the sub-level of the client's communication.
The worker's offer, for example, to provide a concrete
service, or to assume a broker or advocate role, may not
only be meeting the practical need but also saying to client
A, "see, I am willing to give to you," or to client B, "yes,
I recognize and respect your present fear and need for
distance--I'll attend to your concrete need and not expect
too much or too fast, emotionally, from you." This kind
of knowledge of the total person in the total situation, and
ability to intervene and to respond differentially with recognition of the differential meaning to each client of the
worker's superficially similar-appearing response, is today
seen as the sine qua non of individualized and skilled casework intervention.

Towle (143) describes the way the student swings from
one focus to another, before he achieves integration of these
concepts in his understanding and his practice: "(the student)
feels helpless when he gets the full impact of why he has
been unable to, or should not have tried to, reason an individual out of his ills into new ways of feeling, thinking, and
doing.   He may go through a phase of seeing man as more
irrational than he is, until he can encompass the duality--of
man operating consciously and unconsciously, rationally and
irrationally.   This occurs as (the student) experiences the
values of understanding the rationale of the seemingly irrational, unconscious needs and strivings if one is to engage
the individual's conscious, rational self in productive problem-
solving. "

While the worker must be able to diagnose the unconscious significance of the client's verbalizations and behavior,

he responds to these in ways that bring them within the
grasp of the client's conscious and preconscious processes.
The worker seeks always to engage the client's conscious
ego-capacities in the accurate perception of, the thinking-
through, and the problem-solving (Perlman, 100) of his
difficulty. In addition, the caseworker, depending on his
diagnosis of the etiology of the problem, his assessment of
the client's capacities, and the exigencies of the real-life
situation in which both he and his client are embedded (time
considerations, for example), may also attempt to help the
client to see the relationship between selected preconscious
material to his current situation, e. g. , his boyhood relation-
shp with a critical father and his relationship with his
employer now.

Present casework thinking holds that the worker needs
to be aware of and to assess accurately all three of these
topographic systems of his client--conscious, preconscious,
and unconscious.   The degree to which he relates his interventions to one or other of these systems depends on his
total understanding of all the subsystems involved in the
rubric, "psychosocial diagnosis. " With the psychotic client,
his unconscious is all too evident; and here the casework
task is to help strengthen repression and the client's relation
to reality.   With the person in crisis, for whom the stress
has often caused a welling-up of old unconscious feelings and
conflicts and a diminution in the coping capacities of the
conscious ego, the worker's intervention is directed toward
helping the client reestablish stress-shaken capacities for
ego adaptation, or develop new ones.   With another client,
diagnosis may lead to an emphasis in treatment on helping
the client to understand intellectually and emotionally the
connection, based on preconscious material, of what has
happened to him in the past and what he is doing with his
life now--with the ultimate goal of bringing such understanding also into the service of the conscious, thinking, adapting
ego.

Ego Psychology and the Structural Approach

4)   The genetic approach examined the personality
longitudinally, in terms of its history and development; the
topographic in terms of its horizontal "layers"; the structural
approach examines it in vertical cross-section--the relation
to each other and to the outside world of drives (the "id"),
adaptive capacities and mechanisms (the "ego"), and conscience

and ideals (the "superego"). The term "structure" is of
course a conceptual rather than a literal one: it is used
merely to describe a "group of mental contents and processes
which are functionally related to one another" (10). The
topographic dimension orders the data of all the other
dimensions according to this trichotomous classification.
Freud's theory of conflict is a description of the interactions
among these three aspects of personality. Each is continuously related to the others, as all three structures represent
a continuum rather than discrete and disparate entities.

Freud postulated that the id--the mass of primitive
instinctual life-needs of the organism--comprised the total
psychic apparatus at birth. Out of this initial amorphous
reservoir the ego and superego slowly differentiate and assume distinctive identities.

The id is the psychophysiological source and repository
of the drives, the most primitive part of the mind, totally
unconscious, concerned only with the gratification of
instinctual life-needs. Anna Freud (24) pointed out that we
can never know the id directly, but only as it is filtered
through the operations of the ego. It is the biological substratum of the personality, essentially unmodifiable by
experience with the outside world. Its rootedness in the
biology of the organism is indicated by observable changes
in the degree and direction of the pressures it exerts in the
individual, for example in puberty. The term "id" literally
means "it": and is what we mean when we feel "something
(it) wants me to" or "something (it) made me."

The ego develops out of experience and reason; it is the
"executive of the personality," the integrated self. Its
function Freud saw as achieving viable compromise among
the conflicting demands and pressures of its "three harsh
masters" (32): the id's demand for total and immediate
gratification of impulse; the superego's demand for control,
and often for total suppression, of such impulses; and the
demands of the environmental reality. Its task is therefore
to transmute the primitive needs of the organism into social
modes of expression. Although Freud spoke of the ego as
the "executant" and mediator of the personality, and wrote of
it as "the hope of the world" ("where id was, there shall
ego be") (32), he saw the ego as having no energies of its
own, rather only borrowing the energies of id and superego,
and turning these to its advantage by use of what Munroe
(96) calls "tricks," and Anna Freud (24) termed "defense

mechanisms. " The most well-known of these "defenses"
are repression, suppression, projection, sublimation,
rationalization, undoing, regression, reaction-formation--
although the list is still being lengthened.   Freud saw much
of the activity of the ego as designed to ward off anxiety:
realistic threats to the organism from the outside environment; the pressures of the id which the ego has "learned"--
rightly or wrongly--are dangerous; and the self-condemnation
of the superego.

It remained for the neo-Freudian "ego psychologists"--
Hartmann, Kris, Loewenstein, Rapaport (52, 56, 57, 80)--to
conceptualize the ego as more than Freud's innately helpless
mediator whose "superior knowledge of reality and control
of the pathways of attention, memory and action allow it a
measure of expedient action, but only in the service of the
id and superego" (96).   The ego psychologists carried on
the study of the ego as a structure of the personality with
some autonomy and power of its own, primarily in the
development of the secondary process--those aspects of the
ego that are reality-adapted and derive from maturational
processes: locomotion, cognition, memory, perception, and
rational thought and action.   Hartmann and his colleagues
saw these ego capabilities and functions (Hartmann called
them "apparatuses") as essentially "conflict-free, " regardless of how intimately they may be interwoven with id drives
and superego pressures in everyday life.   Freud assumed
that all behavior is derived from instinctual drives, and
that the ego is also drive-connected, its function arising
out of the necessary conflicts among these drives and between them and reality.   In essence, he saw the ego functions
as biologically-determined givens of the human organism.
Hartmann, in contrast, argued that the ego apparatuses have
a "primary autonomy" of their own, representing an inborn
capacity for pre-adaptiveness to the environment (52).   He
saw the functioning of the ego apparatuses as not only conflict-free, but also as pleasurable in their own right: for
the child, mastery of his own body and of his microcosmic
environment, learning and development of his capacity for
comprehension and thought, is as important as the gratification of impulses and drives.

As the child acquires some capacity to cope with himself
and his world through these primarily autonomous ego
functions, patterns of behavior develop which take on a
"secondary autonomy" of their own. The patterns of behavior so established tend to persist beyond the initial

situation and to become elaborated in their own right--e. g. ,
the habit of cleanliness persists beyond the original training
experience and becomes a persistent behavior pattern.   In
Hartmann's terminology, it has been "neutralized. "   The
energy thus made available to the ego for adaptive behavior,
thought processes, etc. has been "appreciably altered from
its original sexual or aggressive character" (89), i. e. , it
has been freed from its instinctual nature.   It has been
neutralized; rather than being employed in direct drive satisfaction, the energy is now available in the service of the
ego.

Hartmann (54) sums up the value of Freud's structural
construct: "... the demarcation lines of the three systems,
ego, id, superego, are geared to the typical conflicts of
man: conflicts with the instinctual drives, with moral
conscience, and with the outside world.   The paramount
importance on neurotic and normal development of these
conflicts, and of the ways to solve them, was one of the
earliest discoveries of Freud and has remained central in
psychoanalytic practice and theory ever since.   ...   The
systematic and objective study of conflict has remained one
of its essential aspects and has proved a necessary and
fruitful avenue to the explanation of human behavior. "

The ego psychologists differed with Freud regarding his
emphasis on the totally biologic matrix of human personality--
his conclusion, for example, that at birth the human being
is nothing more than raw, undifferentiated id.   They posited
an id-ego matrix from birth, i. e. , that some of the ego
functions and capacities are at least germinally present from
the beginning of life.

The thesis of ego psychology is that although complex
ego organizations of behavior come about initially in connection with drive states, and employ ego apparatuses which
tend to develop autonomously (primary autonomy), they also
have a special autonomy (secondary autonomy) in their own
right.   Hartmann (52) writes, "differentiation progresses not
only through the mastery of new demands and tasks by
creating new apparatuses, but mainly by the latter taking
over, on a higher level, functions which were originally
carried out on a lower level. "

The great contribution of the ego psychologists was
their concept of the ego, the part of the client that the caseworker can see and interact with, his id and superego being

largely unconscious and therefore accessible only through
their ego-derivatives. The ego is something to a great
extent, although not totally, learned, a precipitate of life
experience rather than a biologic given, and therefore
susceptible to further learning through life experience,
including the experience with the caseworker. It is through
the ego that the person "learns from experience to weigh
the advantages and disadvantages of his behavior, to force
the outcome of prospective action, and to suppress and
repress needs, drives, and impulses which endanger himself and others. It is through the ego that the individual
learns by trial and error so that he is prone to repeat
experiences in order to rectify the past. Thus he is capable
of repetition for mastery, hence inclined toward progression
in learning, as differentiated from the uncorrected repetitive
activity implicit in regression" (Towle, 144). Towle continues, "learning throughout life is a nurturing process, in
which the individual seeks, participates, contends, aggressive-
ly demands, or passively expects. These primary patterns
will, of course, be reinforced, modified, and ramified by
other experiences and relationships" (145). The casework
situation is for the client such an "experience" and a "relationship"; its goal--as is the goal of all life processes--is
so to "reinforce, modify, or ramify." Bandler (3), for one,
has written perceptively of such a "life model" for casework
practice. The basic difference, of course, is that the professional participant in this life experience of the client's
assumes responsibility for disciplined control of what occurs,
toward the client's benefit.

Ego psychology has clarified the development of the
secondary process, "the development of those aspects of
the ego that seem to derive from maturation of the reality-
adapted aspects of the organism (rational thought and action,
perception, attention, memory, cognition, locomotion, and
the like), and that may be considered conflict-free in essence,
however intimately they may be interwoven with drives
(instincts) in the course of living" (Munroe, 88). This concept has been of pragmatic usefulness to casework: while
the worker is responsible for diagnosing and understanding
the areas and dynamics of conflict of the client, essentially
what he, and the client, have to work with toward solution of
the difficulty is the conflict-free portion of the client's ego.
It is for this reason that casework lays such emphasis on
inclusion of intrapsychic and situational strengths and resources, as well as limitations and pathology, in casework
psychosocial diagnosis.

Stamm (130) terms ego psychology the "link between psychoanalytically oriented personality theory and theory from the social sciences. " Ego psychology has attempted to bridge and to relate both our "knowledge about personality structure and its interrelationship with social reality" (130), and the earlier Freudian understandings of pathological development and behavior, to normal development and functioning. Ego psychology has gone appreciably beyond the older psychoanalytic hypotheses of behavior in terms of impulses, drives, and emotions alone. It is important to note, however, that ego-psychological concepts do not invalidate the earlier constructs; they are based upon them and have developed and refined them further. Boehm (7) notes that "since the ego is conceived of as that force in the personality which brings the internal person into relationship with the outside world, it is the particular concept of personality which needs to be stressed in regard to social functioning. However, the ego needs to be viewed in re- lation to the other two concepts (id and superego) and in terms of its psychogenetic development. Hence, the student has to know how the ego is formed and shaped in the course of the psychosexual development of the human being and how it is affected at various stages in the life cycle through interaction with the superego and the id. "

Stamm suggests that ego psychology is "an integral part of theory about personality structure and functioning, which provides one set of theoretical constructs from which to ex- plain our case findings ... concepts about the functioning ego form a connecting link between concepts about instinctual drives and unconscious conflicts, and concepts about social role and its ties to the structure and functioning of social institutions. Intrapsychic factors determine the psychological meaning of events and circumstances and, at the same time, situational factors influence ego needs, roles, and adaptive patterns" (132).

One of the most important effects of ego psychology on casework theory and practice has been its impetus to return casework to its focus on the person-in-situation constellation, an integration of the pre-professional concentration on situational factors alone and the later concentration on intra- psychic factors alone. The client comes to the caseworker with a problem in psychosocial functioning--usually definable in terms of role functioning of himself, one or more of his significant others with whom he is interacting, or the role dysfunctioning of one or more of the social institutions and

systems set up to meet his needs. He describes the problem,
and he and the caseworker work out ways to solve or ameliorate it in terms of everyday behavior and attitudes; these are
the material of casework intervention.   Stamm points out that
"everyday behavior is a complex psychosocial phenomenon.
We must analyze it in various ways--as a social role and as
family interaction, as an expression of ideals and values, as
physical processes, as an expression of psychological processes, such as instinctual drives and defensive operations.
Casework practice requires that we use all these frames of
reference" (133).   Stamm goes on to propose that ego
psychology constructs offer such a unifying theory for the
diagnosis and understanding of all these frames of reference,
a way of "pulling together" and extracting meaning and perspective from the worker's various discrete sub-diagnoses;
and therefore also a floor for the worker's design or strategy
of intervention.   The worker is seeking to understand
(diagnose) the level of development of the perceptive, executive, and integrative functions of his client--because, in the
last analysis, these are all he has to work with.   Have the
ego's protective functions ("defenses") been overdeveloped
at the cost of its other equilibrium-maintaining resources?
Or is the client's social situation such that these indeed are
vitally necessary adaptations to his environment (as, for
example, in some delinquents, and in some slum residents)?

     Clinical diagnosis of neurosis, psychosis, or character
disorder becomes much more than a sterile labeling, and
takes on immediate implications for the design of intervention, when it is seen as assessment of the client's ego
functioning and capacities.   The crucial task of differentially
diagnosing whether a client is indeed a neurotic as he appears,
or is actually a "pseudo-neurotic schizophrenic"--a psychotic
barely holding on to his grasp on reality by use of obsessive-
compulsive, or hysterical, or other neurotic mechanisms--
becomes easier when the worker undertakes an analysis of
areas of ego capacity and deficit, and of the fluidity of the
client's ego boundaries.   Borderline and pseudo-neurotic
psychotics are people who "leak": while ego functioning may
be quite good in some areas or under certain circumstances,
in other areas it is strikingly deficient by contrast; and the
"boundary" of the ego, that which gives it its integral
character and which is comparatively inviolable normally
from assaults from the unconscious id or superego, has
gaps in the wall--unconscious material leaks through.   The
task for the caseworker, with a client like this, is to support
the ego defenses he does have--neurotic though they may be--

and to foster and anchor his tenuous ability to relate to
reality. If the client were a neurotic, as he superficially
appears to be, casework treatment would be oriented entirely
differently; thus the crucial importance of differential diagnosis,
and the importance for the casework task of the insights of psychoanalytic theory and of ego psychology in making such diagnostic
assessments. Utilizing the concepts of ego psychology, the caseworker understands that he must identify and work with the "conflict-free" areas of the neurotic's ego, and that in addition to
this, he must actively "loan" his own ego and superego capacities
to the client in whom their development is primitive.

The client's functioning, in turn, must be related to his
social situation, to the kind and degree of presses and supports that exist in his physical and human environment. Is
his situation so stress-producing and depriving of the basic
essentials that all his energies must be directed to his
survival needs--should he be helped to "adjust" to this, or
is the situation itself the focus for intervention? Work with
parents takes on a wider dimension when the worker includes
in his psychosocial assessment, not only the presenting problem, but the capacity of this family to provide for the
children's ego growth. The "immature personality" or
"weak ego" of the client becomes more diagnostically comprehensible to the worker when it is related to a detailed
assessment of particularized ego functions, their weakness
or lack of full development, and the areas of conflict-free
functioning and autonomy. It is Stamm again who points
out that "the caseworker sometimes generalizes about ego
strength and weakness without specifying to what functions
he is referring. Do we mean that the ego has insufficient
energy to control instinctual impulses and selectively to
direct the discharge of tension? Are we referring to an
ego dominated by, or at the service of, aggressive impulses
or to a primitive or distorted superego? Do we mean that
the ego makes a poor choice of defensive reactions or defense mechanisms to handle a problem? Do we mean that
such functions as the perception of reality or thought processes are not at a level appropriate to age and constitutional
equipment? Or are we attempting to describe the general
level of ego organization" (134)?

"Ego psychology... has enriched our understanding of
the nature of self reliance and of the underlying forces
tending to promote or inhibit its development. Formerly,
we tended to note only one aspect of ego function, its
conscious adjustment to the outside environment. Now we
recognize that the ego works unconsciously as well as

consciously, that it faces inward as well as outward, and that, confronted with the id, the superego, and reality, it seeks to realize its interests as best it can" (Garrett, 39).

Casework seeks to engage the functioning-ego part of the client's personality, the ego capacities that are autonomous, successfully adaptive, and relatively free of conflict. This is the part of the client's personality which is capable of learning. Many of casework's techniques, some of which existed long before the influx of psychoanalytic or ego-psychology theory but which have been focused and sharpened by them, are educative techniques: "in casework situations, one by one, can be found elements of a complete educational process" (Hamilton, 46). We have given to the "resilience of the human being" (Hamilton, 50), his capacity to adapt and to learn, a new respect as we have sought to engage with him in finding and fostering these capacities.

The superego is the third and last functional subsystem of personality to be developed. Like the id, the superego is also largely primitive and unconscious, sitting as judge and censor ("conscience"), opposing the free expression of id impulses, but operating with "something of the blind power of the instinctual drives" (89). Freud observed that, "for all their fundamental difference, the id and the super-ego have one thing in common: they both represent the influences of the past--the id the influence of heredity, the super-ego the influence, essentially, of what is taken over from other people--whereas the ego is principally deter-mined by the individual's own experience, that is by acci-dental and contemporary events ... " (25). The superego is the means and process by which the individual makes his heritage--cultural, social, religious and human--truly his own. It is his conscience, his inner discipline, his rules for life, the ideals of his culture, and his own "ego ideal, " that is, his concept of himself.

Freud saw the development of superego as a life-long process, but as given its greatest impetus during the period from about three to six years of age, the time of the oedipal conflict and its resolution. He isolated some of the dynamics operating in this development, primarily the child's identification with his parents, resulting in his intro-jection of their images, their standards, their commands and their prohibitions--the literal taking into his self, on an unconscious level, of these aspects of his parents. The parents'--and later, other authority figures'--values and

standards thus become incorporated into the child's own
developing personality.   While recognition of the existence
and importance of a social dimension is implicit in Freud's
psychology, and particularly in this theory of the development of moral sense, it is contained only implicitly and is
not fully developed.   Freud omitted, for example, to give
explicit attention to other matrices of standard- and value-
formation such as the tremendous influence of the peer
group.   Cultural forces in the development of superego are
also only hinted at.

The level and quality of superego development of the
client, i. e. , the way and the strength with which his
internal behavioral monitoring devices operate, is part of
total psychosocial diagnosis.   The client with a critical,
perfectionistic superego is difficult for both himself and his
significant others to live with.   The worker must have some
understanding of how this came about in order to respond
effectively to the client so burdened--is he, for example,
still carrying on his back the criticism, expectations,
domination of parents perhaps long since dead?   If his
earlier learning took place within the context of such a demanding and frustrating relationship, then what kind of
corrective relationship, to permit new learning, does he
need from the worker now?

Since the superego is largely unconscious, the worker's
treatment route to it is via the client's ego processes--in
the case of this kind of client, a relationship that reflects
the kind of acceptance and sustenance that the client cannot
give himself, and that enables him to perceive and identify
with the worker's more reasonable superego expectations--
plus possibly also what Hollis (67) calls "reflective discussion" or "direct influence" concerning the appropriateness
in the light of reality of the client's rigid self-expectations.
Towle (146) makes the essential point that such a person
does not really have an integrated superego of his own: he
has merely grafted on that of others; and Wheelis (152)
points out that the strength of the superego is reciprocal to
the strength of the ego.   To this extent, it is erroneous to
refer to such a client as suffering from a "too-strong"
superego; rather, he has never really developed this aspect
of his personality.   The goal of casework with such an
individual is to provide him with an atmosphere and a
relationship in which he can resume the learning and growth
process that was earlier frustrated.

The client also loosely described as having a too-
rigid superego may reflect a different set of psychodynamic
needs and motivations: the person, for example, who sacri-
fices for others, allows himself to be dominated and exploited
out of an apparent conviction that more is expected of him
than anyone else and he is more deserving of criticism and
censure of less-than-perfect performance, is often in effect
deviously demonstrating his moral superiority. He too has
introjected too-extreme parental expectations, but out of his
resentment has actually gone the parents one better. When
in his life situations he continues to fail his (the parents')
exorbitant standards, there is a ring of childlike "so there"
satisfaction at the same time as he castigates himself for
his inadequacies--almost as if he were saying to parents,
"well, you were convinced I'd never amount to much, are
you satisfied now?" In the backwards sort of way characteristic of neurotics, the client with this kind of superego
problem is actually battling for a sense of his own identity.
For the worker to assume that he needs exactly the same
sort of nurturing, warm, guilt-reducing relationship as the
client in our previous illustration, and to fail to recognize
the unconscious "games" he is playing, will probably produce
only a worker frustrated, puzzled, and angered by the
client's skill in outmaneuvering him in order to maintain his
distorted convictions. What this client needs, in contrast,
is not a focus on the superego problem, which here is only
symptomatic, but on his negativistic but real search for a
sense of himself. Casework treatment would here take the
form of the worker's declining to assume for the client the
responsibility for his behavior that the latter is attempting
to foist upon him.

Or yet another kind of rigid superego problem: the
person who has been traumatized by his relationship with
an authoritarian, often punitive, parent, to the extent that
his only way to protect himself from the parent has been
to become him--to destroy and at the same time retain him
by assuming the authority role. These are the men, for
example, who are punitive and brutal to their sons, but who
describe their own hatred and fear, as children, of a father
just like themselves. This client's need to be the petty
martinet is his way of expressing his love and hate for the
original authority in his life; all that he has suffered himself must be suffered also by those whom he dominates, and
he must demonstrate his love for his father by becoming
just like him. This client sees any relationship in terms of
a power struggle; and this struggle the worker must win--but

not in the same way and by the same means as the client attempts to do. This client respects only strength, and he must be convinced that the worker is strong, that he cannot dominate or bully or corrupt him. If the client can come to perceive the worker as strong but not cruel, authoritative but not authoritarian, unable to be controlled but not controlling, this is the "corrective experience" for this client.

It is therefore not enough merely to label: the worker must be able to identify not only deficits in superego functioning, but also to understand the why of it for each unique client.

Underdevelopment of superego, or superego "lacunae" as found in the character disorder, some borderline personalities, some delinquents and addicts, needs to be as accurately diagnosed, and responded to by the worker's actively loaning some of his own better-developed and integrated ego and superego capacities. This may take the form, in some instances such as protective services to abusing or neglectful parents, of intervening very directly in the social reality and by use of authority and social control.

One of the reasons why Freud's clinical case material seems today rather foreign to our own case experience, is that the kind of patient he dealt with in fin de siècle Austria is comparatively rarely met in practice today. Pollak (107) argues that the conditions of our present-day American culture tend to create, not Freud's classic anxiety hysteric for whom repressed and distorted sexual needs seemed to be the root of psychic evil, but the character disorder--the client characterized not by an excess of repression but by its deficiency, impulse-ridden, whose problems and symptoms are ego-syntonic rather than painfully experienced as ego-dystonic, suffering from gaps in ego development and lacunae in superego structure. Pollens (109) notes that Freud experienced most of his successes with patients suffering from symptom neuroses, and failed with psychosis, character and behavior disorders; and suggests that this was because he focused on oedipal pathology and kept distance from the preoedipal disturbances. Spotnitz (129) holds that "preverbal patterns are responsive only to symbolic, emotional, and reflective interventions. Affective nonverbal communications ... give the preoedipal personality freedom to grow."

Someone has said that sex was once the "dirty little
secret" that many of us carried guiltily buried; today it is
the wish to make money. Today sex is considered "not only
a virtue but almost an obligation" (58); the sexual repression
so evident in some of Freud's patients has lessened in
contemporary America, but one may question whether "compulsive sexual activity is fundamentally more healthy than
compulsory sexual repression" (58). The free expression
of violence and aggression is coming to be perceived as a
right. The American social scene of today seems to be
characterized more by a sexual and aggressive diarrhea,
than the sexual and emotional constipation of Freud's day.

The caseworker's treatment response to either kind of
client--the neurotic or pseudoneurotic psychotic with overly-
rigid superego, or the client whose superego functions on a
primitive level or with appreciable "gaps," is at base the
same although the worker's specific activities may indeed
vary greatly. In essence, the worker is offering to each
client a socializing and learning experience within the context of the casework relationship--a time-compressed re-
capitulation of the kind of giving but expecting relationship
with parental figures years earlier that, if he had then been
provided with it, would have provided the matrix for more
normal superego development. The worker is providing a
"corrective emotional experience," a matrix of carefully
controlled conditions within which the client may resume the
interrupted process of growth--to greater or lesser extent,
and always with realistic goals in terms of overall psychosocial diagnosis.

As social casework has integrated more some of the insights of the social sciences, it has developed increased
sophistication about the way in which cultural, class, and
other social group expectations shape its clients' view of
themselves and the world--their superegos; and the way in
which such conditioning is also shaping the middle-class
practitioner's perception of what is "right" and expectable
behavior (see, for example, Kluckhohn, 79).

A Black welfare mother's, or Puerto Rican, or Mexican-
American client's perception of time, or of "responsibility,"
may be very different from (and possibly philosophically and
pragmatically superior to) the worker's. Without a perceptive-
ness of broader social and cultural conditioning influences
on his and his client's value orientations, the worker may
erroneously diagnose inadequate superego development in a

client whose superego is quite adequate--just different. It
may well be that this kind of client should have help in recognizing and modifying some of his own culturally-derived perceptions and behavior when these are clearly inappropriate
for functional use in his present social reality--when his
different regard for time, for example, or the "responsibility"
owed to an employer, endangers the job he wants to keep.
The worker must, however, have a comprehensive grasp of
the meaning to the client of his cultural and social referents,
to enable him to do so and yet hold on to his cultural
identity. The worker must also be sensitively aware that
life is very different for many of his clients than it is for
him, that patterns of behavior and reaction that would be
considered dysfunctional or pathological in the worker's
personal world may be highly functional in the survival-
oriented world of the client.

    5) The economic dimension of Freud's theory of
personality holds that all behavior is regulated by, and its
function is to dispose of, psychological energy. In this,
Freud presaged Cannon's (13) idea of "homeostasis"--the
tendency of the organism to maintain a state of equilibrium;
and some of the concepts of modern General Systems Theory,
particularly those of "entropy" and "feedback. "

    The economic is therefore a quantitative dimension,
treating of the internal quantity and transfer of energies.
Qualitatively there may be little difference between normal
and pathological processes or even conflicts; it is the
quantities, the economy, of the shifting internal equilibrium,
the strength of a particular force or of its counterforces of
ego repression, superego prohibition, etc. that tip the balance
for the individual toward psychic stability or instability.
The kind and manner of this upset or disequilibrium will be
determined by a number of factors: the previous structural
levels of development and structural alliances of the personality; the operational efficiency of such structures as ego and
superego; the adaptive ego-devices that have been learned
from previous life experiences; the quantity and quality of
libidinal and aggressive demands of the organism (for example, the heightening of these in adolescence); "fixation" at
an earlier level of psychosexual maturation, or around some
"trauma" that has caused intense cathexis; or the impingement of exogenous interpersonal or social circumstance.

Rapaport (111) points out that psychological energies "cannot be expressed in the mathematical formulas in which physics expresses its energy concepts, yet they are referents of phenomena which seem to abide by the laws of energy exchanges--conservation, entropy, least action. " He compares the principle of conservation of energy to the psychoanalytic proposition that cathexes (energy) are never lost, and are "traceable in the expenditures and transformations of cathexes involved in psychological forces. " The principle of entropy Rapaport sees as implicit in "the much misconstrued pleasure principle: drive energy tends toward discharge (i. e. , diminution of tension). "   And the principle of least action is subsumed in the Freudian formulation that "processes involving cathexes other than those of basic drives operate so as to expend the least amount of cathexis. "

The human psychic organism can thus be viewed as an open "system" (4), in which psychological energies, derived either totally from the organism's own innate biologic drives, or from the interaction of its drive-needs with the demands and opportunities of the environment, are expressed, discharged, dammed up, stored, or transformed into thought and action by means of what Freud conceptualized as the various structures, layers, and apparatuses of the personality. Ego operations perform, in part, as the "boundary" of the system, "whose function is to filter or select inputs and outputs" (5).   Both ego and superego functions serve to provide "feedback loops" and "storage" (6).

The economic aspect of internal personality integration, and the economics of the personality's transactions with its social environment, are implicit in casework theory and practice but have not been explicitly focused upon in casework literature to any great extent.   Yet we know from empirical practice experience that the operative dynamics of a person, or of a client group such as the family, may shift dramatically with varying quantitative pressures from within and without.   Such a perspective on the economic aspects of human functioning underlies, for example, Hollis' notion (73) of the "press" and "stress" in the person-in-situation gestalt, casework integration of crisis theory (99), and such casework treatment modalities as family therapy. Casework students sometimes have difficulty initially in seeing beyond the need merely to identify forces, functions, mechanisms that are operating within the client or the family, to the need to assess the relative weighting and balance of these, the dynamic fashion in which they interact--"the

psychodynamics of the case." Perspective has returned to
casework in assessing the relative force of situational press
impinging on the client, and the dynamic economics of how he
perceives and reacts to that press so that it becomes either
stress or challenge. Economically, the psychotic is being
swamped by his unrepressed id and superego unconscious
forces; the integrity of his ego boundaries has been broached
and there is not a sufficient quantum of ego energies as
counterforces to hold the flood at bay. The obsessive-compul-
sive neurotic has too tight and rigid an ego and superego,
dynamic energies are too narrowly constricted and bound
down, there is not enough free flow of energies within the
personality.

   Implicit, therefore, in all casework study, diagnosis,
and intervention is an economic perspective of the client,
his situation, and the dynamic interaction between them.
Recognition of this relative weighting of forces and resources,
both within and without, directs the caseworker's clinical
judgment as to the point on the person-situation continuum at
which to intervene, and shapes the specific mode of intervention. Assessment of the economic weightings and equilibria involved in the client's intrapsychic functioning, his
interpersonal transactions, and his interactions with his
social environment, helps to answer such practice questions
as: what is the relative force and weighting of libidinal and
aggressive needs? Of their ego and superego counterforces
in this individual? What is the equilibrium in this marriage
or this family, what are the economics of the pushes and
pulls among the members? If the relationships were better
at some earlier time, how and why did the balance change?
Is the problem of this child in the family actually not only
an expression of a total family dysfunction, but perhaps also
a way for other members, individually, or for the total
family group, to maintain its homeostasis? What will happen
to the rest of the family if one member changes and disturbs
the equilibrium? Does this welfare mother, burdened and
harassed by a destructive reality situation, have sufficient
quantity of inner resource so that she can "make it" if the
worker can provide some relief from the external pressures?
And since, by virtue of the caseworker's entry into the
client/situation configuration, a new component has been
added to the system, how can the worker use his dynamic
role as part of the client's or client group's system to bring
about change in that system's economic equilibrium?

Psychoanalysis as a Method of Treatment

Certain concepts and techniques are seen as central to the psychoanalytic method of psychotherapy: "free association," the therapist's role as a "blank screen," the recovery of the repressed," interpretation of dreams, insight development and "working through," resistance, and the handling in treatment of the "transference neurosis." Some are not relevant to casework's focus and goals; others are relevant only with modification to fit them into casework's unique practice; and some have had a major impact upon both our theory and our practice.

Free association is the "basic rule" of psychoanalytic therapy: the requirement that the patient verbalize every stream-of-consciousness thought, feeling, and memory that undirectedly arises, regardless of how apparently insignificant, embarrassing, or painful. The treatment situation is structured so as to "leave the patient ... alone with his thoughts" (92) as much as possible; the therapist (both by his physical position out of sight behind the couch and by his attitude) is an outside interpreter rather than a realistic participant. Freud's experience with this technique was that it tended to encourage the emergence of repressed memories and other unconscious material ordinarily not available to the ego processes of consciously controlled thought.

Free association is patently not an appropriate technique for social casework, which never is focused on the deliberate bringing into consciousness of such repressed material, but rather on the conscious ego capacities of the client and his real-life situation. Our intellectual knowledge of the psychoanalytic technique and its effects may have had some influence, however, on the pre-Freudian predilection of casework for a barrage of questions as the style of social study; we learned something about how to listen. We learned that, for many people in our hectic time and culture, to have found someone who is able and willing to listen responsively is "therapeutic" in and of itself. We learned that, for all but the most disturbed client, as he talks he hears himself talking; and he is placed in a position of assessing, weighing, judging what he is saying--in short, his own ego capacities are brought to bear. Fenichel (21) says, "the verbalization of unclear worries alone brings relief," because an ego can face verbalized ideas better than unclear emotional sensations. "

Inexperienced caseworkers sometimes have difficulty in
handling silences in the casework interview, until they learn
how to listen to the silence and what it means, to "hear"
the kinds of two-way nonverbal communications that are very
actively transpiring. There are angry silences, fearful
silences, teasing or awkward or comfortable or thoughtful
silences. The worker's silence can also speak to the client,
sometimes more loudly and more convincingly than the
spoken word.

Ruesch (120) termed communication the central ingredient
in all "mental healing. " We learned from psychoanalysis,
and then refined in our own practice, that there are many
more forms of communication than words. For some
clients--children, the deprived, some psychotics, some immature personalities--action by the worker indeed "speaks
louder than words" and such a client is often not even able
to hear the worker's words unless he has first been communicated with, reached, on the nonverbal level that is
meaningful to him.

New caseworkers often struggle also in learning how to
focus, learning to what extent to permit and encourage the
client to talk in his own way, at his own pace, and about
what he wants to talk about--and to what extent the worker,
as the professional "other" in the transaction, is still
responsible for focusing the interview and keeping it on
track. Both of course obtain, as the exigencies of the case
situation and the particular interview require; but one of the
things we learned from psychoanalysis was that in the last
account (with the obvious exception of concrete needs which
the worker has it in his power to meet by use of services
or social resources), the client "owns" his problem, and
that he will solve it in the way that is right for him. Caseworkers learned not to move in too fast with queries, or
advice, or reassurance; to let the client "tell it like it is"
in his way and at his pace, and so to provide an atmosphere
in which he begins, as he talks and describes his situation,
how he feels about it and how he would like to change it, to
bring his own ego capacities to bear, to begin to see it in
different and more accurate perspective, and so to take the
first step toward handling it more constructively. The caseworker's ability to question, selectively, at appropriate
points in the interview and in a way that helps the client to
maintain focus, is one of the basic skills of casework.

The blank screen concept of the helping person is also
not applicable to casework. It is a sine qua non of casework
that a real worker is involved with a real client concerning
a real-life situation; and that the casework experience is itself a slice of real, alive, pulsating life between two flesh
and blood human beings interacting with each other on a
meaningful human level. Casework's whole focus on reality,
on the real problem and the actual current capacities and
resources of the client and his situation, militates against
the wholesale importing of such a therapeutic technique into
our practice.

We learned something here too, however: to look critically and honestly at our need to "save," to be the giver, the
solver, the source of all help. There are case situations
where to swamp the client with the worker's "warmth" and
need to demonstrate helpfulness means to snuff out what are
perhaps his first efforts to come to grips with his situation
himself; or clients who are frightened by the worker's attempt
to come too close to them emotionally; or clients who, because of experience that has bred mistrust in human relationships, are rendered all the more suspicious and hostile.
And there are casework situations where the worker needs
to move in with just this kind of emotional sustenance, and/
or its concrete expression in terms of services or assumption
of a brokerage or advocacy role. "Relationship" is the
essential basis of all casework intervention, the medium on
which all our treatment techniques--psychological or social
--are "floated." Boehm (8) paraphrases Hollis to the effect
that "the only criterion of the value of a treatment method
is its appropriateness, i. e. , what is most likely to help in
a given situation ... hence, one treatment method is not
inherently superior to another." The treatment technique
and the use of the relationship are differential: they hinge
on differential diagnosis of who this client is, what is his
situation, and what he needs of the worker.

Freud's other major technique for acquiring access to
the unconscious of his patients was dream analysis, which
he considered so important that he termed it "the royal road
to the unconscious." In psychoanalytic therapy, the two
techniques focused on unconscious material are combined:
the patient reports and describes his dreams, and then is
asked to free-associate to them. Since every dream is
always the "product of highly idiosyncratic unconscious
systems" (90), and is multiply-determined, it can be understood on many levels simultaneously, and may indeed offer

the analyst and the patient insight into the latter's more buried needs and conflicts.

Since casework does not deal with such "buried" material directly, but only as it is expressed via ego-derivatives, dream analysis has not been a technique appropriate for social casework. This does not mean that on occasion a caseworker may not discuss some dream material with a client if this has been disturbing to the client (as in our earlier illustration); and the worker may indeed ask the client what is his perception of and reaction to the dream experience. The difference lies in the distinctive ways the psychoanalyst and the caseworker would handle such material: the caseworker's focus is on relating the dream content to a reality and ego-accessible focus, rather than emphasis on interpretation of the unconscious content itself. It is crucial that the worker be aware of some of the unconscious meanings of the material--but he would probably respond to the hypothetical client in our illustration by "universalizing" that her experience is not as shocking or unusual in reality as she perceives it, that most parents at times get tired of the worry and responsibility of parenthood and a dream such as she describes seems--in the sleep state--an easy way to obtain relief; and then would use the situation as a springboard, to different degrees and depth depending on the client, for discussion of her confusion between what she may feel is the magical power of her wishes and thoughts and the reality difference between this and what she actually does, or her anger and guilt toward her child, or whatever is germane to the needs of this particular client at this time. The focus in casework is always on the worker's diagnostic understanding of the meaning, conscious and unconscious, of the client's verbalizations and behavior; but response to the client is in terms of what is "ego-handleable" and reality-oriented.

Recovery of the repressed as a goal of psychoanalytic therapy is implied in the above techniques of free association and dream analysis. Little need be added at this point other than the obvious that this also is not a goal of social casework, which respects the ego defense of repression, is aware that since it is a deeply unconscious mechanism, it is therefore not accessible to casework techniques anyway; and which has recognized from its practice experience that the goal of casework--for example, with the psychotic or borderline client--is often to strengthen the forces of repression rather than attempting to dilute them. Even with the better-integrated client, the experienced casework practitioner recognizes that so primitive and deep-seated a defense of the personality exists for a purpose, is helping to maintain inner equilibrium, and should not be tampered with.

With certain more psychologically disturbed clients, who spontaneously produce unconscious material, or with some clients as the result of the transference situation despite the worker's attempts to control transference (and the kind of client who develops such an intense, unconscious-releasing transference is often quite disturbed), the worker's response is still directed toward helping the client to focus on reality and to reinstate repression.

Interpretation of the psychodynamic meaning of the patient's thoughts, feelings, and attitudes, especially in terms of their psychogenetic origin, is the hallmark of psychoanalytic therapy. Its goal is the development of "insight." "Psychoanalytic therapy started with catharsis and shifted to insight" (Alexander et al, 2). This technique has been adopted in modified form by casework, for those clients for whom it is appropriate. We venture to submit that casework's recognition that the proportion of clients for whom this technique and goal of help are appropriate is comparatively small, was in advance of the later similar recognition by psychoanalysis and other schools of "insight" therapy.

The focus of insight treatment is to "broaden the ego so that a portion of it can stretch away from the other portions to attain enough distance for an observing function to emerge and look at the experiencing functions" (Hammer, 51). Its goal is to help the individual achieve more understanding and control of himself, by his conscious, reasoning, directing ego. (Erikson referred to this aspect of psychoanalysis as the "first systematic and active consciousness-expansion" (17).) As such, interpretation by the worker aimed toward development of insight by the client, is an extremely useful technique of casework--but only when properly defined in the casework context, and when appropriate to the individualized needs of the client.

Hamilton (47) subsumes what she terms "clarification" under interpretation, oriented toward "giving (the client) insight into her feelings, but not their motivation. Unconscious material is not provoked or elicited, but unconscious derivatives are handled in relation to reality. Specific defenses are commented upon from time to time." Interpretation at one level or another is implied in three of Hollis' (68) treatment classifications: "reflective consideration of the current person-situation configuration," reflection by the client on "the dynamics of his response patterns and tendencies," and "procedures for encouraging the client to think about the development of his response patterns or tendencies."

In casework, interpretation aimed at development of insight by the client may be geared toward a variety of foci, or at several different levels. It may involve helping a character-disordered client to recognize that he does have a problem--the neglectful mother, for example, or the client who is inappropriately unconcerned about his pattern of losing jobs because of his conviction that it is always the boss's fault--aimed toward making ego-alien what has been ego-syntonic, and toward generating some focused appropriate anxiety for use in treatment. Interpretation may concern patterns of communication--the marital partners who seem unaware of the way one or both speak for the other, or cut each other off, or engage in "double-bind" communication. It may involve helping a family group to recognize what they are saying and doing to, and asking from, each other. Interpretation may be directed toward a client's defensive behavior of rationalization, intellectualization, avoidance, defensive hostility, etc. It may be oriented toward helping a client recognize that the perfectionistic, self-critical standards of his severe superego are much harsher than those of other people. Interpretation may be used to draw to the client's attention patterns in the characteristic ways he relates to other people, or seems to expect the worst of himself, or tends to withdraw when frightened or under stress. Or it may be related to helping the client to see the associations and links between the past and the present so he can better understand and control some of his behavior and attitudes-- the wife, for example, who unleashes on her mother-in-law all the pent-up resentment she has felt for years but has never dared express toward her own critical, ungiving mother. Interpretation, on a very simple level, can be enormously helpful to the confused psychotic who literally does not know that the painful internal upset he is experiencing is called "feeling sad" or "being mad at," and which therefore is a common human experience and something that makes him more like, not different from, other people. Or interpretation may be related to helping the defeated, hopeless client perceive that he does have strengths and abilities with which he is not crediting himself.

Inexperienced practitioners, and students, often become confused about the proper place of interpretation in casework treatment. Some will not risk anything that smacks of "confrontation" for fear that such might damage the relationship--not recognizing that a relationship this wobbly wasn't much to begin with; or that they are intruding into psychiatric territory; or that their role with the client is always to give and to support, never to expect or to challenge. More intellectualized students, on the other hand, who have done some reading on their own or perhaps have had a therapeutic experience themselves, attempt to impose upon the casework situation with their clients a preconceived notion that only achievement of insight by the client into the genetic roots of his difficulty is truly "therapeutic," this based on the naive misperception that insight-oriented intervention is "better" than other forms of treatment, or somehow carries more status. These students need to learn that understanding of psychodynamics is for the worker, not necessarily the client; and that they do not have to share everything they know with the client. They need to learn, too, that casework is a more difficult art than the mere parroting back to the client of what they have learned.

Some of this confusion concerning the proper place in casework of interpretation has to do with the artificial dichotomy sometimes made in casework literature between "supportive" and "insight-oriented" treatment. This tends to give the impression that, when "supporting" a client, one must never interpret; and that in "insight-oriented" intervention the worker is not also supportive. The practitioner experienced with clients, however, knows that in every case there is some mixture of both nurture and expectation in varying proportions according to the needs of the client, the goals, and the timing. Differential balancing of these two components may indeed vary with the same client within the same interview. Students sometimes achieve the misperception that "supportive treatment" means "being nice" to the client; it takes time, and experience, for them to see that "support" is a transitive verb and therefore takes an object--they must be clear about specifically what they are supporting, and why.

The concept of interpretation, borrowed from psychoanalysis, has, like some other aspects of that theory and technique, sometimes been shallowly understood and thus misapplied. Inexperienced practitioners, or those who have identified closely with psychiatric mentors, might see inter-

pretation as inherently "superior" to other forms of intervention, and set insight as the "best" goal of treatment.
This ignores the crucial intermediary step of diagnosis--of
who this client is and what he needs. If such interpretive
techniques are erroneously "applied" (like a mustard plaster)
to a client for whom they are not appropriate, and who needs
something else from the worker, then at best the result may
be an aborted case, and at worst a cruelly unhelpful experience for a client who has asked for bread only to be given
a stone. Boehm (8) speaks to this misperception in the
field, which he sees as rather common: that the closeness
of casework ". . . to the psychoanalytic model and the implication that psychologically caused problems can best be
treated by psychological means has facilitated the impression
frequently held by students and practitioners that treatment,
to be effective and lasting, needs to seek internal changes.
Perhaps the phrase 'changes brought about within the individual' has given rise to the assumption that in the last
analysis all problems of social functioning can be traced
and, ideally, should be traceable to psychological causes,
that only limitation of skill and knowledge, as well as of
time, agency function, and facility in practice, cause the
use of other methods thought by definition to be less thorough.
This position also has given rise to a frequently held notion,
often explicitly stated, that treatment activities directed toward other than internal changes are less worthwhile--hence,
the prestige of settings and methods of treatment where
psychotherapeutic techniques are thought (often erroneously)
to be in use. This position in some instances has actually
caused workers to view clients' needs as requiring psychotherapeutic activities, another example of the self-fulfilling
prophecy. "

    Sometimes agencies become caught up in the kind of
circular reasoning to which Boehm refers, with the result
that the diagnosis and treatment plan may be, in effect, pre-
set and determined before the client ever gets to the agency.
If the mind-set of an agency or clinic is that all problems
of all clients are caused by intrapsychic pathology alone,
and that the treatment for intrapsychic pathology must be
"intensive long-term psychoanalytically oriented psychotherapy, " then this is the diagnosis and treatment plan
imposed on the client, regardless of what he describes as
his problem, and regardless of whether this is what he
needs or whether it will do him any good. Since everyone
has some intrapsychic pathology of some sort and degree
and/or many things can be made to fit this rubric, material

which emerges in the course of therapy is then used to justify the diagnosis and treatment.

"Interpretation, " as narrowly and technically defined by psychoanalysis, does refer to making conscious the un-conscious, to helping the patient to recognize consciously and to deal with his "id-bits. " This narrow semantical use of the term is perhaps part of the reason why confusion has arisen as to its appropriateness in casework treatment. As used in casework, its meaning is much broader--as in the examples noted above--and caseworkers are more experienced with the flexible use of interpretation with many different kinds of clients, and in many different ways, than are psycho-analysts.

Casework has known for years (but did not effectively communicate to practitioners of other disciplines) that people are effectively helped by techniques other than interpretation and insight; that these are not appropriate for all clients or perhaps even for the majority; and that sometimes real personality change is observed as a result of a casework experience that did not include interpretive techniques by the worker or achievement of insight by the client. The notion that only through insight can change in functioning or solution of a life problem come about, is now under increasing criticism by both psychoanalysts and practitioners of other psychotherapeutic schools. Hobbs (59) avers, "... the accept-ance of insight as the sovereign remedy for all neuroses re-presents both an unwarranted extrapolation from Freud's position and a failure to take into account the kinds of neuroses generated by Viennese life at the turn of the century and by American or European life today. Freud could not have been more explicit in insisting that his method worked best, if not solely, in cases of massive repression with accompanying conversion symptomatology. Contemporary culture often produces a kind of neurosis different from that described by Freud ... characterized not so much by repression and conversion as by an awful awareness and a merciless raw anxiety. " Hobbs criticizes the therapeutic benefit to the patient of the therapist's inter-pretations (as defined psychoanalytically): "... the occurrence of an insight merely means that the client is catching on to the therapist's personal system for interpreting the world of behavior. The therapist does not have to be right; he mainly has to be convincing" (59). He points out that psychothera-pists of very different theoretical persuasions, whose inter-pretations to their patients therefore reflect these quite

different frames of reference, seem to get just about the
same results. Hobbs' definition (60) of insight is that it is
"manifested when a client makes a statement about himself
that agrees with the therapist's notions of what is the matter
with him"; and concludes that this "is not a particularly useful formulation." Psychoanalyst Allen Wheelis (153) takes a
more moderate view, and reflects the usefulness of interpretation and insight for casework intervention: "insight will
never again appear to (the psychoanalyst) as the irresistible
instrument of personality change which once it seemed, but
it will always be a useful tool to have near at hand".

Casework uses interpretation when, in the worker's
clinical judgment and according to his differential diagnosis,
he decides that this will be of use to the particular client.
Casework, however, has a much broader role repertoire to
offer the client than the narrow role set borrowed from
psychoanalysis of interpretive therapist only. The "social
therapy" component of casework as a psychosocial method
of intervention has until recently been derogated in favor of
the psychotherapy component; we are today learning anew
that engagement by the worker in a variety of practice roles
other than the psychotherapeutic model, such as broker,
advocate, mediator, teacher, social parent, guide, normative
model, family system participant, demonstrator--in short,
active intervener and participant in the client's life systems--
is often more effective in many situations. The client who
has secured the wherewithal for a decent level of life when
this is lacking, or who has experienced the active participation and guidance of the worker in his healthy struggle
against a noxious environment may have been helped far
more effectively--subjectively in terms of his feeling about
himself and his enhanced ego capacities for coping, as well
as objectively--than if he had spent weeks relating only to
his subjective inner life. The client who has grown within
the context of a relationship with a worker who served for
him as a parent, a normative model, and a teacher, may
have done so without one interpretation having been offered.

We are by no means derogating the importance of understanding and relating to the person in the person-situation
configuration (a real danger that exists, it would seem, in
our present emphasis on situational factors alone); to the
contrary, we are underlining the subjective, personality-en-
hancing, and ego-fostering effects on this "person" of an
experience with the worker in which he finds that worker
acutely concerned with him as a person and with the realities

of his life, willing to become involved with both, and not
needing to fit him into some preconceived model of "proper"
treatment but sensitively responsive to what is needed.

Casework has been in advance of psychoanalytic therapy
in its recognition that for most of the clients with whom we
deal, it is the relationship with the worker that serves as
the "corrective experience," and as the basis for any other
techniques of intervention that are brought to bear. We know
that the relationship itself is for most clients the aspect of
the experience with the worker that he "takes home with
him," more important than any insight he may have picked
up along the way. At the least, the relationship is an
experience for the client--perhaps one of the few such he
has had--that he is entitled to what playwright Arthur Miller
claims as the basic right of every individual: "attention
must be paid." An experience in which he is treated as a
person entitled to respectful attention and thoughtful concern,
and the total commitment of the worker's skills and brain
and experience, is "therapeutic" in itself for many clients.
For many, the "corrective emotional experience" of what
Hobbs (60) describes as a "sustained experience of intimacy
with another human being without getting hurt" is what is
meaningful to the client, and what frees him to grow and to
cope better with his life. For many others, the experience
with the worker is a laboratory in which to try out new ways
of relating to others and of perceiving themselves, as this
is lived out through the relationship with the worker itself.

A component of the casework process which has not been
explored and developed to any extent is treatment as an
educational process. The further development of learning
theory and its integration by casework into our current
understanding of ego psychology and into the body of casework theory itself, may be a needed next step in our professional development. Behavior modification theory and
practice have a place here, although they are excessively
narrow. Certainly, however, every casework experience
that is a "good" one for the client, meaning effective, is a
learning experience; but we have not looked in a focused
way at precisely what are the educational and learning components in the process: to use sociobehavioral nomenclature,
how are some of the activities and responses of the worker
"reward" or "punishment," "extinction" or "shaping"? What
other components of the way that people learn, i. e., the way
that the ego grasps, digests, and assimilates new knowledge
or new mastery, are characteristic of casework treatment?

Hobbs (61) implies this question, and in effect echoes
Boehm: "Faced with a breakdown of personal functioning,
we seem to assume that the development of understanding
itself is a sufficient intervention to correct the difficulty.
If a person can be helped to understand the origins and
current manifestations of his neurotic behavior, particularly
if he feels deeply while he is gaining this insight, the
neurotic behavior should disappear. A good rational question
is: Why should it disappear unless appropriate learning
experiences follow?"

We may perhaps sum up the utility of interpretation and
insight for casework by quoting Wheelis (154) to the effect
that "psychoanalysis has only insight to offer"--but casework
has, not only insight for those for whom it is appropriate,
but much more.

Working-through is a valuable concept that casework has
borrowed from psychoanalysis. It means simply that people
learn slowly, that it takes time to integrate new ways of behaving, to give up some of the ingrained expectations and
attitudes engendered by past experience. The client characteristically moves ahead two steps, and falls back one.
The same issues, fears, decisions, must often be "worked
through" over and over before the client can really assimilate
them and make them his own. This concept is related somewhat to the foregoing concerning interpretation: the client
will not and does not accept the worker's suggestions or
interpretations merely because they are the worker's (although he may indeed appear to, out of a need to be com-
pliant, fear of displeasing the worker, emotional bribery, or
any other of a host of reasons). The worker's interpretations
or advice or clarifications must be made his own by the
client. Most caseworkers have had the experience of a
client expounding to them about a decision or idea, or
attitude or insight that he is sure is totally original--but
which the worker recognizes as something he suggested
weeks before, and which the client perhaps even resisted
vigorously at that time.

Working-through is a learning process, and we have only
recently begun to look at casework treatment as a learning
experience for the client. We do know that in social work
education (see, for example, Towle, 142), learning demonstrates this "backing and filling" process, and that there
are times when the student seems to have hit a plateau at
which all learning and integration appears to cease. We

have learned from educational experience, however, that this
phenomenon is much like the physiological plateau of the
young child who loses his appetite for days or even weeks
at a time; but he is not ill, has not stopped growing, is
merely marshaling his physiological resources, integrating
the gains he has made previously, in preparation for the
next big push of growth that is soon to come and that his
body is instinctively preparing for.

We also know--or at least suspect--that the integrative
or learning process in maladaptive and adaptive behavior is
much the same (see, for example, the classic attempt to
apply learning theory to psychotherapy of Dollard and Miller,
14). To some extent, then, the casework experience may
be, partially at least, an unlearning experience for the client
in its initial phases, before he can move on to re-learning.
Towle (147) notes, "often the learning task implied in (the
client's) current experience has become traumatic, sometimes
even to the extent that goal-striving has broken down. In
these instances the initial charge on the social worker is
that of helping the client find new goals, adapt old goals, or
resume pursuit of abandoned goals." Hobbs (61) also speaks
of the therapeutic experience as one of "specific and concrete opportunities for learning new ways of responding, new
ways of relating to other people, and new ways of perceiving
oneself. The stress is on immediate experience and specific
behaviors."

Resistance, as technically defined in psychoanalysis,
refers to the patient's efforts to maintain repression against
emerging unconscious material and forces; in effect, against
the analysis which is attempting to loosen the repression.
More broadly defined, resistance refers to the paradoxical
proclivity of human beings to reject irrationally with one
part of themselves that which they also rationally and consciously desire. ("Each man kills the thing he loves.")
Like transference, resistance is often a less-than-conscious
phenomenon; and the two concepts are often closely related
in practice. The client, for example, who rejects the
worker's help because of the negative transference in which
he is caught up, and which leads him to perceive the worker
as "just like" his critical, dominating mother, is manifesting
resistance. Or the client who with one part of himself does
want help, but finds himself struggling against it because it
seems to him that otherwise he will be swallowed up, will
lose his identity and be forever dependent. The Rankian
("functional") school of casework contributed some valuable

insights in understanding the ways in which ambivalence and resistance are manifested in a treatment situation. Virginia Robinson (119) propounded the perspective of that school in understanding resistance: "this principle for which every name is misleading, call it will, ego, or self, is fundamentally resistive to change from without and is even slow to recognize as its own and accept responsibility for any process of change from within. Its fear of loss of its own identity and control may inhibit even its normal growth process. "

It is obviously crucial to distinguish such irrational resistance from rational factors such as the initial reluctance or inhibition of many clients to involve themselves in a process they do not know about and are unsure concerning what it may require of them, lack of understanding or misunderstanding of the worker's and agency's role and purpose, etc. Resistance, as used in casework, can refer to more conscious misperceptions of the client such as the resistance of the adolescent to a process which he did not himself request and into which he has been forced by parents, or the resistance of the long-hospitalized patient to help with planning for discharge. Or resistance may reflect an ego burdened and eroded by too much stress or anxiety: the protective functions of the ego then take over, at the expense of the integrative functions. Obviously, as with any other piece of behavior of the client, it is not sufficient to diagnose "resistance" in a given client situation; the worker must understand what kind of resistance it is, whence it comes, and what functions it serves.

The understanding of the phenomenon of resistance has proven of great pragmatic usefulness to casework. It helped us to understand why our efforts with some clients were unavailing, sometimes the more so the harder we tried; and it gave us more of a sensitive grasp of how the process of help seems to the client--how he perceives it.

In this area also, however, there may have been some misapplication in casework, due to lack of full understanding of the underlying psychoanalytic theory. Sometimes behavior of the client is labeled resistance, and handled as if it were the unconscious phenomenon, when it is not: the Black ADC mother from the rural South, for example, who cancels and comes late to appointments is clearly "resisting"--but perhaps

because "talking treatment" just does not make much sense
to her, and her and the worker's divergent goals and role
expectations have never been clarified. Here one might
question whether it is the client who is resistant, or whether
what is operating rather is the worker's imposition of a
process which is resisting the client, instead of understanding her perceptions and tailoring a plan of help that is meaningful to her.

Sometimes resistance is defined only as a negative,
rather than as the common human phenomenon which it is,
and which contains seeds of health and growth (as the
"functionalists" so well understood). A client's apparent
lack of resistance, overtly at any rate, is often greeted as
an index that a "good relationship" has been established and
the case is moving well. Perhaps it does mean this; but we
might also question the meaning of such a client's compliance
and total acceptance of the worker's suggestions and interpretations. We do not always remember that since man is
a creature of polarities, that "resistance" of one kind or
another must exist in every interpersonal situation. Love
and hate co-exist in every relationship--the reaching for, and
the pulling away from. Without such recognition, we cannot
work with resistance productively.

Inexperienced caseworkers sometimes respond in terms
of trying to get rid of what they see only as a block to treatment, without first seeking to diagnose its meaning to the
client. Such efforts to batter down, or reason away, the
client's resistance as aften as not only compound it. Strean
(136, 139) has written perceptively of the need, rather, to
join the client's resistance, recognizing its validity in terms
of his perception of the situation, and starting from there--
from "where the client is. "

The concept of transference has had perhaps more far-
reaching influence on casework than any other. Transference
is defined by Hamilton (48) as "irrational elements carried
over from other relationships, particularly in the past, now
displaced upon the therapist... " Hollis (70) enlarges this
definition to include "any distorted way of relating to people
that has become a part of (the client's) personality, whether
or not he identifies the worker in a direct way with early
family figures. All of these unrealistic reactions can be
positive or negative (in the sense of warm or hostile), and
they may represent id, ego, or superego aspects of the
personality. "

Countertransference is the obverse: the worker's like unrealistic emotional reactions or attitudes toward the client.
Hollis (71) feels that this definition also has been broadened
in casework to include the worker's realistic responses to
the client that are, however "countertherapeutic. "

Like resistance, transference is a universal human
phenomenon that occurs in every relationship. Simply put,
it means that since man is capable of both intellective and
affective memory, he brings with him to every new experience
and relationship in his life the sum weight of all his earlier
experiences and relationships; and tends to interpret the new
in terms of its real or seeming analogy to the old. Such
"transfers, " indeed, are how we learn.

The client who was overprotected and indulged as a
child, encouraged, out of the parent's need, to remain a
dependent child, may relate to the caseworker as if the latter
were yet another nurturing, all-giving parent who will give
all and expect nothing but compliance and gratitude. Or the
woman whose history recounts a series of relationships with
men in which she was exploited and emotionally or actually
abandoned, will tend to relate to a male caseworker as if he
is like all the others, the latest of the line.

The handling of transference phenomena is different in
casework than in psychoanalysis. In the latter, extensive
regression in the transference is encouraged to the point of
development of the "transference neurosis. " In casework,
by contrast, the focus is not on unconscious material in
terms of encouraging its production, or on planned regression
of the client, or on fostering of such an intense transference
reaction that it approaches the dimensions of transference
neurosis. The statement is made in casework that the worker
"works within the transference but not with it. " We would
take issue with this, as it seems to imply that the worker
accepts the transference as a given and does not use it as
one of the major dynamics in treatment. Rather, the skilled
caseworker actively works with the transference itself. The
client is not encouraged actually to relive incidents and feelings of the distant past. Positive reality and transference of
the client toward the worker are, within some limitations,
usually encouraged and not interpreted. Yet the worker is
acutely aware of transference implications, and his treatment
must include them. With the dependent, childlike client described above, the worker may utilize his understanding of
the transference manifestations in the client's attitudes and

behavior, to gear treatment toward an experience in frustration for this client, the normal experience of frustration that she did not receive earlier from parents. A certain amount of dependency gratification must be provided, since this is the only basis on which such a client understands relationship; but the effort is then made to move treatment toward a weaning and growth experience. With the second client, whether or not the transference is "interpreted," the worker would gear treatment toward providing this woman with a corrective relationship with a different kind of man who is not exploitative, not sexually corruptible, and who will not abandon her. In both situations, the worker is actively working with the transference.

Overt negative transference is relatively easy to identify. Not so easy always is a kind of pseudo-positive transference of the client's: for example, the dependent woman previously described whose dependence on and appreciation of the worker may be so ego-gratifying to him that treatment degenerates into a mutual-admiration situation in which each participant is engaged in meeting the other's emotional needs.

A risk in the misapplication of psychoanalytic theory concerning transference is in labeling as negative transference a reality reaction of the client's: perhaps he does have good reason to feel resentful toward the worker or the agency. Casework students are taught to examine the reality situation before leaping to conclusions concerning transference.

The notion of countertransference, that the worker can be controlled by irrational emotional needs and attitudes as much as can the client, is a rather disturbing one. Littner (82) discussed the "impact of the client's unconscious on the caseworker's reactions": the ways in which the client's unconscious transference needs and expectations can be communicated to the caseworker on the same unconscious level, and can in effect "supervise" or control his responses--unless the worker is aware of what is happening. We all prefer to see ourselves as always rational and controlled, always objective and acting in the interest of the client. It is perhaps for this reason that obvious negative countertransference manifestations--active feelings of dislike, for example--have received more attention as deleterious to the worker-client relationship than positive countertransference. (Negative countertransference includes, however, subtle depressed expectations of the client, racially discriminatory attitudes of which we are not totally aware, etc.) As deleterious to treatment as negative countertransference can be the worker's need to be seen by the client (and himself) as "warm" and "giving," to be liked and appreciated, and to have a "successful" case. In such an atmosphere, the client is effectively boxed in: he is forced to adopt role behavior complementary to the worker's countertransference-determined behavior, and thus is subtly but effectively forbidden to be himself and to dare risking himself.

Countertransference is sometimes spoken and written of in casework (and in psychoanalysis) as if it were an unmitigated evil, something to be avoided at all costs. This would seem to deny the basic principle involved--that transference manifestations are an inevitable, and not necessarily destructive or pathological, part of every human relationship. The caseworker's countertransference reactions can be one of his most useful tools in diagnosis and treatment, but only if they are recognized and so used. In his own reactions, the worker has an invaluable aid to understanding, for example, the client who inspires in him warm and protective feelings, or the client whom the worker finds vaguely irritating and disturbing. Diagnosis can assume much sharper dimensions if the worker is able to look at, not only his own possible emotional needs that have sparked his inner response, but also what about each of these clients makes him feel as he does. "Hunches," or intuitive responses on the part of the worker, are often the product of his countertransference, his unconscious having recognized something in the situation with which his more conscious processes have not yet caught up. Emotional reactions, hunches, and intuitions are not sufficient in themselves, of course; they must be later taken apart by the worker, relived in slow motion as it were, and understood. If so understood, they are then available for use.

EVALUATION

The influence of psychoanalysis on social casework has, on balance, been more positive than otherwise. Its intellectual penetration of casework was the single most important influence in the professionalization and scientific ordering of the casework method. Most of its concepts, and some of its therapeutic techniques, have been absorbed so totally into casework theory and practice that they could not be dispensed with now without leaving major gaps. Many of the ideas of psychoanalytic theory have proved of immediate, pragmatic value to caseworkers in going about their task of effectively helping individuals and families. Psychoanalytic concepts have been of major influence in giving structure, rationale, and focus to the casework processes of study, diagnosis, and intervention. And finally--and perhaps this has been its most weighty contribution--psychoanalysis has sharpened and strengthened casework's focus on the person: the unique, never-to-be-duplicated "one. " It helped us to recognize that we had to focus on the person as well as the situation. It helped us to recognize that, while there may be loose types and classifications of individuals, and types and classifications of the social problems that impinge upon and erode individuals, casework, when it was dealing with this client or this family, was not addressing itself to "the problem of alcoholism" but to this man who has a drinking problem, and how it affects him and his family. Casework's place within the methods of social work has always been based on this dedication to the individual who is lost in the aggregate group or is falling through the cracks of even the best designed mass program.

Yet the picture is by no means unblurred. Psychoanalysis, both personality theory and therapeutic technique, has been accused of non-eligibility to rank as a science (Eysenck, 19 and Sears, 123). Some of its assumptions and concepts have proven empirically verifiable, but many are not accessible to verification. According to the usually-applied criteria for a science, psychoanalysis does not merit admission. Yet it must be remembered that Freud--who had started as a neurophysiologist and who strove to apply scientific method to his work--did not himself consider his product a science. At best, psychoanalysis can be considered a "protoscience"--the forerunner of a science. Its major value lies in the web of ideas about human personality and the functioning of the mind that may some day serve as the nucleus, either by positive validation or by being discarded, for the comprehensive personality theory that at present does not exist. The unverifiability of psychoanalysis is as much a function of the present inadequacy of the state of knowledge and research method, as it may be of the essential invalidity of the theory itself. At present we just do not know; and all of the psychological and behavioral sciences, and applied practice disciplines, based on this non-existent comprehensive and validated personality theory, must live with such a state of uncertainty, for now. For casework, this means that while it is recognized that psychoanalysis as a theory has "holes, " it is the best we have to date; and casework has always been a most pragmatic art, willing to use inventively whatever tools are at hand.

Casework's history of appropriation of a variety of ideas and theoretical constructs from a variety of sources evidences also, not only its weakness in its failure to date to construct a real casework theory of its own, but also paradoxically its strength--its recognition that the broadness of its charge to serve many different kinds of individuals and families in many different situations with many different problems, and this by utilization of the broadest range of helping techniques found in any discipline, attests to its recognition, in advance of other disciplines, that human phenomena that have existence and structure at multiple levels call for multiple theories. The intellectual demands made of the casework practitioner (by the needs of his practice, not necessarily academic) are enormous: to work effectively with his clients, he must have a usable grasp of personality theory, small group theory, role theory, systems theory, communication theory, cultural anthropology, etc., etc. It is perhaps, therefore, understandable that psychoanalytic theory and technique have at times in the past been too totally and un-critically accepted as dogma by casework: they purported to offer a sure anchor. It was forgotten, by some psycho-analysts and caseworkers both, that psychoanalysis is no more than what Kasin (75) calls the "first draft of a method to investigate the meaning of mental disorder. As frequently happens, the use of a tool reveals something yet unknown about the problem to be solved. Increased knowledge of the problem suggests new tools. In turn, these illuminate new aspects of the problem, and eventually a great many new un-solved problems must be handled with as yet undevised tools. What has happened, however, is that the operation can be continued in a richer, broader context. From the study of symptoms, and diagnosis of particular varieties of neurosis, we were led to the elucidation of character structure, to the general structure of personality, to the adaptive nature of mental illness, to the illness of society, and to considerations of identity and values in the life of each man... "

As this kind of "first draft," Freud's system of organiz-ing the processes of personality functioning has not yet been surpassed, although it has been deepened and enriched by later theorizers. Whiteman (155), for example, relates the tale of a recent research study in which "a large battery of personality tests and inventories was subjected to a factor analysis. After an enormous amount of mathematical toil,

the data seemed to be comfortably reduced to or at least
accounted for by three factors. To the consternation of the
investigators who had undertaken the study with quite different
theoretical predilections, the factors appeared to have an
almost agonizing resemblance to id, ego, and superego!"

The error, however, of assuming psychoanalysis to be
more than it (or at least its originator) purported it to be,
and of failing to recognize that it is no more than this web
of ideas, has had some fairly serious disadvantageous effects
for casework. Some of its proponents tend to develop an
almost religious devotion to its concepts; this perception of
theory as if it were dogma brings about closure of other
points of view and results in narrowness and constriction.
Another most serious effect for the professional development
of casework has been the establishment of a superior-inferior,
master-pupil role relationship between psychoanalytic psychiatry and casework, in which psychiatry is deferred to, not
questioned, and in which its narrow area of concern and its
goals are adopted unthinkingly as relevant and sufficient for
casework. This has served, at some times and places, to
establish the role of casework as ancillary to psychiatry.
Caseworkers have sometimes needed to narrow their practice
role repertoire to the comparatively very narrow role set
of the psychotherapist, meaning a consequent diminution in
effectiveness of the practitioner and the agency, since not
every client needs psychotherapy and many need much more
than psychotherapy. The agency, and its clients, are deprived of the full range of knowledge and skill that should
characterize the social worker. Because of this kind of
historic relationship with psychiatry, caseworkers have not
always assumed their responsibility to share with and teach
other disciplines casework's insights and expertise. An
example of this latter was Pollak's (108)--a sociologist, not
a social worker--underlining for child guidance clinics that
the child in treatment had a family and a social situation that
were crucially relevant; but the concept of "family focus"
has been basic to social casework ever since Mary Richmond
stated that the focus of the case is all who share the family
table. Caseworkers have dealt for years with the kinds of
clients who are not appropriate for psychiatric treatment and
with whom psychiatry would not know how to intervene; but
casework does know how to intervene. Yet we have not
sufficiently or well enough taught what we know; one negative
result of the alliance with psychiatry is that we became used
to a recipient role.

One of the reasons for the still to be found misperceptions and misapplications of psychoanalytic theory in casework practice, is the fact that many practitioners do not
know psychoanalytic theory (or any other personality theory)
well.   Towle (148) describes how "fragments of theoretical
formulas, such as 'maternal rejection, ' 'castration complex, '
'oedipal conflict, ' 'acceptance, ' 'supportive, ' 'insight therapy, '
etc. become the basis of easy generalizations, which connote
pretensive adequacy when there is not an adequate intellectual or emotional grasp of concepts ...   This atomistic
tendency not only has been the student's means to deal with
complexity, but often it has been the instructor's easy
adaptation. " And Fraiberg (23) writes of her concern that
"students emerge from their introduction to psychoanalysis
with a terminology that seems to have very little meaning
for them.   The student knows the terms 'ego, ' 'id, ' 'superego, ' 'oedipal complex' and 'libido. ' He has learned the
names of defense mechanisms with the same dutiful feeling
that he once learned the Latin names for plants and with as
little expectation that the knowledge will do him any good.
He often misuses this terminology in ways that reveal his
uncertain grasp of concepts. "

The anti-psychoanalytic feeling among some practitioners,
generated partly by this misperception and misapplication of
the theory, is sometimes reflected in the practitioner's or
student's disclaimer, "you know, I'm not very psychoanalytic"
or the statement, "I'm eclectic. " What this sometimes
means is that the practitioner is not very anything--he has
no frame of reference.   Studies of the efficacy of psychotherapy among practitioners of different theoretical persuasions seems to indicate that "success" rates do not vary
that much among the various schools of thought; the crucial
variable, rather, is that the therapist have some frame of
reference which he knows well and which serves for him as
a referent.   Without such a referent, he has no way of
ordering data, no way of putting it together into a cohesive
formulation in order to guide his intervention, and no orderly
way to objectify and draw on his own and others' past
experience with like situations.   In effect, he is starting
"cold" with each new case, whatever experience and knowledge he brings to the task a relatively untappable, because
unorganized, subjective mass.   Pollak (108) noted in his
study of clinic practice that observations tend not to be used
or even comprehended until there is such a frame of reference
into which to fit them.

A major limitation of the usefulness of psychoanalysis
for casework is its failure to focus explicitly on the social
dimension.   That Freud was not unaware of the crucial impact on the person of his human and social environment,
seems demonstrated by the implicit inclusion of this dimension in some aspects of his theory, e. g., his theory of early
psychosexual development deals with the child's social transactions with parents.   Psychoanalytic theory, however, has
little to offer casework in terms of understanding the social
situational component of the person-in situation constellation.
It may tell us much about the individual members of a family,
or a marriage, or a counseling group, but little about the
interactional processes that are occurring, and which are the
focus of work with any group rather than the one-to-one
worker/individual interaction.   The ideas of psychoanalysis
have little to offer casework in our attempt to understand so
as to modify effectively where needed, the causal relationship of dysfunctional societal institutional structures to
individual dysfunctioning.

It remains for the social sciences to develop an integrated and complementary social theory, a task that was
begun only after the impetus to social science of World War
II.   In the comparatively few years since, there has been
a fantastic proliferation of new knowledge in this area, but
as yet it is not well coordinated or cohesive.

Casework has had long experience with "environmental
manipulation," as all such techniques of social therapy were
so lumped until fairly recently.   We have known from case-
by-case experience that to focus on the client's subjective
reality when he is drowning in a destructive objective reality,
is not only professionally irresponsible but cruel.   Stamm
(135) takes Hollis' (69) classification of casework treatment
to task, as "a continuum with measures designed to reduce
environmental stress at one end, measures to support and
strengthen adaptive functioning somewhere in the middle, and
finally, at the other end a precious therapeutic segment
dedicated to the resolution of instinctual conflicts. "   "Environmental manipulation" has sometimes been referred to as if
it were easy, something that untrained caseworkers do because they are not educationally equipped to do "real" casework.   Yet we know from practice experience that environmental manipulation is often the most difficult and the trickiest
of all, demanding the greatest amount of diagnostic acumen:
not only in terms of the skill needed to effect some change in
a seemingly impermeable environment of welfare bureaucracy,

poor housing, racial discrimination in the schools, etc., but also because it is often a "go-for-broke" technique. The worker who errs in making an ill-timed or outright wrong verbal interpretation to his client about the latter's psychodynamics can, in most instances, recoup his losses: words can be retracted, partially at least. But action cannot be undone. Although psychotherapeutic techniques in casework have been extensively explored and fairly well standardized for use in certain kinds of client situations, sociotherapeutic techniques, despite their long history in casework, have not been so analyzed and explicated. We do not know the processes and dynamics involved in, for example, advocacy, in the same way as we know the processes and dynamics involved in psychotherapeutic intervention. This is a pressing need for the field, and may perhaps be the current "growing edge" of casework. Casework's concentration over the last generation on the honing of its psychological understandings and skills was perhaps a necessary developmental phase toward its eventual full professional stature. We need now to devote the same intensive analysis and study to the processes subsumed under the "social" portion of our psychosocial art, but now illuminated by what we have learned about the person in that situation since Richmond's day.

We seem to have returned to the controversy of years ago between what Mary Richmond called then the "wholesale or the retail" perspective on the best way to meet human need. Strean (137) comments that "... recently too many caseworkers and other social workers seem to feel that they must make a choice and either be situational workers, social activists, reformers, or else be completely 'the clinician.' If casework is to be genuinely psychosocial, each caseworker must synthesize both elements and be a 'situationalist' and a clinician--i.e., working with the person and situation, and moving back and forth from the individual to the family group, to the community and back to the individual again.... What the new practice modes have had a tendency to do, at times, is to demean and diminish the individualizing process--such an important part of the caseworker's armamentarium. At times we have become so 'situational' in our approach, so 'crisis-oriented' that we forget that there is a person in the situation and a person in the crisis and we fail to address ourselves completely to his unique and subjective needs."

We learned a great deal from psychoanalysis. We learned too, it is hoped, that casework has need of every

new learning and insight that it finds pragmatically useful
for its responsible task of helping individuals and families
in trouble; that some theories are of greater moment and
relevance to this task than others; that none is in itself
sufficient; and that the task of welding a truly cohesive
theory to undergird social casework is still before us.

References

1. Alexander, Franz, Our Age of Unreason, rev. ed.
    (N. Y. , Lippincott, 1951), p. 7.

2. _____ and T. M. French, Psychoanalytic Therapy,
    (N. Y. , Ronald, 1946).

3. Bandler, Bernard, "The Concept of Ego-Supportive Psycho-
    therapy" in Ego-Oriented Casework, Howard J. Parad
    and Roger Miller (eds.) (N. Y. , FSAA, 1963).

4. Berrien, E. Kenneth, General and Social Systems (New
    Brunswick, N. J. , Rutgers University Press, 1968),
    p. 16.

5. Ibid. , p. 32.

6. Ibid. , pp. 34-47.

7. Boehm, Werner W. , The Social Casework Method in
    Social Work Education, Vol. X, Social Work Curricu-
    lum Study (N. Y. , Council on Social Work Education,
    1959), pp. 102-103.

8. Ibid. , p. 30.

9. Bowlby, John, Maternal Care and Mental Health (World
    Health Organization, 1952).

10. Brenner, Charles, An Elementary Textbook of Psycho-
    analysis (Garden City, N. Y. , Doubleday, 1955),
    pp. 1-15.

11. Ibid. , p. 59.

12. Bruck, M. , "Behavior Modification Theory and Practice:
    A Critical Review, " Social Work, April 1968.

13. Cannon, Walter B., The Wisdom of the Body (N. Y., Norton, 1939).

14. Dollard, John and Neale Miller, Personality and Psychotherapy: An Analysis in Terms of Learning, Thinking, and Culture (N. Y., McGraw Hill, 1950).

15. Erikson, Erik, Childhood and Society (N. Y., Norton, 1950).

16. _____. "The Problem of Ego Identity," Jour. Amer. Psychoanalytic Assoc. (1956) 4: 56-121.

17. _____, quoted in Emmanuel Hammer, "The Role of Interpretation in Therapy" in Use of Interpretation in Treatment, E. Hammer (ed.) (N. Y., Grune and Stratton, 1968), p. 8 fn.

18. Eysenck, Hans J., Uses and Abuses of Psychology (Harmondsworth, Middlesex, England, Penguin, 1954).

19. _____, The Effects of Psychotherapy (N. Y., International Science Press, 1966).

20. _____ and Stanley Rachman, The Causes and Cures of Neurosis (San Diego, Knapp, 1965), p. 62.

21. Fenichel, Otto, The Psychoanalytic Theory of Neurosis (N. Y., Norton, 1945).

22. Flavell, F. H., The Developmental Psychology of Jean Piaget (Princeton, N. J., Van Nostrand, 1963).

23. Fraiberg, Selma, "Psychoanalysis and the Education of Caseworkers" in Ego-Oriented Casework, Howard J. Parad and Roger Miller (eds.) (N. Y., FSAA, 1963), p. 253.

24. Freud, Anna, The Ego and the Mechanisms of Defense (London, Hogarth Press, 1937).

25. Freud, Sigmund, An Outline of Psychoanalysis, Standard Edition, Vol. 23, p. 148.

26. _____, Beyond the Pleasure Principle, Standard Edition, Vol. 18, p. 38.

27. Ibid., p. 64.

28. _____, Civilization and Its Discontents, tr. by
    Joan Riviere (London, Hogarth Press, 1930).

29. Ibid., p. 47.

30. _____, "Instincts and their Vicissitudes" in
    Collected Papers of Sigmund Freud, Vol. 4 (London,
    Hogarth Press, 1948), p. 63.

31. _____, New Introductory Lectures in Psycho-
    analysis (N. Y., Norton, 1933).

32. Ibid., p. 112.

33. _____, Standard Edition, Vol. 14, p. 297.

34. Ibid., p. 279.

35. Ibid., p. 282.

36. _____, Standard Edition, Vol. 21, pp. 111-112.

37. _____, The Future of an Illusion, Standard Edition,
    Vol. 9.

38. Garrett, Annette, "Modern Casework: The Contributions
    of Ego Psychology" in Ego Psychology and Dynamic
    Casework, Howard J. Parad (ed.) (N. Y., FSAA,
    1958), p. 4.

39. Ibid., p. 42.

40. Gramlich, Francis W., "On the Structure of Psycho-
    analysis" in Psychoanalysis, Scientific Method, and
    Philosophy, Sidney Hook (ed.) (N. Y., New York
    University Press, 1959), p. 298.

41. Hall, Calvin S. and Gardner Lindzey, Theories of
    Personality (N. Y., Wiley, 1957), p. 540.

42. Ibid., p. 128.

43. Ibid., p. 55.

44. Hamilton, Gordon, Theory and Practice of Social Case-
     work, 2nd ed. (N. Y., Columbia University Press,
     1951), p. 207.

45. Ibid., p. 205.

46. Ibid., p. 9.

47. Ibid., p. 258.

48. Ibid., p. 256.

49. _____, "A Theory of Personality: Freud's
     Contribution to Social Work" in Ego Psychology and
     Dynamic Casework, Howard J. Parad (ed.) (N. Y.,
     FSAA, 1958), p. 26.

50. Ibid., p. 22.

51. Hammer, Emmanuel, "Interpretation: What Is It?" in
     Use of Interpretation in Treatment, Emmanuel Ham-
     mer (ed.) (N. Y., Grune and Stratton, 1968), p. 4.

52. Hartmann, Heinz, "Ego Psychology and the Problem of
     Adaptation" in Organization and Pathology of Thought,
     David Rapaport (ed.) (N. Y., Columbia University
     Press, 1951).

53. _____, "Psychoanalysis as a Scientific Theory" in
     Psychoanalysis, Scientific Method, and Philosophy,
     Sidney Hook (ed.) (N. Y., New York University Press,
     1959), p. 11.

54. Ibid., pp. 10-11.

55. Ibid., p. 6.

56. _____, and Ernst Kris, "The Genetic Approach in
     Psychoanalysis" in The Psychoanalytic Study of the
     Child, Vol. I (N. Y., International Universities Press,
     1945), pp. 11-29.

57. _____, and Rudolph Loewenstein, "Notes on the
     Theory of Aggression" in The Psychoanalytic Study of
     the Child, Vols. III-IV, (N. Y., International Universities
     Press, 1949), p. 21.

58. Hendrick, Ives, Facts and Theories about Psycho-
    analysis, (N. Y. Knopf, 1948), pp. 92-93 (quoted in
    Towle, op. cit. , p. 41).

59. Hobbs, Nicholas, "Sources of Gain in Psychotherapy" in
    Use of Interpretation in Treatment, Emmanuel Hammer
    (ed.) (N. Y. , Grune and Stratton, 1968), p. 14.

60. Ibid. , p. 15.

61. Ibid. , p. 19.

62. Hollis, Florence, Casework: A Psychosocial Therapy
    (N. Y. , Random House, 1964), p. 25.

63. Ibid. , pp. 181-182.

64. Ibid. , p. 188.

65. Ibid. , p. 75.

66. Ibid. , p. 131.

67. Ibid. , p. 225.

68. Ibid. , pp. 65-82.

69. Ibid. , Ch. 4.

70. Ibid. , p. 154.

71. Ibid. , p. 155.

72. Ibid. , p. 15.

73. Ibid. , pp. 179-180.

74. Kadushin, Alfred, "The Knowledge Base of Social Work"
    in Issues in American Social Work, Alfred J. Kahn
    (ed.) (N. Y. , Columbia University Press, 1959),
    p. 77 fn.

75. Kasin, Edwin, "Interpretation as Active Nurture: An
    Interpersonal Perspective" in Use of Interpretation in
    Treatment, Emmanuel Hammer (ed.) (N. Y. , Grune
    and Stratton, 1968), p. 197.

76. Kennedy, Gail, "Psychoanalysis: Protoscience and Metapsychology" in Psychoanalysis, Scientific Method, and Philosophy, Sidney Hook (ed.) (N.Y., New York University Press, 1959), p. 277.

77. Kinsey, Alfred, Sexual Behavior in the Human Female (N.Y., Saunders, 1953).

78. Klein, Melanie, The Psycho-Analysis of Children, 2nd ed. (London, Hogarth Press, 1937).

79. Kluckhohn, Florence, "Variations in the Basic Values of Family Systems," Social Casework, Feb.-Mar. 1958.

80. Kris, Ernst, "The Nature of Psychoanalytic Propositions and their Validation" in Freedom and Experience, Sidney Hook and M.R. Konwitz (eds.) (N.Y., Cornell University Press, 1947), p. 241.

81. Leitch, M., and S.K. Escalona, "The Reaction of Infants to Stress: A Report on Clinical Findings" in The Psychoanalytic Study of the Child, Vols. III-IV (N.Y., International Universities Press, 1949), pp. 121-140.

82. Littner, Ner, "The Impact of the Client's Unconscious on the Caseworker's Reactions," in Ego Psychology and Dynamic Casework, Howard J. Parad (ed.) (N.Y., FSAA, 1958).

83. Maier, Henry W., Three Theories of Child Development, rev. ed. (N.Y., Harper and Row, 1969), p. 220.

84. Op. cit.

85. Masters, William and Virginia Johnson, Human Sexual Inadequacy (Boston, Little, Brown, 1970).

86. Mittelman, Bela, "Motility in Infants, Children, and Adults: Patterning and Psychodynamics" in The Psychoanalytic Study of the Child, Vol. IX (N.Y., International Universities Press, 1954), pp. 142-177.

87. Munroe, Ruth, Schools of Psychoanalytic Thought (N.Y., Holt, 1955), p. 224.

118   Social Casework

88. Ibid., p. 90.

89. Ibid., p. 107.

90. Ibid., p. 303.

91. Ibid., p. 62.

92. Ibid., p. 301.

93. Ibid., p. 72.

94. Ibid., p. 75.

95. Ibid., p. 77.

96. Ibid., p. 89.

97. Nagel, Ernest, "Methodological Issues in Psychoanalytic Theory," in Psychoanalysis, Scientific Method, and Philosophy, Sidney Hook (ed.) (N.Y., New York University Press, 1959).

98. Odier, C., Anxiety and Magic Thinking (N.Y., International Universities Press, 1956) (quoted in Maier, op. cit., p. 9).

99. Parad, Howard J. (ed.), Crisis Intervention (N.Y., FSAA, 1965).

100. Perlman, Helen Harris, Social Casework: A Problem-Solving Process (Chicago, University of Chicago Press, 1957).

101. Ibid., p. 176.

102. Ibid., p. 164.

103. _____, "Casework and 'The Diminished Man,' " Social Casework, April 1970.

104. Piaget, Jean, The Language and Thought of the Child (N.Y., Harcourt, Brace and World, 1926).

105. _____, The Construction of Reality in the Child (N.Y., Basic Books, 1954).

106.　　　　　, "The General Problems of the Psychobiological Development of the Child" in Discussions on
Child Development, J. M. Tanner and B. Inhelder
(eds.), Vol. IV (N. Y., International Universities
Press, 1960), pp. 3-28.

107. Pollak, Otto, "Social Factors Contributing to Character
Disorders," Child Welfare, April 1958.

108.　　　　　, Integrating Sociological and Psychoanalytic
Concepts (N. Y., Russell Sage Foundation, 1956).

109. Pollens, Bertram, "The Analyst's Role: To Interpret
or to React?" in Use of Interpretation in Treatment,
Emmanuel Hammer (ed.) (N. Y., Grune and Stratton,
1968).

110. Rapaport, David, "The Structure of Psychoanalytic
Theory: A Systematizing Attempt," in Psychology: A
Study of a Science, Sigmund Koch (ed.), Vol. 3
(N. Y., McGraw Hill, 1959), p. 112.

111. Ibid., p. 111.

112. Ibid., p. 86.

113. Ibid., pp. 90-91.

114. Ibid., p. 122.

115. Ibid., p. 97.

116. Ibid., p. 87.

117. Ribble, Margaret, The Rights of Infants (N. Y.,
Columbia University Press, 1943).

118. Roazen, Paul, Freud: Political and Social Thought
(N. Y., Knopf, 1968), p. 217.

119. Robinson, Virginia, Supervision in Social Case Work
(Chapel Hill, University of North Carolina Press, 1936).

120. Ruesch, J., Therapeutic Communication (N. Y.,
Norton, 1965).

121.   Sears, Robert R. , "Social Behavior and Personality
       Development, " in Toward a General Theory of Action,
       Talcott Parsons and E. A. Shills (eds.) (Cambridge,
       Harvard University Press, 1951), pp. 465-478.

122.   _____ , "A Theoretical Framework for Personality
       and Social Behavior, " Amer. Psychologist, (1951) 6
       (9):   476-483.

123.   _____ , Survey of Objective Studies of Psycho-
       analytic Concepts (N. Y. , Social Science Research
       Council, 1942).

124.   Seeley, John, The Americanization of the Unconscious
       (N. Y. , Lippincott, 1967).

125.   Siporin, Max, "Social Treatment: A New-Old Helping
       Method, " Social Work, July 1970.

126.   Spitz, Rene, "Anaclitic Depression", The Psycho-
       analytic Study of the Child, Vol. II (N. Y. , International
       Universities Press, 1946), pp. 313-342.

127.   _____ , "Autoerotism: Some Empirical Findings
       and Hypotheses on Three of its Manifestations in the
       First Year of Life, " The Psychoanalytic Study of the
       Child, Vols. III-IV, (N. Y. , Inter. Univ. Press, 1949),
       pp. 85-120.

128.   _____ , "Hospitalism: An Inquiry into the Genesis
       of Psychiatric Conditions in Early Childhood, " The
       Psychoanalytic Study of the Child, Vol. I, (N. Y. ,
       International Universities Press, 1945), pp. 53-74.

129.   Spotnitz, Hyman, "The Maturational Interpretation, " in
       Use of Interpretation in Treatment, Emmanuel Hammer
       (ed.) (N. Y. , Grune and Stratton, 1968).

130.   Stamm, Isabel, "Ego Psychology in the Emerging
       Theoretical Base of Casework, " in Issues in American
       Social Work, Alfred J. Kahn (ed.) (N. Y. Columbia
       University Press, 1959), p. 80.

131.   Ibid. , p. 86.

132.   Ibid. , pp. 87-88.

133.   Ibid. , 87.

134.   Ibid., p. 95.

135.   Ibid., p. 84.

136.   Strean, Herbert, Paradigmatic Interventions in Seem-
       ingly Difficult Therapeutic Situations," in Roles and
       and Paradigms in Psychotherapy, Marie Nelson, et al
       (ed.) (N.Y., Grune and Stratton, 1968).

137.   _____, "Recent Developments in Social Casework
       Theory and Practice: A Social Work Educator's
       Evaluation," Presentation to the Conference for the
       Advancement of Private Practitioners in Social Work,
       Vancouver, British Columbia, June 17, 1970 (mimeo.).

138.   _____, "The Social Worker as Psychotherapist,"
       Keynote Address to N. J. NASW, Oct. 30, 1970
       (mimeo.).

139.   _____, "The Use of the Patient as Consultant,"
       Psychoanalytic Review, Summer 1959.

140.   Thomas, Edwin, Behavioral Science for Social Workers
       (N. Y., Free Press, 1967).

141.   _____, "Selected Sociobehavioral Techniques and
       Principles: An Approach to Interpersonal Helping,"
       Social Work, Jan. 1968.

142.   Towle, Charlotte, The Learner in Education for the
       Professions (Chicago, University Chicago Press,
       1954).

143.   Ibid., p. 104.

144.   Ibid., p. 54.

145.   Ibid., p. 65.

146.   Ibid., p. 58.

147.   Ibid., p. 87.

148.   Ibid., pp. 108-109.

149.   Wheelis, Allen, The Quest for Identity (N. Y., Norton,
       1958).

150.   Ibid., p. 77.

151.   Ibid., p. 30.

152.   Ibid., p. 164.

153.   Ibid., p. 235.

154.   Ibid., p. 157.

155.   Whiteman, Martin, "A Conceptualization of Freudian Psychology," Columbia University School of Social Work (mimeo.).

156.   Wolff, P.H., "The Developmental Psychologies of Jean Piaget and Psychoanalysis," Psychological Issues, (1960) 2:1 (quoted in Maier, op. cit., p. 9).

157.   Wolpe, Joseph, Psychotherapy by Reciprocal Inhibition (Stanford, 1958).

Chapter 3

The Systems Model and Social System Theory:
Their Application to Casework

Irma L. Stein

The System Concept

The idea of system is not a new one but it has developed
through cross-disciplinary research and application to many
fields of study and has emerged as a pivot in modern scientific thought. A voluminous body of systems theory[1] literature has developed in various fields, including social work.
This literature includes a variety of definitions of the term
system and discussions of the origins and developments in
general systems theory; it explicates the various significant
sub-theories, concepts, principles, and properties of general
systems theory; and it addresses itself to the practical applications to diverse fields such as engineering and social work
and suggests implications for the future developments of
these disciplines and fields of practice.

Definitions of system reviewed by this writer reveal
similarities but also reflect different emphases that have
some import. The "founder" of general systems theory,
Ludwig Von Bertalanffy, defines systems as "sets of elements
standing in interaction" (7, p. 2). James Miller, another
system theorist, defines system as a "set of units with
relationships among them. " The word "set" implies that the
units have common properties. The state of each unit is
constrained by, conditioned by, or dependent on the state of
other units" (34, p. 200). Allport states that "a system is
any recognizable delimited aggregate of dynamic elements
that are in some way interconnected and interdependent and
that continue to operate together according to certain laws
and in such a way as to produce some characteristic total
effect. A system, in other words, is something that is
concerned with some kind of activity and preserves a kind of
integration and unity; and a particular system can be recognized as distinct from other systems to which, however, it

may be dynamically related" (1, p. 469).

Hall and Fagen's definition of system is similar to Bertalanffy's: "A system is a set of objects together with relationships between the objects and between their attributes." They go on, however, to say that their definition "does imply, of course, that a system has properties, functions or purposes, distinct from its constituent objects, relationships and attributes " (20, p. 81). Ellis and Ludwig take a somewhat different emphasis in their definition of a system that "is something that accomplishes an operational process; that is, something is operated on in some way to produce something " (15, p. 3). Gross has pinpointed the difference in emphases of these definitions when he points out that many people define a system structurally in terms of a set of interrelated elements. "Others [like Ellis and Ludwig] think of a system in terms of performance, particularly input-output activities . . . . These two approaches can be brought together in the concept of a system as a set of interrelated elements with a capacity for certain kinds of performance. The concept of system capacity (or capability) helps bring together both the structural and performance approach." Gross also notes, however, that in either of these approaches the system is regarded as something "environed"--that is located in, or involved in transactions with an environment composed of other systems (19, p. 370).

Grinker summarizes the nature and basic principles of systems. In his words:

> a system is considered to be some whole form in structure or operation, concepts or functions, composed of united and integrated parts. As such, it has an extent in time and space, and boundaries. A system has a past which is partly represented by its parts, for it develops or assembles from something preceding. It has a present, which is its existence as a relatively stable or what might be called resting form, and it has a future, that is its functional potentiality. Its space form, structure, and dimensions constitute a framework which is relatively stable and timeless, yet only relatively so, for its constituents change during time but considerably slower than the novel or more active functions of the system. To view the change of these functions through time, the frame or background may be artifically considered as stable (18, p. 370).

Grinker, like others, deals with the important notion of the system and its environment. He notes that "the dividing line between the system and environment is partly conceptual and to that extent arbitrary. . . . Thus, a system is the whole complex of the organism and environment. Environment is composed of those variables whose changes affect the organism and which are changed by the organism's behavior. Thus, both the organism and environment are two parts of one system" (18, p. 371). [2] Hall and Fagen offer a similar statement regarding the system and its environment. They add, however, that

> the statement invites the natural question of when an object belongs to a system and when it belongs to the environment; for if an object reacts with a system in the way described, should it not be considered a part of the system? The answer is by no means definite. In a sense, a system together with its environment makes up the universe of all things of interest in a given contest. Subdivision of this universe into two sets, system and environment, can be done in many ways which are in fact quite arbitrary. . . . From the definition of system and environment . . . any given system can be further subdivided into subsystems. Objects belonging to one system may well be considered as part of the environment of another subsystem (20, p. 83, 84).

The fluidity of the system-environment and system-subsystem concepts lead into a discussion of closed and open systems and the distinction between the physical-chemical model and the organismic-organic model. Explication of the closed and open systems, however, should be introduced by a brief presentation of the origins and developments of general systems theory.

General Systems Theory and Model

General systems theory structures the similarities of sub-theories or theories of particular systems into formal isomorphies. This global theory is described by Bertalanffy as "the formulation and derivation of those principles which are valid for 'systems' in general" (6, p. 139). He has also stated that "the isomorphy is a consequence of the fact that in certain aspects, corresponding abstractions and conceptual models can be applied to different phenomena. It is

only in view of these aspects that system laws will apply.
This does not mean that physical systems, organisms and
societies are all the same" (7, p. 2). In 1962 Bertalanffy
stated that "general systems theory was conceived as a
working hypothesis; being a practicing scientist [he] sees the
main function of theoretical models in the explanation, pre-
diction and control of hitherto unexplored phenomena" (8,
p. 17).

Many writers have dealt with the fact that general
systems theory provides a model, and stress the particular
significance of the model for practititioners. Initially (1947),
Bertalanffy focused upon the concept of system as an entity
rather than a summation of parts. The founder of the organismic viewpoint in biology (Bertalanffy), as well as other
system theorists, saw the need for the expansion of conceptual schemes that would deal with the multi-variable problems of the biological, behavioral and social sciences. 3
Thus, it was Bertalanffy's contention that physics is but one
model dealing with certain aspects of reality and that it is
necessary as well as possible to introduce other models
dealing with other aspects of reality. It should be recognized
that general systems theory was "one within a group of
parallel developments. " Some of these other developments
include cybernetics (which uses the feedback model), information theory, game theory, and decision theory. There
is much overlapping of these "parallel" theories. While
different conceptual tools predominate in the individual fields,
all these parallel theories have some common features.
First, they are concerned with problems characteristic of
the behavioral and biological sciences that are not dealt with
in classical physical theory. Second, they introduce new
concepts and models, as for example, the concept of information compared to energy in physics. Third, they are concerned with multi-variable problems. Fourth, "these models
are inter-disciplinary and transcend the conventional fields
of science. " While these parallel theories have common
features, it is noted that the various "systems theories" also
are models reflecting different aspects of reality. They are
not mutually exclusive and are often combined in application.
This implies "the hope for further synthesis in which the
various approaches of the present toward a theory of 'wholeness' and 'organization' may be integrated and unified" (8,
p. 13-14).

General systems theory thus, as a global theory encom-
passing sub-theories, has model-building attributes. As such,

according to Boulding,

> it lies somewhere between the highly generalized
> constructions of pure mathematics and the specific
> theories of the specialized disciplines . . . . At a low
> level of ambition but with a high degree of confidence
> it aims to point out similarities in the theoretical
> constructions of different disciplines where these
> exist, and to develop theoretical models having appli-
> cability to at least two different fields of study.   At
> a higher level of ambition, but with perhaps a lower
> degree of confidence, it hopes to develop something
> like a 'spectrum' of theories--a system of systems
> which may perform the function of a 'gestalt' in
> theoretical construction (10, p. 197).

Stated somewhat differently,

> general systems theory is a set of related definitions,
> functions, and propositions which deal with reality as
> an integrated hierarchy of organizations of matter
> and energy . . . . [It deals] with the structural and
> behavioral properties of systems.   The diversity of
> systems is great.   The molecule, the cell, the organ,
> the individual, the group, the society--all are examples
> of systems.   These systems differ in their level of
> organization; they also differ in other crucial aspects
> (34, p. 193).

While the distinction between open (and all living systems
are open) and closed systems is considered to be of crucial
import, Rapaport states that "systems that are living in the
common sense of biological sense of the word, share many
features with systems that are not; and these common features derive from the way systems are organized.   This
suggests a generalization of the concept of 'organism' to the
concept of 'organized system'. " Any organized system,
living or non-living, may be viewed from three perspectives
which thus encompass the broadest scope of general system
theory.   All organized systems thus are studied in terms of
"the structure of the system, in particular the means by
which it is enabled to receive, to store, to process and to
recall information; . . . . the functioning of the system, in
particular the way in which, by means of processed and
stored information, the system responds by 'behavior outputs'
to 'sensory inputs' from the environment; and finally, . . .
the evolution of a system type" (39, p. xx).   Rapaport goes

on to say that having recognized that structure, function, and evolution (being, acting, and becoming) are fundamental aspects of all organized systems, the concept of organism may be expanded to include not only individuals but "whole complexes of living organisms" and societies (39). Like Bertalanffy, Vickers and Haire, Rapaport defends the "organismic analogy." Haire, for example, states that "the biological model for social organizations--and here, particularly for industrial organizations--means taking as a model the living organism and the processes and principles that regulate its growth and development. It means looking for lawful processes in organizational growth" (8, p. 30).

In light of the above discussion it is interesting to consider Walter Buckley's statements concerning the need to replace outmoded models of society with a more viable and appropriate conceptual framework. While Buckley also views a system as a complex of elements or components related in a causal network such that each component is related to at least some others in a more or less stable way within any particular period of time, he gives considerable emphasis to the varying degrees of "systemness" and varying degrees of "entitivity." The central key to systems or entities is the organization of their components into systemic relationships. It is this organization which imparts to the aggregate characteristics that are not only different from but often are not found in the parts. Thus, the fact that the system is a whole which is more than the sum of its parts also means to Buckley that the sum of the parts must be taken to mean not their numerical addition but their unorganized aggregation. While systems are phenomena of widely differing kinds, a crucial distinguishing feature of a system is the particular nature of the relations of the parts. Buckley points out that whereas the relations of parts of an organism are physiological, involving complex physio-chemical energy interchanges, the relations of parts of society are primarily psychic, involving complex communicative processes of information exchange. This involves a shift from the organismic model to the organic model and finally, to the psycho-social model. That is,

> as we proceed up the various levels (from organic to socio-cultural systems), the relations of parts become more flexible and the structure more fluid with process as the set of alternative behaviors open to the components increases. The interrelations characterizing higher level systems depend more on transmission

of information [than the transmission of energy] (11, p. 47).

Thus, Buckley distinguishes between the organismic model and the psycho-social model, unlike Bertalanffy and others who apply the organismic model to personality as well as to complex societies. Also, in his psycho-social model information theory replaces concepts of psychic energy.

Living systems are one type of concrete system, as contrasted with conceptual systems. They have boundaries which are at least partially permeable, thus permitting transmissions of matter-energy or information to cross them. [4] They are made of matter and energy organized by information; they require matter-energy in certain forms and amounts (34). The subject of matter-energy and information is an important one in the development and application of general systems theory. The nature and "place" of matter-energy and information are related to the system level-- simple to complex--and also to concepts of structure, process and function which apply to all organized systems. Further comments regarding these basic concepts may elucidate the notion of system change, which is at the core of social work practice.

Basic Concepts and Principles

The definitions given above of system and environment and their distinctions indicate that any given system can be further divided into subsystems. (It might also be said that the elements of a system may be systems of lower order-- often referred to as the hierarchical order of systems.) The structure of a system is the arrangement of its subsystems and components in three-dimensional space at a given moment of time. [5] The structure may remain relatively fixed over a long period or it may change from moment to moment, depending upon the characteristics of the processes in the system. All change over time of matter-energy or information in a system is process. Process also includes history, less easily reversed changes such as mutations, birth, aging. Historical processes alter both the structure and function of the system. Thus there is a circular relation among the three aspects of systems--structure changes momentarily with functioning, but when such change is so great that it is essentially irreversible, an historical process has occurred, giving rise to a new structure (34, p. 209).

Bertalanffy has observed that "what are called structures are
slow processes of long duration, functions are quick processes
of short duration" (9, p. 234).

Structure, process, and function of organized systems
may be understood also in terms of the three basic principles cited by Grinker; the principle of stability (which for
some includes change, growth, and evolution), the transactional principle meaning a reciprocal relationship among
all parts of the field and not simply an interaction which is
an effect of one system or focus on another, and the principle of the process of communication of information (varying
from signals characteristic of biological systems to symbols
characteristic of social systems) (18, p. 372).

The development of general systems theory led to the
important distinction between closed and open systems. "A
system is closed if there is no import or export of energies
in any of its forms such as information, heat, physical
materials, etc. , and therefore no exchange of components,
an example being a chemical reaction taking place in a
sealed insulated container" (20, p. 86). By contrast, open
systems have a permeable or at least partially permeable
boundary so that such systems exchange materials, energies,
or information with their environments. Within the system,
the material taken in from the environment undergoes reactions which partly may yield components of a higher complexity. Living systems are open and they have innate
capacities for growth and elaboration and, as suggest above,
are capable of increasing differentiation and specialization.
Closed systems are characterized by increasing entropy, that
is, increasing disorder and de-differentiation. Open systems
can maintain themselves at a high level and evolve toward an
increase of order and complexity (negative entropy) as a
result of their capacity for exchange of materials with their
environments and specifically the transfer of matter into the
system from the environment.

Particular attention must be given to the open system
because it permits a focus on a system or subsystem in the
hierarchic order (molecule to society) and the relations or
connections of that system or subsystem to other systems
and subsystems in the field. 6   First, the characteristic of
wholeness in contrast to summativity has been stated. The
significance of this is that a change in one part of the system
will cause a change in all of them and in the total system.
This characteristic of wholeness has been described also in

terms of the transactional principle, that is, reciprocal relationships among all parts of the field. Non-summativity,

> as a corollary of the notion of wholeness, provides a negative guideline for the definition of a system . . . . It is necessary to neglect the parts for the gestalt and attend to the core of its complexity, its organization. The psychological concept of gestalt is only one way of expressing the principle of non-summativity; in other fields there is great interest in the emergent quality that arises out of the interrelation of two or more elements (49, p. 125).

One example of this at the physiological level is the "Moiré patterns"--optical manifestations of the super-position of two or more lattices. At the personality system level guilt may be considered as an emergent property (31). The emergent properties have a complexity for which the elements, considered separately, could never account. Moreover, the slightest change in the relationship between the constituent parts is often magnified in the emergent quality. Non-summativity and the emergent quality are essential to communication theory. Thus, if behavior is communication, "it follows that communication sequences would be reciprocally inseparable; in short, that interaction is non-summative" (49, p. 126).

A second concept or property of open systems is tension, strain, or conflict. It has been argued that tension does not occur only occasionally or residually as a "disturbing" factor, but rather that some level of tension is characteristic of and vital to complex adaptive systems, though it may manifest itself in either destructive or constructive ways (11). The source of the tension in open systems may be in its matter-energy composition, in structural changes or incompatabilities, or because external disturbances require that the system find ways of dealing with such disturbances. According to Chin,

> we find built-in differences, gaps of ignorance, misperceptions or differential perceptions, internal changes in a component, reactive adjustments and defenses, and the requirements of system survival generating tensions. Tensions that are internal and arise out of the structural arrangements of the system may be called stresses and strains of the system. When tensions gang up and become more or less sharply

opposed along the lines of two or more components,
we have conflict (13, p. 204).

System theory per se does not prescribe or attribute positive
or negative values to tension and conflict. Indeed, while
tension reduction, relief of stress and strain and conflict
resolution are frequent working goals of practitioners, there
is growing attention to "the possibility of increasing tensions
and conflict in order to facilitate creativity, innovation, and
social change" (13, p. 204). 7

Miller defines the concepts of stress, strain, and threat
in terms of transmissions in open systems:

> An input or output of either matter-energy or infor-
> mation, which by lack or excess of some characteris-
> tic, forces the (system) variables beyond the range
> of stability, constitutes a stress and produces a
> strain (or strains) within the system. Input lack and
> output excess both produce the same strain--diminished
> amounts in the system. Input excess and output lack
> both produce the opposite strain--increased amounts.
> Strains may or may not be capable of being reduced,
> depending on their intensity and the resources of the
> system . . . . The relative urgency of reducing each of
> these specific strains represents the system's 'hier-
> archy of values. '

> Stress may be anticipated. Information that a stress
> is imminent constitutes a threat to the system. A
> threat can create a strain. Recognition of the mean-
> ing of the information of such a threat must be based
> on previously stored (usually learned) information
> about such situations . . . . Processes--actions or com-
> munications--occur in systems only when a stress or
> a threat has created a strain which pushes a system
> variable beyond it range of stability (34, p. 224).

Miller notes that a system and its environment are each
changing and the two at all times fit each other. That is,
outside stresses or threats are mirrored by inside strains.
After some period of interaction the system and its environment (particularly its immediate environment, the suprasystem) in some sense become a mirror of each other. At
the personality level, the individual has a cognitive map of
the organization of his environment, of greater or lesser
accuracy--stored information, memories, which are essential

for effective life in that environment (34). [8]

Like Chin, Miller sees conflict as a special sort of strain; namely, when the system receives directions to carry out two or more actions which are incompatible. An effective system usually resolves such conflicts by giving greater compliance to the command with higher priority in terms of the system's values. Other sorts of adjustment processes are also used to deal with system conflict (31). Chin believes that the concept of system tension has major utility in that the dynamics of the system are exposed for observation. The system responds to tensions with activities that do not affect the structure of the system (dynamic operating processes), and activities which directly alter the structure itself (system change) (13).

It may be useful to cite several cross-level hypotheses (formulations that apply to two or more systems) to explicate further the concepts of stress and strain. One such hypothesis is as follows: as stress increases, it improves system output performance above ordinary levels and then worsens it. What is extreme stress for one subsystem may be only moderate stress for the total system, the more components of it are involved in adjusting to it. When no other components with new adjustment processes are available the system collapses. A third cross-level hypothesis is: the larger the number of subsystems or components in conflict, the more difficult will be resolution of the conflict. Two other hypotheses are: 1) the greater the resources available to a system, the less likely is conflict among its subsystems or components; 2) as average information input rate increases, the costs (measured in energy, time, etc.) remain more or less constant for a period of time and then finally increase rapidly near the point where the performance curve begins to decrease from the maximum because the system is overloaded (35, p. 401-405).

A third characteristic of the open system is that it "will attain a steady state in which its composition remains constant, but in contrast to conventional equilibria, this constancy is maintained in a continuous exchange and flow of component material" (8, p. 18). Although some writers use the terms steady state and dynamic homeostasis or dynamic equilibrium interchangeably (Chin and Miller), others such as Bertalanffy and Buckley believe that the term homeostasis should be utilized in its narrower but well-defined sense because it reveals certain limitations, namely that while the homeostasis concept "acknowledge directiveness in self-regulating circular processes, it still adheres to the machine theory of the organism . . . . The organism [in the homeostasis concept] is essentially envisaged as an aggregate mechanism for maintenance of minimum cost" (8, p. 18). Furthermore, in the concept of homeostasis the organism is essentially viewed as a reactive rather than proactive or a spontaneously active system.

Fourth, the steady state of open systems is characterized by the principle of equifinality which means achieving identical results from different initial conditions. Stated differently, if a system is open it can be shown that the final state will not depend on the initial concentrations. It will be determined entirely by the properties of the system itself, that is, the constants of proportionality which are independent of the conditions imposed on the system. "Such a system will appear to exhibit 'equifinality' or, metaphorically speaking, to have a 'goal of its own'" (39, p. xviii). The importance of the concept of equifinality for social work theory and practice is evident in the literature (22, 44). The concept of man as changing and creative, and as affecting his environment as well as being affected by it, is consistent with social work values and goals. The fact that the system can achieve independence of initial conditions has also been of interest to behavioral and social scientists as well as to other professional disciplines concerned with change strategies. Buckley, in referring to those processes which tend to elaborate or change a system's given form, structure, or state (morphogenesis), suggests an opposite principle called "multifinality." The latter means that similar conditions may lead to dissimilar end-states. Thus, initial conditions in either the personality or the environment may or may not be relevant or causally dominant (11).

Two additional properties are related to the concept of steady state. The first, which has been referred to above, is the dynamic interplay of the subsystems operating as functional processes. Each subsystem has its function or functions to perform, and it does so in relation to all of the others (22). Bertalanffy has made the point that in development and evolution dynamic interaction of processes of open systems precedes mechanization or structured arrangements such as feedback. This second property, feedback, is considered a secondary regulation of the steady state superimposed upon the dynamic interplay of open system processes.

"In systems terms, feedback refers to some of the consequences of outputs--consequences which are fed back into the input and processing to affect succeeding outputs" (27, p. 52). Although Bertalanffy states that the feedback scheme is represented by the concept of homeostasis in the living organism, Wiener defines feedback as the "property of being able to adjust future conduct by past performance. It may be simple as the common reflex, or it may be a higher order feedback, in which past experience is used not only to regulate specific movements, but also whole policies of behavior. Such a policy-feedback may, and often does, appear to be what we know under one aspect as a conditioned reflex, and under another as learning" (50, p. 33).

Negative feedback maintains the steady state of the system (for example, maintenance of a constant body temperature) while positive feedback alters the variables of the system and destroys the steady state. Thus positive feedback can initiate system changes--if it continues and is unlimited it may destroy the system. 9 Amplification feedback may operate in both negative and positive feedback. In amplification feedback energy is both derivative and redirected; "that is, no energy arises from the local source, but instead an additional source of energy is exploited and utilized in some particular way. Any chain reaction mechanism is an illustration of this phenomenon" (22, p. 47). The deviation-amplifying process may be non-adaptive--for example, the "looking-glass self" at the personality system level, the cycle of poverty and the "vicious circle" theory of racial discrimination at the socio-cultural level. The deviation-amplifying process challenges the uni-directional cause and affect analysis. Rapaport has argued for "explanation in terms of 'efficient' causes operating here and now, and not of 'final' causes . . . . We can treat 'purpose' causally in the former sense of forces acting here and now; if we can build a model of purposefulness, we can explain it" (11, p. 52). 10 As noted, negative feedback maintains the steady state of the system. However, feedback control always exhibits some oscillation and always has some lag. If the extent or degree of the oscillation or lag is great, or there is some faulty operation of feedback mechanisms the system is under stress and pathological conditions may develop.

Feedback mechanisms are involved in the process of "progressive mechanization" which accompanies the process of "progressive segregation" or differentiation. These regulatory processes are life maintaining but they also:

> impose constraints upon the free interplay of the
> functional subsystems of the system, in which case
> they would seem to impose a limit upon the degree
> to which the system may achieve its potentiality. . . .
> The fact that the fixing of arrangements, the imposing
> of constraints, while a necessary condition of organ-
> ization, limits the extent to which the organism may
> realize its potentiality, is perhaps at the basis of the
> social work principles of maximizing self-regulation
> and self-determination and of keeping manipulation by
> external agents to a minimum (22, p. 49).

As stated above, feedback mechanisms may be of a simple
order, such as the reflex arc or they may be as a higher
feedback mechanism such as cortical learning.   Indeed, the
feedback concept has been used to attack the basic under-
pinnings of traditional psychology, namely the reflex arc and
the behavioristic stimulus-response conceptions, as inadequate to explain the learning and functioning of higher organisms.   A stimulus cannot be defined as independent of the
subject on whom it acts; it is not possible to know what the
stimulus or the response is without a good understanding of
the total feedback transaction.

> What is relevant to an organism and its behavior is
> not simply some external event, or solely some in-
> ternal state, but rather the transaction whereby certain
> aspects of the external stimuli are 'sampled' by the
> organism and matched against selected internal
> states. . . .   'Meaning' is generated during the total
> transaction and ceases to exist when the transaction
> is terminated. . . .   The human can rehearse a total
> transaction entirely on the covert level, and thus can
> continually generate meaning and meaningful behavior
> apart from the concrete events symbolized (11, p. 54).

In addition to the impact on traditional psychology, Buckley,
Deutsch and others believe that cybernetics, based on the
principle of feedback, will restore the problem of purpose
to a fuller share of attention in scientific fields and professional disciplines.   "It will help us to make a much needed
distinction between the attainment of actual external goals,
and the reduction of goal-drive merely by internal readjust-
ment that provides an ersatz satisfaction (or short-circuit),
such as scapegoating, drug addiction, or other so-called
'mechanisms of control'" (11, p. 57).

Vickers cites three main groups of problems concerned with adaptation. How does the system know what action is needed? How does it decide what to do? How does it make its decisions effective? He describes the regulating process which continually adjusts behavior so as to preserve the desirable state; and equally adjusts the desirable state so as to keep ways of behaving within the limits of the possible:

> The problems for R [a regulating process] is to choose a way of behaving which will neutralize the disturbance threatening the maintenance of E [a desirable state]. Success means initiating behavior which will reduce the deviation between the actual course of affairs and the course which would be consonant with E; or at least preventing its nearer approach to the limit of the unacceptable or the disastrous.
>
> This decision is a choice between a limited number of alternatives. Men and societies have only a finite number of ways of behaving, perhaps a much smaller number than we realize; and the number actually available and relevant to a given situation is far smaller still. It is thus essential to regard these decisions as the exercise of restricted choice.
>
> These decisions are of four possible kinds. When the usual responses fail, the system may alter itself, for instance by learning new skills or reorganizing itself so as to make new behaviors possible; it may alter the environment; it may withdraw from the environment and seek a more favorable one; or it may alter E. These are possible, if at all, only within limits; and altogether may prove insufficient.
>
> It remains to ask how men and societies choose from among these alternatives, when choose they must. In brief, the answer is 'by experience', but experience operates in various ways, none of them perfect; and they demand some closer enquiry (47, p. 223).

These characteristics and properties of open living systems may enhance understanding of dysfunctional or pathological conditions which confront the practitioner. Thus, for example, there may be an insufficiency of input to maintain the system or the input may be of a kind that cannot be utilized by the system; there may be excessive tensions within the system or in the system-environment interchange; there

may be disturbances in the operation of a particular subsystem or in the interplay of dynamic system processes;
there may be faulty feedback mechanisms; there may be too
great a "cost" in establishing a new steady state--that is,
the system resources cannot absorb the cost in making the
transition to a new steady state (22, p. 49-50).

Systems Theory and Personality and Social Systems

There is ample documentation of the significance of
general systems theory, and specifically the theory of open
systems, for personality and social system theories.   It
appears to this writer that general systems theory has provided further "evidence" for several groups of psychologists
and sociologists to oppose the dominating or traditional
tenets in both fields; that is, Freudian psychoanalytic concepts and the Parsonian structural-functional model.   Such
opposition is of particular import because the structural-
functional model of social systems developed by Parsons incorporates and/or is complementary to psychoanalytic concepts of personality.   Moreover, social work literature has
utilized these two theories primarily in application to social
work practice (e. g. , Lutz, 31).   Indeed, recent articles devoted to the relationship of social casework and systems
theory utilize illustrations that demonstrate the congruence
of psychoanalytic concepts, for example, the psychic
structure of id, ego, and superego, and the congruence of
social system concepts, for example, role, status, social
structure and function with general systems theory and with
the goals, values, and method of social casework (44, 23,
26).

Hollis states that "the familiar id, superego, and ego of
Freudian personality theory can be viewed as such structural
components of the personality"--in accord with the systems
theory notion of interacting structural parts (23, p. 192).
Sister Mary Paul Janchill points out that "in general, caseworkers have not explored psychological theories for different
interpretations of insight and have tended to keep its definition
within the psychoanalytic model, " but she later shows how
both psychoanalytic theory and structural-functional analysis
may be drawn upon to explicate or implement systems concepts of importation of energy, through-put, and output.   She
also notes that homeostasis is a crucial concept in psychoanalytic theory and that recent studies of dreams have contributed to its validation (44, p. 76, 78-79, 80).

Family theorists as well as family therapists in social work and allied professional disciplines have extensively utilized the Parsonian structural-functional model. Bell and Vogel's analysis of nuclear family interaction and organization is based on Parson's more abstract model concerning the four "problems" or "requisites" that every social system must meet to maintain itself (4). Many family studies, with implications for family treatment, have been rooted in the Parsonian model. Klein has written about a project focused on the family as the client-system in which structural-functional categories were employed in family diagnosis and treatment. He concludes that "any practice which predicates intervention in the structural-functional aspects of the family, but which does not include the personality systems [of the family members] will not be able to reach a viable family treatment objective. " He further states that "those who sub- scribe to this premise must remember that Talcott Parsons was explicit in pointing out that the personality systems of the members of the social system are interpenetrating with the social and cultural systems" (26, p. 9). Lutz also notes that according to Parsonian theory, the personality is the mediator of the other three--biological, social and cultural-- systems (31).

With this recognition of the utility of general systems theory for personality and social system theories, some consideration should be given to notions that challenge the Freudian psychoanalytic and Parsonian social system models. These notions essentially refer to concepts of change and deviance.

Before proceeding, however, it should be stated ex- plicitly that general systems theory is applicable to both personality and social systems. Bertalanffy believes that general systems theory is abstract and general enough to permit application to the personality as a system--that is, to psychological phenomena (8, p. 24). And Gordon Allport writes that "whatever also personality may be, it has the properties of a system" (3, p. 109). Similarly, Gross views social system theory as a special application of general systems theory--

> it deals with systems ranging from single formal
> organizations of various types up to urban, regional,
> national, and international territorial entities. It may
> be applied to the family and the individual personality
> system. It is 'general' in the sense that it is not

partial, that is, it is capable of dealing with all
aspects of organizations and territorial entities (19,
p. 369).

He also cites the "vigorous boost to the study of social
systems provided by the fundamental . . . work of James
G. Miller across all levels of living systems" (19, p. 366).

The personality may be understood as an open system
in interchange with its environment, characterized by wholeness, steady state, tension, differentiation and specialization,
and the hierarchic order of parts or processes.   The personality system of man is "symbol-creating and symbol-domi-
nated" and cannot be reduced to drives or instincts (5).
Grinker points out that the understanding of disease is based
on how the psyche as a system develops and organizes into
a comprehensive whole (18).   In systems theory, the psychotic regression is essentially disintegration of personality;
that is, de-differentiation and de-centralization.   The mentally
ill individual "has an ego boundary that is at once too fluid
and too rigid" and frequently has disturbances of symbolic
functions (5, p. 713-714).

Bertalanffy and others emphasize the usefulness of the
concept of the organism as a spontaneously active system.
Even without external stimuli, the organism is not passive
but intrinsically active.   The spontaneous, internally-based
activity and the inherent tensions of the individual account
for much of man's social and cultural creativity.   In fact,
it is considered a symptom of mental disease that spontaneity
is impaired (5).   As noted earlier, the "active organism"
concept attacked the stimulus-response scheme and the original homeostasis principle associated with the "law of inertia"
and the system "seeking" tension reduction.   In this regard,
Bertalanffy states that "the homeostasis scheme is not applicable 1) to dynamic regulation, that is, regulations not based
upon fixed mechanisms but taking place within a system
functioning as a whole . . .   2) to spontaneous activities,
3) to processes whose goal is not reduction but building up
of tensions, and 4) to processes of growth, development,
creation and the like" (5, p. 710-711).

The question of the equilibrium concept in personality is
one often raised by theorists and practitioners.   While it is
true that equilibrium has been a basic tenet in Freudian
theory of personality, it is also true that developments in
ego psychology (within psychoanalytic theory) have dealt with

the "active organism" and the proactive nature of personality,
e. g. , the primary autonomous functions of the ego.   Moreover, Lutz, presenting the Parsonian view of the concept of
equilibrium in personality, states that "the personality seems
to seek not merely a dead level of equilibrium or the complete discharge of all tensions.   Rather it seeks the maintenance of some levels of tension pleasant to itself and the
exercise of its own abilities" (31, p. 32).

Allport is one of the leading figures in the field of
psychology who has attacked the "static view" of personality.
He states that

> to be sure it [personality] is an incomplete system,
> manifesting varying degrees of order and disorder.
> It has structure, but also unstructure, function but
> also malfunction.   As Murphy says, 'all normal people
> have many loose ends. '   And yet personality is well
> enough knit to qualify as a system--which is defined
> merely as a complex of elements in mutual inter-
> action (3, p. 567).

Allport cites the two major criteria of open systems--materi-
al and energy exchange and the steady state--which are incorporated in most current theories of personality and thereby "they emphasize stability rather than growth, permanence
rather than change, 'uncertainty reduction' (information
theory) and 'coding' (cognitive theory) rather than creativity.
Most personality theories emphasize being rather than becoming; . . . they are biologistic in the sense that they
ascribe to personality only these two features of an open
system that are clearly present in all living organisms"
(2, p. 345-346).   He rejects the "functionalism" current in
psychology and social science because its emphasis is always on the usefulness of an activity in maintaining the
"steady state" of a personality or social or a cultural
system.   "'Functional' theories stress maintenance of present direction allowing little room or not at all for departure
and change" (2, p. 350).

Many biologists and most personality theorists, according to Allport, neglect two additional criteria of open systems.
Certain personality theorists, however, have recognized and
utilized the third criterion; namely, "the tendency of human
personality to go beyond steady states and to strive for an
enhancement and elaboration of internal order even at the
costs of considerable disequilibrium" (for example, Goldstein's

conception of self-actualization, post-Freudian ego psychology, Woodworth's behavior-primary vs. need theory, Robert White's emphasis on competence, and Erikson's "search for identity"). The fourth criterion derived from the theory of open systems is the recognition of personality as part of the context of the social-cultural environment. Allport himself takes the somewhat conservative position that the personality theorist should be able to cast the individual's behavior in its situational context and in terms of role theory and field theory, but that he should not define personality per se in terms of interaction, culture, or roles. He accepts the transactional criterion of the open system but cautions that it is not to be applied so as to lose the personality system itself (2, p. 346-348).

It is of interest that Allport not only qualifies the use of the transactional criterion of the open system, but that he also stresses the danger of using general systems theory which seeks formal identities between physical systems, the cell, the organ, the personality, small groups, the species, and society. In attempting to unify science, closed or only partly open systems become our model. In other words, rather than seeing the open system as part of general systems theory, Allport proposes that open-systems theory be utilized in opposition to general systems theory. From this perspective, he reduces all sharp controversies in personality theory "as probably arising from the two opposed points of view--the quasi-closed and the fully open" (2, p. 348-349).

In the light of this discussion, it should be understood that general systems theory does include the four criteria specified by Allport; moreover, it does not, by being a "holistic" theoretical model which attempts to establish formal identities between the different system levels, utilize the closed or quasi-closed model where the open model is indicated. That is, the organismic model as used by Bertalanffy and others is an open system model--whether it be concerned with the cell or societal system level. Furthermore, while there is no living system that is completely closed, there is no living system that is completely open in all areas. "Certain areas of open systems become somewhat isolated from the whole and thus tend to function more like closed systems" (22, p. 55). Allport himself, in defending his concept of functional autonomy (i.e., motives may become functionally autonomous of their origins), indicates that there is preservative autonomy which applies to the relatively closed part-systems within the personality, and propriate

functional autonomy which applies to the continuously evolving
structure of the whole (2, p. 349).   Hearn indicates that the
question of whether a system is open or closed can be
answered by assuming that it is both.   At any point in time
a system, especially an organismic system, possesses some
degree of both openness and closedness (e. g. , the schizophrenic individual).   It may also be postulated that the openness of organismic systems "is only temporary and transitory, "
that is, a system will die; negative entropy will cease and
positive entropy will reign.   The usefulness of the concepts
of open and closed systems is that they define "the manner
in which the open and closed aspects of organismic systems
can be expected to function" (22, p. 57).

     Similar challenges of the Parsonian structural-functional
theory have been made by social scientists.   It is claimed
that the Parsonian model, like the classical equilibrium
model, has a "conserving orientation. "   "The boundary of
the [social] system is defined in terms of 'constancy
patterns' that are based upon a harmonious set of common
norms and values and mutually supporting expectations.
Equilibrium in turn is defined in terms of the boundary-
maintaining system of constant, harmonious, mutual, common,
reciprocal, complementary, stabilized, and integrated
patterns. "   The Parsonian system thus "excludes, or includes
only residually, structured strains and deviant patterns which,
however, may be constant, mutual, and reciprocal within
themselves and to a great extent in relation to the dominant
structure" (11, p. 28).   The Parsonian system includes
mainly those determinate relations making up an "institutionalized" dominant structure of conformity to role expectations.   This is the fixed point of reference and other structural patterns or latent consequences are viewed as potentially
disruptive and posing "problems" of control (functional imperatives) of the system.   Deviance and strains of various
kinds (e. g. , neurotic symptoms, delinquency and criminal
behavior, organized social movements) are not only residual
in the model but they must be treated as dysfunctional for
the system.   This model, therefore, lends only to a consideration of adjustive processes and deviance control aimed
at adaptation of the actor to a given dominant structure and
does not provide for mechanisms that adapt or change the
system structure to accomodate the actor and maintain the
total system.   Social change, it is said, is also residual in
the Parsonian model since it implies that the sources of
change are always external to the system (11, p. 29, 30). [11]

Buckley points out that these inadequacies of the Parsonian model were noted earlier by the sociologist Selznick and the social psychologist, Newcomb.   Selznick has written that:

> in Parson's writing there is no true embrace of the idea that structure is being continuously opened up and reconstructed by the problem-solving behavior of individuals responding to concrete situations. ... Social structure is something to be taken account of in action; cognition is not merely an empty category but a natural process involving dynamic assessments of the self and the other (11, p. 23).

And Newcomb, in 1948, wrote that:

> from a psychological point of view the process of learning to respond in certain ways to other people is the same whether the end result is a conforming or a deviant role.   In either case the process is one of goal-directed behavior involving perception, performance, thought and affect.   The goal toward which behavior is directed while institutionally prescribed roles are being acquired is not necessarily "to acquire the prescribed role" (11, p. 28).

Buckley presents the thesis that the general systems approach provides a more holistic orientation to the problem of complex organization than does the Parsonian model. Like Miller and Bertalanffy, he believes that systems theory "promises to develop a common language unifying the several 'behavioral' disciplines. ...   In its focus on 'relations' rather than 'entities,' it emphasizes process and transition probabilities as the basis of a flexible structure with many degrees of freedom."   Finally, it permits "an operationally definable, objective, non-anthropomorphic study of purposiveness, goal-seeking system behavior, symbolic cognitive processes, consciousness and self-awareness, and socio-cultural emergence and dynamics in general" (11, p. 39).

The foregoing review of some of the implications of general systems theory for personality and social system theories reflects the trend toward models that account for change and deviance.   It poses important questions for the practitioner as well as the theorist.   Such questions relate to the definition and meanings attributed to general systems theory; they include the question of whether the theory of

open systems is separate from or incorporated in general
systems theory, whether the organismic model is valid for
the personality and social systems and whether general
systems theory does or should utilize the "organismic
analogy." Finally, the question regarding the utility of the
structural-functional model for change-agents depends on
whether one accepts this model as incorporating change or
deviance or whether another theoretical model that does
justice to these concepts is required. In attempting to answer
these questions one must take into consideration whether
there are semantic or real differences, whether the meanings
of concepts have changed over time, and most importantly,
it must be remembered that the concepts are part of a total
theoretical frame of reference and "stance" and cannot be
dealt with in isolation except for purposes of analytic exploration. The terms functional and dysfunctional have particular
significance here because systems may often be classified
for purposes of intervention or treatment either as healthy
("normal") or pathological, functional or dysfunctional. [12]
The terms functional and dysfunctional may be applied with
respect to the system's relation to the suprasystem, to the
relations of the system parts, or to the system as a whole.
This then involves the transactional view of system parts-
whole and systems in the field.

Application of Systems Theory to Social Casework: Background

It is not possible within the scope of this chapter to give
a complete presentation and analysis of the implications of
general systems theory for social casework. The writer
will attempt to make explicit those implications incorporated
in the foregoing theoretical material and to suggest additional
points regarding the implications of general systems theory
for social casework within the context of social work practice.
The following discussion, therefore, draws upon the selected
concepts and principles elucidated here (and in other writings)
as they may be applied to the social casework process; it
also gives some consideration to the limitations and "dangers"
involved in the use of systems theory by social casework
practitioners.

Some explanatory introductory comments to such a discussion are in order. First, it should be noted that general
systems theory is highly abstract and cannot be applied to
the casework process in the same way as role concepts, the
family as a unit of attention, small group theory, and the

like; that is, middle-range theories are more readily operationalized. Systems theory overarches these middle-range
theories and concepts, and incorporates them. However, it
also gives these concepts enchanced meaning and usefulness.
It has been suggested, for example, that the role concept,
when isolated from the system of which it is a part, i. e.,
an analysis of the system and its environment or field,
limits the utility of the concept and may distort the goal of
the social worker (45). General systems theory, thus, has
not been concretized in systematic application. It has been
written about--in terms of suggested implications for practice
and the congruence of systems theory with social work values
and principles--but it has not been tested by caseworkers.
Nevertheless, the great interest in systems theory has led
to some application of selected concepts or principles both
in literature and in practice. Carlson applied the concepts
of feedback to explain the dynamics of a riot situation in a
correctional institution (12). Shulman demonstrated the idea
that behavior observed at one level could be applied to behavior at other levels of human organization (43). These
two illustrations, however, are not applied to casework per
se and--while the behaviors of individuals are involved--the
application is at the "social" level rather than at the indi-
vidual-personality level of intervention. [13] Moreover, most
of the literature provides suggestive notions for utilization,
rather than accounts of actual experience in the application
of systems theory.

In 1958 Hearn wrote that "a very great deal remains to
be done before the tangible contributions of general systems
theory toward the illumination and refinement of social work
practice are clearly demonstrated." He cites three tasks
to be undertaken. The first task "is an objective study of
the human realities with which we are dealing in social work
practice. The second is model-building--the development of
models capable of conceptualizing these human realities.
And the third is the testing of the validity and utility of our
models by determining whether their application leads to new
insights for practice and ultimately to the rendering of better
service." Hearn offers some suggestions regarding macro-
scopic and microscopic studies--similar to this writer's remarks above--and indicates that the testing and utilization of
the model should include a variety of social work clients,
i. e., client-systems such as the individual, family, small
group, organization and community (22, p. 73-76). In sum,
the application and testing of systems theory in social casework is still left to the future.

Second, most of the literature concerning the application of systems theory is not only suggestive rather than documented, selective rather than comprehensive, but is essentially concerned with the goals, nature and focus of social work and the development of a practice theory, rather than with the casework process of study, diagnosis and treatment. This is not to say that such discussions do not have implications for the casework process "trilogy," and in fact, these are sometimes pinpointed specifically. However, references to the study, diagnosis and treatment procedures are offered primarily as illustrations of the value of systems theory for the social work method and social work theory as a whole. While some have written about systems theory solely in terms of the casework method (22, 41), many writers view systems theory as the key to a holistic conception of social work practice and the development of social work generalists (42). In the latter view, systems theory is intended to encompass the seven levels of practice. It is a means of counteracting or "dissolving" the compartmentalizations of practice methods. It is expected to move "social work practice into a unified whole and link that whole to the behavioral sciences generally; and to wider bodies of knowledge . . ." (27, p. 62).

Third, the application of systems theory must be considered in relation to the client-system of social casework. As Strean states, a major concern of social casework is the individual and it utilizes its unique method in relating to the individual. But he also comments that the method and function of social casework changes with the times and the society and culture within which it exists (46). Thus, social caseworkers may also be family therapists and group therapists. Their interest in working with families and small groups has led them to draw upon family and small group theory so as to facilitate their therapeutic practice.

There has been much debate, as well as much confusion, regarding the caseworker's client-system. Klein differentiates between the family treatment model, typically utilized by social caseworkers, and the systems approach to family treatment. He makes the point that in the former the goal is to effect change in the individuals as they function in the family group, whereas in the latter, the goal is to bring about change in the family system itself. Consequently, in the former, treatment centers around psychic motivation, non-verbal communication, neurotic interaction and maladaptive coping devices, whereas in the systems ap-

proach treatment is directed to the processes, structural-
functional categories, and elements which compose the system
and their interaction. By elements Klein means "belief,
goal, norm, rank, power, sanction, and so forth" (26, p. 6).
Hollis, on the other hand, believes that treatment of the
individual will affect the family system as a whole. In
systems theory this issue is reflected in the conceptualization
of the system level and the notion of system-environment;
specifically, the hierarchic order of human systems, system-
environment interchange, and the common properties that
apply to each system level. The interrelationship between
the system and its environment may be interpreted as the
fact that each of two systems is part of the external situation
of the other, or that two systems are integrated structurally,
e. g. , personalities are integrated into the roles of the social
system (31). Systems theory, however, may not be used as
a vehicle to reduce one system to another. The primary
system (for intervention) must be determined through systems
analysis and the system must be understood in terms of its
structure, function and process and its transactional field.

The Relationship Between Systems Theory and Social Casework Theory

Systems theory thus has not been systematically applied
to the casework process. However, there are implications
and limited demonstrations that the casework process of
study, diagnosis and treatment can be enriched by systems
concepts and that systems theory is compatible with the
existing framework of casework. A review of the literature
reveals general consensus that systems theory is congruent
with the basic concepts, construct, values and principles of
social casework.

First, systems theory is compatible with and supportive
of the notion that casework is psycho-social, that problems
are to be understood in terms of both internal and external
factors, and that the caseworker's focus is on the person-in-
situation configuration. All writers appear to agree that this
concept is at the core of casework (and social work) practice.
Hollis speaks of the person-situation configuration; Sister
Mary Paul Janchill similarly specifies the person-in-environ-
ment; Gordon cites the person-in-his-life-situation complex,
a simultaneous dual focus on man and environment; Polsky
is concerned with the client and his environment; and Lathrope states that a system cannot be understood apart from

the network in which it is imbedded (23, 44, 17, 38, 28).

This basic concept in casework points to the interdependence of the person and his environment and is tied to the
concept of the open system; for example, there is interchange
of energy and information of the person-system with its
environment, the system seeks an adaptive relationship to
its environment (steady state), and a change in the system
affects its environment and vice versa. Despite the wide-
spread acceptance of this casework concept there has been
dissatisfaction with "a persistent pattern of dichotomizing
internal and external dimensions" that is reflected in the
methods and goals of casework treatment as well as in the
study-diagnostic process (44, p. 75). It is of interest, however, that the utilization of systems theory as a means of
bringing phenomena and events (internal and external) into
dynamic relation to each other, has led to some differing
interpretations or conclusions regarding the implications for
casework practice. Hollis emphasizes the value of working
primarily with the individual to effect change in himself and
indirectly cause changes in others in his environment. Other
writers, however, believe that one of the consequences of
utilizing general systems theory will be to focus special
attention on the environment (22, 38, 17). Also, by using
the open system concept it is recognized that there will be
greater choice in selecting the primary system (the unit of
attention) as well as relating that system to other systems
in the field, and will call for a wider ranger of method,
knowledge and skill.

Second, systems theory, and particularly the open system
concept, provides a scientific framework for the long-stand-
ing values of social casework, namely, respect for the uniqueness of the individual and his self-determination. "The
qualitative as well as quantitative potentials for individual-
ization and development are implicit in this concept of open
system and its dependence on a supporting environment" (44,
p. 78). In 1958 Hearn pointed out that the concept of equifinality is very important in social work theory, particularly
the underpinning notion that it is of the nature of human
beings to be creators.

> On the basis of equifinality[14] it follows that humans,
> regardless of their experiences, will strive to main-
> tain a steady state around a condition that permits and
> fosters creativity. Humans, by nature, are not con-
> tent merely to adjust to their environment. They have

an inner compulsion to influence it and shape it in
ways that create ever more complex relationships
between themselves and their environment (22, p. 45).

Hollis similarly emphasizes the proactive nature of human
systems and their capacity for differentiation. She refers
to the purposive quality of personality systems as the innate
tendency to develop with direction. It is "this aspect of
systems theory that parallels and supports casework's insistence from its own experience upon the uniqueness of the
individual and the importance of working with it rather than
acting as if the individual were merely to be acted upon,
persuasively, or by suggestion" (23, p. 192).

The inherent drive of the organism to have effect may
be related to the concept of negative entropy which is the
basis of the system's growth and differentiation (44, p. 80).
Gordon suggests that the concept of entropy be a guiding
principle in social work; that is, "to reduce entropy in
systems with which we work and influence its extraction and
exportation into the environment in such a way, and in such
a form, that it can be imported into the other systems, depending upon that environment, to promote their growth and
decrease their entropy" (21, p. 65-66). It was noted earlier
that the processes of progressive segregation and progressive
mechanization hold entropic forces in check. They are life
maintaining but they also impose constraints upon the system
and thereby may limit the degree to which the system may
achieve its potentiality. This is relevant for casework
practice which is based

upon the idea that human beings are continually in a
state of approaching, but never reaching, their full
potentiality. The fact that the fixing of arrangements
[e. g., certain feedback mechanisms], the imposing of
constraints, while a necessary condition of organization
limits the extent to which the organism may realize
its potentiality, is perhaps at the basis of the social
work principles of maximizing self-regulation and self-
determination and of keeping manipulation by external
agents to a minimum (22, p. 49).

Lathrope suggests that the systems paradigm--input plus
processing equals output, including the feedback loop--may
help the client-system, whether individual, group, or organization, exercise the effective choice and goal-fulfillment
implicitly conveyed by the idea of self-determination. He

also states that "the systems concept of equifinality lends
practical support to the self-determination tenet, for it implies that there is a wide range and variety of possible
combinations of habits of mind and feelings and of lines of
behavior which can be put together to achieve desired output
and to constitute a person's, or group's or organization's
life style" (27, p. 59). In a like vein, it has been proposed
that the principle of equifinality be "a subject for renewed
cathective interest by caseworkers that should lead to the
creative experimentation in methods by which human growth
and happiness may be influenced and achieved" (44, p. 81).

    Third, systems theory is compatible with but gives
greater breadth and scope to the goals of social casework.
Typically, the casework objective has been phrased only in
terms of the individual. That is, it may be expressed as
enhancing social functioning or social competence, or as
improving ego functioning. As Hollis states, the casework
process is shaped by its objective of helping the individual
to solve his current problems in such a way that he will
have increased his capacity for meeting other problems (23,
p. 190). Polsky, in applying social system theory to client
needs, defines the goal of the social work system as enabling
the client to become more autonomous, to increase his
mastery over his situation and himself in and through the
social work process itself (38). This goal of self-fulfillment
may be recast in systems terms; namely, to "produce the
change from an initial state to the goal state, to assist the
client in maintaining a steady state (in dynamic relation to
his environment) and to overcome what is impeding and to
foster the attainment of that steady state" (42, p. 31; 22,
p. 33). Shafer calls attention to the fact that "prevention
and restoration of equilibrium fall within the function of social
work. Reduction of the causes of conflict as well as the
treatment of consequences of disturbed human relationships
are the purposes to which social work has addressed itself"
(42, p. 33). The emphasis in these goal-purpose statements
is on the "matching" of the system and its environment; to
develop a correspondence between internal and external
relations (21, p. 67). Despite the similarities in these goal
statements, those given by caseworkers tend to focus on
changing the client-system to match the external-system
whereas writers of the systems approach emphasize change
in client-system and also the external systems impinging on
the client-system. The latter also refer to a wide range of
client-systems (individual, family, small group, organization,
community), whereas caseworkers tend to limit their focus

to the individual or family as the client-system.

Thus, while there is congruence between the values and goals of social casework and systems theory, the latter suggests implications for new dimensions for social casework method, the role of the caseworker, and the client-worker relationship. As noted, social work proponents of systems theory view the analogistic aspect of general systems theory, the common properties of systems, and the hierarchical order of open interacting systems as the conceptual basis for the development of a holistic theory of social work and for replacing method specializations of casework, group work, and community organization with a generic social work process. Social casework would be incorporated in a social work method that encompasses "a continuum of interactional approaches constituting a range of modalities." In this context, the role of the social worker will be expanded and the social worker's practice will "occur in the region between the system and its environment" (21, p. 30, 68). For example, Gordon writes that "the central social work focus is placed at the interface between or the meeting place of person and environment--at the point where there is or is not matching with all its good and bad consequences for person and environment. The phenomenon of concern at this interface is the transaction between person and environment.... Transaction is an action intersystem between the person-system and the environment-system" (17, p. 7). The helping system is the mediator between society and the impaired individual (38, p. 19). Thus, while social work activity is focused inside, outside, and at the boundary between the system and environment, emphasis is placed upon activities in the boundary region (21, p. 69).

Systems theory refocuses the locus of social work activity and recasts the role of the social worker as a change-agent. The social worker's role cannot be isolated from the system of which it is a part and it must be recognized that society often shapes social work systems in ways that may not be helpful to clients. Moreover, change in the client involves not only his personality and family system but his helping system and his role in the helping system. We must take into account not only the response of the client-system to the helping system but what the client-system does in its own behalf (22). It is considered important "to enable the client to change by effecting a change in the force-field surrounding him" (21, p. 70). The helping system changes as the clients become better-functioning individuals. With this view of the role of the social worker and the goal of the worker-client relationship, Polsky suggests that we "create temporary insitutions and maximally involve clients in a change process by joining them in overhauling the systems that we have created and excluded them from initially because of their impairment" (38, p. 19). [15] While social casework has always incorporated the notion of client participation, systems theory enlarges the scope and nature of this participation and thereby has significance for the role of the caseworker and the client-worker relationship (including the concept of self-awareness). [16] Systems theory provides a model in which social workers as part of helping systems can facilitate change in the client, the helping system, and the larger society (38, 45).

The system-environment concept has relevance for conceptualizing the worker-client relationship. Whereas Polsky has the notion of creating temporary helping institutions, Hearn states that "the social worker comes into relationship from out of the client's distal environment when a need for service arises, and goes back, not into the distal but into the proximal environment when his function has been served. That is, he is 'out' of the client's life although available should need for service arise again" (22, p. 53). Using casework as an example, he describes the sequence of a typical relationship,

> beginning with the worker as part of the client's distal environment from which he usually moves fairly quickly into the proximal environment. As the relationship continues, . . . the worker and client become welded, . . . at least to some extent, into a dyadic system, manifesting all the characteristic properties of such. Later, in the termination process, the worker tries to move back into the proximal and ultimately into the client's distal environment. Social workers know how important it is for them to assess correctly where the client perceives them to be at various stages in the relationship and to capitalize fully upon these perceptions in the helping process (22, p. 62).

Finally, Hearn suggests that as the client-system becomes progressively more complex so does the social work process. However, "work with lower levels in the hierarchy of human systems may be more complicated, for one is likely to be involved with a system at a deeper level and will likely be helping it to cope with more complex problems" (22, p. 71).

A Model for the Casework Process

The foregoing discussion of systems theory and the role
of the caseworker and the worker-client relationship raises
the question of the utility of an intersystem model which involves two open systems connected to each other. Chin advocates this intersystem model for practitioners because it
includes the change-agent and his relationships as part of
the problem and because it:

> exaggerates the virtues of autonomy and the limited
> nature of interdependence of the interactions between
> the two connected [client and worker] systems . . . .
> The change-agent built into an organization . . . does
> not completely become a part of the client-system.
> He must remain separate to some extent; he must
> create and maintain some distance between himself
> and the client, thus standing apart "in another
> system" from which he re-relates (13, p. 207).

Intersystem analysis furthers understanding of the connectives,
conjunctive and disjunctive, between the two systems and
poses the issue of the internal system of the change-agent.
"Helpers of change [tend] not to see that their own systems
as change-agents have boundaries, tensions, stresses and
strains, equilibria, and feedback mechanisms which may be
just as much parts of the problem as are similar aspects
of the client-systems." In an intersystem model, thus,
relational issues are more available for diagnosis (13, p.
208).

It appears to this writer that the concept of system as
an entity, as open, and as part of a hierarchical organization
of systems allows for the kind of analysis that Chin seeks
in an intersystem model. In fact, it was noted above that
social work itself may be considered as an action intersystem, thereby focusing on connectives between the client-
system and other systems in the field, including the helping
system. Client and worker may be part of the helping
organization but the system model implies that they are also
systems in themselves, with all the basic characteristics and
properties of systems. In addition, the analogistic aspect
of general systems theory facilitates analysis of the system
and its relations to other systems. Hearn's description of

the sequence of the worker-client relationship over time is more adequately represented by the system model presented here than the intersystem model. 17   That is, his formulation suggests that the worker is part of the environment-field and that the client-system and helping system move in relation to each other.   For purposes of analysis and intervention it would seem that, at a certain point in the relationship process, client and worker may be conceptualized as a dyadic system of interaction.

General systems theory provides a framework and conceptual tools for the psycho-social problems confronting social workers.   Typically, the concepts of steady state and stress, strain and conflict have been cited to describe the problems of individuals and groups to which social casework (and all social work practice) has addressed itself.   Thus, it has been stated that social workers "are confronted with people whose capacity to maintain steady states through effective responses to coded (i. e. , informational) inputs is impaired. " Systems theory is useful in explaining "variations in the client's capacity to maintain or return to stable states in both normal and pathological environments" (42, p. 33). Stated differently, social work "service is rendered to clients who are experiencing or may experience the disequilibrating effects of stressful situations" (22, p. 69).   The dynamic aspect of steady states of open systems suggests that the system under stress--through new inputs--may reorganize toward a new level of steady state; in other words, stress may lead to new adaptations.   This is the key idea in crisis intervention.   Many of the cross-level propositions formulated by Miller contain explanatory and predictive knowledge regarding system processes that maintain or disturb the steady state, including adjustment processes used in maintaining variables in steady states, growth, cohesiveness, and integration, and pathology.   Additional systems concepts incorporated in these propositions include input and output, differentiation, decentralization and interdependence of subsystems and components, and system-subsystem boundaries (35).

Systems theory, its concepts and hypotheses, have implications for use in the casework process as a whole and in the study, diagnosis and treatment dimensions of this process.   Before specifying some implications for the study-diagnosis-treatment process, the overall utility of general systems theory as a model of human systems with which caseworkers work, should be stressed.   While models are

means of theory building, they have practical value in conceptualizing the psycho-social problems of client-systems.
The system model enables us to organize existing knowledge
from many scientific disciplines, to point to gaps and inconsistencies in this body of knowledge, to generate new
knowledge, at the same time that it enables us to work with
the concrete case.   The practitioner utilizes a conceptual
or analytic model[18] as he constructs the working model of
the concrete problem-situation.   He sees where congruities
and discrepancies occur between the conceptual model of the
system and the actual events.   "He becomes . . . the observer, analyzer and modifier of the conceptual model he is
using" (13, p. 201).   In his article on the nature of clinical
evidence, Erikson points out that the practitioner "must
maintain a constant inner traffic between his often dramatic
observations and his conceptual models however crude they
may be" (27, p. 49).

    Conceptual or analytic models of systems may be applied
to different units of human interaction.   The system model
can "bring into common perspective what initially appears on
the basis of surface manifestations to be unrelated or disparate phenomena and complexities" (28, p. 1).   It contains the
protocols of observation and action to guide the practitioner.
It provides mind-holds; it identifies what factors are taken
into account and the relationships among them; it lessens the
danger of overlooking the indirect effects of a change of a
relationship (27, p. 49; 13, p. 201-202).   As a way of thinking and analysis, says Helen M. Lynd, systems theory makes
"a difference in the kinds of questions to which attention is
directed, the kinds of experiences considered important for
study, the kinds of hypotheses entertained, the models and
analogies considered appropriate, and the range of human
variations and possibilities envisaged" (42, p. 35).   Chin
suggests that the theoretically minded practitioner examine
his conceptual model for its usefulness in effecting change.
The questions he raises for this purpose are: First, does
the model account for the stability and continuity in the
events studied at the same time that it accounts for change
in them?   Second, where does the model locate the source
of change?   Third, what does the model assume about how
goals and directions are determined?   Fourth, does the
model provide the change-agent with levers or handles for
affecting the direction, tempo, and quality of these processes
of change?   And a fifth question running through the other
four is: how does the model "place" the change-agent in the
scheme of things?   (13, p. 211-212).   In sum, general systems

theory as a holistic theory has sub-theories and incorporates a wide range of theories from different disciplines. The system model thus provides a broader scientific base for practice and offers the caseworker a disciplined framework for investigation and analysis of the client-environment systems; it enhances predictive ability while it fosters the utilization of more diverse and creative interventions.

There appears to be consensus that the application of systems theory to casework practice leads to a diagnostic approach that has a larger view of symptom or problem behavior and avoids unidirectional cause-effect thinking; it requires a synthetic--rather than piecemeal--analysis that focuses on the study of relations rather than of entities per se; it facilitates the formulation of alternative solutions to problem situations, the identification and selection of appropriate points for intervention, and permits a wider scope of change strategy and innovative techniques. Typically, systems theory literature explicates systems concepts and suggests the way the practitioner may be guided by them. That is, systems concepts are not integrated into the casework format of study-diagnosis-treatment. It may be useful, thus, to present a brief summary statement of the conceptualization of the casework (or, more accurately, social work) process in systems terms and illustrate the ways in which systems concepts may be applied to the study-diagnosis-treatment procedures. Particular systems notions that have theoretical and practical significance for the casework process are discussed below.

A Systems Conceptualization of the Casework Process

Systems theory directs us to look at all systems in the field. The practitioner identifies the system-environment complex, locates the boundaries of the client-system, and assesses the degree of openness and closedness of the system. [19] The notion of human organizations as hierarchic open systems composed of interrelated subsystems (e. g., the biological and psychological subsystems of the individual) focuses the practitioner's perception on the mutual interrelations of system parts, the system-environment interchange and the interrelationships among the systems in the field. The worker views the system-environment interchange and relational factors in terms of the goal directedness and the steady state of the client-system. His inquiry includes such questions as: what are the conditions conducive

to the maintenance or achievement of a steady state representing the best possible relationship between the system and
its environment; what parts of the system are stable or precarious, rigid or fluid?   Identifying and locating such system
factors provide guides for reestablishing or reorganizing the
steady state of the system. The concept of steady state is
interwoven with concepts of system tension, strain, and conflict, on the one hand, and adjustive processes on the other.
Does the system resist or deny outside impingments?   What
parts or subsystems show readiness to change?   "Which
part of the system gives you the maximum overall change
in system performance for the least or smallest change in
the subassembly structure?" (18, p. 279).   How do tensions
operate in the system and what type of change (dynamic or
structural) do they lead to? (13).   Such questions imply that
the steady state of the system is related to restorative resources within and outside the system, to systems strains
and tensions, and to stresses from systems in the environment.   Since the system's steady state is related to entropic
processes as well as to progressive systematization (wholeness), the practitioner is concerned with entropy transfer
between the system and its environment.   Stated differently,
the consequences of transactions between system and environment may be assessed in terms of entropic processes.   Growth,
development, and differentiation of the system are related
to the decrease in the entropic process (negative entropy)
which is dependent on the environment and the transaction
intersystem at the organism-environment interface.   The
practitioner needs to determine whether, and in what way,
the transaction intersystem accomplishes a substantial redistribution of entropy between the organism and environment systems (17).

    Transmission processes maintain and change the steady
state of the system and also influence system performance.
Thus, the practitioner examines: a) the nature of input to
the system--what is available in the environment and what
is selectively utilized by the system; b) what the system does
with the input, that is, its conversion or processing; c) what
is the output of the system into the environment; and d)
what are some of the consequences of outputs that are fed
back into the system and tell the system how it is doing. [20]
The worker utilizing this perspective appraises environmental
imports into the system "such as income . . . and material resources, interpersonal interaction with significant others, . . .
communicative acts involving objective, cognitive communication and intimate, cathectic communications" (27, p. 53).[21]

The worker attempts to evaluate the system's sensitivity and responsiveness to the environment and its capacity to convert the resources in the environment into input. What resources is the client-system unaware of and why? How does the system choose its imports and what does this choice preclude in terms of alternate imports? What resources as potential input does the worker know about and control? What input would alter the system's processing and output in the desired direction? (27). In sum, the amount, nature, and form of input, past or current, will aid the practitioner's understanding of the client-system and problem situation and guide his intervention strategy.

General systems theory gives particular attention to environmental inputs that enhance the system's performance. Caseworkers, however, are most familiar with the concept of input in terms of the worker's communications within the "casework relationship." Hollis, for example, states:

> through our input, casework communications, we
> hope in some instances to enable the client's ego to
> develop greater capacity to test reality. By bringing
> about this change in one structure--the ego--we ex-
> pect to modify the interaction between ego, id, and
> superego which in turn modifies what system theorists
> call the system's emergent qualities and what we
> would call the individual's functioning. This change
> in turn enables the client to respond differently in
> other systems of which he is a part--his family, his
> work, and so on. On the other hand, if the case-
> worker presses too hard--interprets too quickly,
> challenges defenses, or sets too high expectations--
> the client experiences anxiety and may regress to an
> equilibrium less adequate for his interactions with
> his social environment (23, p. 192-193).

Klein writes about the family therapist who identifies and clarifies family communication processes, "Particularly those that interfere with effective communication and personal validation, . . . [and who] facilitates and develops interrelations within the family and helps them use each other for facilities and for mutual need-meeting" (26, p. 8).

The practitioner is concerned with the ways in which the system uses its imports and the relation of the imports to the system's output. The way the system responds to energy and information may be referred to as processing activities, coding, or through-put. Mechanisms of defense, for example, can be understood as through-put at the psyche system level; role interaction at the interpersonal level can influence internal processing activities (44, p. 79). It is suggested that the concept of primary task--the central organizing idea by which activities are governed--assists the worker in understanding the complexities of processing. This requires that the worker explore what is happening to input and also disturbances in expected task accomplishments, for example, learning difficulties and non-productive behaviors. The client-system may not be working on an appropriate life task or it may be using inappropriate and problematic ways of coping with life tasks and thereby may fail to achieve its own aims and those of the social-cultural systems of which it is a part (27). Systems propositions may clarify some aspects of internal processing that have relevance for the practitioner. One such proposition of James C. Miller states that "there is always a constant systematic distortion-- or better alteration--between input or energy or information into a system and output from that system." Another proposition states that "the distortion of a system is the sum of the effects of processes which subtract from the input to reduce strains in the subsystems or add to the output to reduce such strains" (33, p. 525-527). Hearn points out that social workers are familiar with distortion of communication between themselves and their clients; if they understand the source of such distortion workers may be able to predict the form and direction which it may take (22).

The practitioner has to be aware--and at times make the client-system aware--of the kind of internal processing being carried on and its relation to the output produced. Outputs in problem situations confronting the caseworker are likely to include anxiety states, disturbances in role performance, interpersonal difficulties. In systems analysis, depression as an "output symptom" may be interpreted within psychoanalytic theory as object loss, or using social science concepts as patient control of environmental systems such as the family and employment, that is, its latent functional consequences (44, p. 80).

"The nature, polarity, and degree of feedback in a system have a decisive effect on the stability or instability of the system" (20, p. 87). As a response to the client-system's output, feedback is most often viewed as an adjustive process that steers the system's operations in a goal-directed way. However, faulty feedback mechanisms may disturb the steady state, may throw the system into non-productive or self-destructive oscillation (27, p. 51). Feedback processes may be reflected, for example, in the client-system's feeling of rejection; a deviation-amplifying feedback system may lead to delinquent behavior. The practitioner utilizing systems theory attempts to determine the client-system's feedback procedures and their adequacy. Is there a lag in feedback; is it intermittent or continuous? What is it that blocks effective use of feedback mechanisms?

Gordon's formulation gives breadth to the feedback notion. He states that:

> transaction as an intersystem is . . . linked to organism-environment exchange provisionally through feedback to both organism and environment.... The idea is consistent with the well-known fact that encounters between organisms and environment leave both changed. Also, organisms that do not have corrective linkages between their inputs and outputs fare poorly. Environments that do not have restorative structures below their surfaces may also be adversely affected through transaction (17, p. 8).

Deutsch, writing about socio-cultural systems, identifies three kinds of information supporting feedback effectiveness which also has applicability to work with person and group systems. He states that:

> a . . . system must continue to receive a full flow of 1) information of the world outside; 2) information from the past, with a wide range of recall and recombination; 3) information about itself and its own parts. Three kinds of feedback which make use of these types of information include: 1) goal-seeking--feedback of new external data into the system net whose operational channels remain unchanged; 2) learning--feedback of new external data for the changing of these operating channels themselves; that is, a change in the structure of the system; and 3) consciousness, or "self-awareness"--feedback of new internal data via secondary messages, messages about changes in the state of parts of the system itself . . .(11, p. 56).

The change-agent can help a client-system increase its diagnostic sensitivity to the effects of its own actions upon

others (13). For example, the caseworker may utilize
negative feedback in allowing the client to locate his problems and test their source or he may utilize a deviation-
counteracting process to interfere with problem-creating
behavior (44, 37). Lathrope points out the importance of
feedback loops for the social work practitioner's interventions
and Chin cites programs in sensitivity training which attempt
to increase or unblock the feedback processes of clients
and thereby have long-lasting significance for them (27, 13).

This discussion of the social work process in systems
terms contains references to interventions or change strategies as well as approaches to study-diagnosis. It may be
helpful, however, to review some of the ideas that pertain
specifically to the practitioner's treatment. First, systems
theory does not suggest that we only intervene in one system;
it does not preclude simultaneous strategic interventions in
one or more systems or subsystems. The practitioner is
concerned about the relevance of a particular entry for effecting change or alteration in the operation of all the interrelated systems whether it be a person-system or a social-
system (40). Klein states that the systems approach to family
treatment prescribes the involvement of all aspects of the
system in treatment--he includes the individual, family,
social group, community and broader social systems as well
(26).22 Second, cross-level propositions of general systems
theory may be used by the practitioner to apply knowledge
of behavior at one level of the system to behavior at other
system levels and thereby guide the practitioner's strategy
for inducing change (43, p. 39). Third, systems theory
suggests that the practitioner intervene in selected para-
meters of the environment and system variables to establish,
maintain, and reorganize the steady state of the system (22).
Activity with regard to resistance is based upon an assessment as to whether it reduces unstablizing inputs or threats
and maintains the "best possible" relation of the system and
its environment, or whether, by reducing threatening input,
adaptive change in the system is endangered (42). Fourth,
systems theory guides the practitioner's activity in facilitating the optimum distribution of entropy in the transaction
intersystem; that is, the practitioner intervenes to promote
the growth and development of the client-system and simultaneously intervenes to ameliorate the environmental systems
(17). Fifth, systems theory propositions that elucidate the
nature of responses to stress and the ways in which the
system employs defenses against stress may guide the practitioner's interventions in crisis situations as well as in situ-

ations in which stress is prolonged over time.[23] Sixth, general systems theory encompasses notions about information and communication nets and has particular relevance for the practitioner's interventions in the system's transmission processes including input, internal processing, output, and feedback. In sum, this discussion of the application of general systems theory to the social work process suggests that the wide range and combinations of its sub-theories and concepts should become part of the practitioner's knowledge base.

ISSUES FOR CASEWORK PRACTICE

Four aspects of systems theory which pose significant issues for casework practice have been selected for presentation. In the following discussion, the notions of system model, system boundary, feedback loop and deviation-amplifying system, system tension and conflict are explored with regard to their conceptual and empirical implications.

System Model

The choice of model used to represent the casework process raises interesting ideas for diagnostic and treatment practices. It has been suggested that general systems theory replace the disease model implicit in the study-diagnosis-treatment formulation employed by caseworkers. Unlike general systems theory with its focus on a synchronic analysis of interacting systems, the study-diagnosis-treatment formulation presupposes pathology at the outset (44, p. 81). Others, however, view general systems theory as congruent with and providing a broader framework for these casework procedures (e. g., Hollis). Those who support the use of the structural-functional model for casework practice apparently view it as compatible with the study-diagnosis-treatment format (38, 26, 40).[24] Some confusion, however, seems to exist in regard to the relationship of the structural functional model to the systems model and both of these models to the disease model of medicine. Involved in this issue are the varying conceptions of the systems model and the structural-functional approach interchangeably, implying that they are synonymous or identical (26, 44); whereas others imply that the structural-functional approach is compatible with or incorporated in the systems approach (38, 19); and still others view the structural-functional model as incompatible with and superseded by the systems model (2, 5, 11).

Questions raised with respect to both these models concern causal analysis and the normative pivot of pathology. These relate to concepts of stability and change, purpose and goal-seeking. A brief examination, thus, of the structural-functional model and the systems model with respect to these questions (causality and pathology) is indicated. First, the assumption that the structural-functional model broadens the base of causal analysis (in contrast to the disease model reflected in the study-diagnosis-treatment format of casework) may not be valid. This model seeks to understand and explain a present behavior or phenomenon in terms of the function it has for another system or subsystem (and not simply for the system in which the behavior exists) but it does so mainly in terms of the continuity, maintenance and stability of the larger system of which it is a part. Stated differently, whereas the traditional causal analysis focuses on a time sequence of prior cause and present effect, functional analysis focuses from present to future events. "But explanation must always translate functions into 'efficient causes'; that is, prior or current states of a system rather than presumed future effects unless some presumption of automatic adequacy or self-regulation can be supported" (11, p. 76). Moreover, functionalism has also been attacked on the basis that it fails to deal with the causal priority of some parts of a system over others; that is, as noted earlier, it does not deal with problems of development and change. Finally, because functional analysis tends to focus on system "needs" it is inadequate in dealing with the concept of system purpose and goal-seeking. Analysis of manifest and latent consequences does not recognize that "most social patterns are a complex emergent product of both purposive and unintended consequences" (11, p. 78).

The systems model, however, does adequately deal with causal analysis, particularly through its concepts of equifinality and feedback. These concepts indicate that different initial conditions may lead to similar results or that similar initial conditions may lead to different results. In this way, the systems model challenges unidirectional cause-effect thinking and clarifies the ways in which transactions operating between the client-system and external systems may generate a deviant outcome. As pointed out earlier, the initial conditions in either the client-system or the external system may or may not be relevant or causally dominant. [25] In contrasting systems analysis with functionalism, Buckley states that "the concepts of teleology and purpose have been

made more respectable or precise by rendering them into
'efficient causes,' or more particularly, into specifiable
mechanisms involving feedbacks" (11, p. 79). Furthermore,
systems analysis does provide the conceptual tools for understanding self-regulation, development, and disintegration of
the system and does not assume automatic regulation or
"mechanisms of control" for any system. Thus, thinking
and learning, particularly as they are manifested in decision-
making, are given an important place in systems analysis.
The systems model is best suited to deal with the problem
of the complex open, adaptive system which depends not
simply on mutual relations of parts, but on certain kinds of
mutual interrelations. In other words, the systems approach,
unlike the traditional causal analysis (which is the type of
analysis frequently utilized in the disease model) or functional analysis, gets at "the full complexity of the interacting
phenomena--to see not only the causes acting on the phenomena under study, the possible consequences of the phenomena, and the possible mutual interactions of some of
these factors, but also to see the total emergent processes
as a function of possible positive and/or negative feedbacks
mediated by the selective decisions, or 'choices,' of the
individuals and groups directly or indirectly involved" (11,
p. 80).

Second, the assumption that both the systems model and
the structural-functional model replace the disease model
which assumes system pathology "at the outset" should be
examined. The issue perhaps is not whether pathology is
assumed but rather what the notion of pathology means and
the way this notion is dealt with in a conceptual scheme.
It should be remembered, for example, that the medical
model was formulated with reference to one system level,
although it has been applied to other system levels as well.
According to Bertalanffy,

> the system concept provides a theoretical framework
> which is psycho-physically neutral.... Causality is
> a category applied to bring order into objectivated
> experience reproduced in symbols.... However,
> causality . . . is but one instrument to bring order
> into experience--and there are other 'perspectives'
> of equal or superior standing (5, p. 716-717).

Thus, it is not that systems theory when applied to a client-
system presumes pathology, but rather that system-theo-
retical notions, by providing a theory of personality, also

provides a consistent framework for psycho-pathology.   If
mental illness is understood as a disturbance of system
functions, isolated symptoms or syndromes do not define the
disease entity.   Psychopathology will be appraised with respect to such notions as the active organism and spontaneous
activity, differentiation and de-differentiation, centralization
and progressive mechanization, symbolic activities and so
forth.   The answer to the question whether an individual is
"mentally sound or not is ultimately determined by whether
he has an integrated universe consistent within the given
cultural framework" (5, p. 715).

        In applying the structural-functional model the practitioner
"starts with dysfunctional clients and a system functional to
clients' dysfunctioning" (38, p. 17).   In functional analysis,
according to Harold Falding (as quoted by Polsky, 38, p. 17):

> evaluating social arrangements as functional or dys-
> functional is equivalent to classifying them as normal
> or pathological.   This is a necessary preliminary to
> the search for causal explanation. ...   Distinguishing
> normal from pathological cases is one of [the physio-
> logist's] assignments and precedes causal knowledge
> of the conditions of normal or pathological functioning.
> Social systems are more complex than livers, of
> course, but the two things are alike in this respect.

Thus, judgments as to whether the system be classified as
functional or dysfunctional is a diagnosis of its normality
and pathology.   However, it is recognized that such an
evaluation is based upon a system of values as well as a
body of knowledge.   Obviously, there are difficulties and
complexities in deciding whether a system is functional or
dysfunctional, particularly when such a decision depends
upon which system or subsystem is being evaluated and
where the observer is located.   By and large, theorists
and practitioners are guided by such notions as autonomy,
self-realization and fulfillment which must be operationalized
with respect to each system-environment complex.   A basis
for distinguishing functional from dysfunctional human organization (or as Hearn states, "up from down, a better from
poorer human condition" (21, p. 65)) may be suggested by
the system concept of entropy.   As Gordon attempts to show,
this concept "constitutes the link between the organism and
environment and delineates the nature of the relationship that
must exist between them if that relationship is to be growth-
producing" (21, p. 66).

System Boundary

As stated earlier, a system as an entity must have
boundaries and living open systems have semi-permeable
boundaries. Thus, boundaries are ultimately dynamic. The
exchange of matter-energy and information between the system
and environment causes boundary change; there is boundary
change with time in growth, maturation, and learning (18,
p. 361). The practitioner, thus, must identify the boundaries
of the system, subsystem, and environmental system in the
transactional field that will be the focus of investigation and
intervention. We do not as yet have criteria for locating
boundaries and selecting action systems but social workers
are familiar with these activities in practice; such activities
are often guided by the use of psychological and social
science concepts. Grinker points out that "boundaries in the
psychological universe always involve an interpersonal process for which communication is necessary. However, there
are symbols common to cultural, social, personality and
somatic systems" (18, p. 361). Bertalanffy states that "in
psychology, the boundary of the ego is both fundamental and
precarious. . . . It is slowly established in evolution and
development and is never completely fixed" (5, p. 713).

The practitioner not only focuses his activity at the
boundary--whether it be the biological and psychological subsystem boundaries of the individual or the boundaries between the person-system and the environment-system--but
he also works "with" the boundary; that is, he explores and
"tests" boundary characteristics and he uses his efforts to
support and maintain boundaries. He is concerned about the
integrity of the ego boundary, especially since it must receive information from other subsystems of the person-
system and from the environment-systems and must translate and utilize this information in such a way as to maintain
system autonomy as well as system adaptiveness. Emotionally disturbed clients may have ego boundaries that are too
fluid with respect to messages from other subsystems of the
system and from external systems, or that lack sufficient
permeability to new inputs causing the system or subsystem
to become "encapsulated" or partly "closed off" from its
environment and thereby limit the development of system
potentialities. The practitioner seeks to establish a relationship with such a client-system as a means of enhancing
boundary dynamics and strengthening boundary stability.

Social workers serve a boundary-maintaining role in the identification, treatment and correction of non-conforming or deviant behavior. Kai T. Erikson points out that "deviance is not a property inherent in certain forms of behavior, it is a property conferred upon those forms by the audiences which directly or indirectly witness them," and he shows how the labeling of some behavior as deviant effectively serves as a boundary maintenance mechanism. The boundaries of social systems marked by the behaviors of its participants, and deviants, by their non-conforming behavior, best perform this function. In this view, according to Erikson,

> transactions taking place between deviant persons on the one side and agencies of control on the other are boundary maintaining mechanisms. They mark the outside limits of the area within which the norm has jurisdiction, and in this way assert how much diversity and variability can be contained within this system before it begins to lose its distinct structure, its cultural integrity.... Thus deviance cannot be dismissed simply as behavior which disrupts stability in society, but may itself be, in controlled quantities, an important condition for preserving stability... (28, p. 10).

The role of the helping system is to label and treat deviants so as to protect society against them. The helping system carries out its "control" mandate from society, but the social worker should give attention to the negative consequences of this role for the non-conforming or deviant client-system. This may be an arena for change in the helping system as it seeks to enable the client-system to further its own development and autonomy. Caseworkers are attuned to the scapegoat child's behavior as a boundary maintaining mechanism for the parent subsystem and the family system as a whole. Perhaps they will use this understanding in their activities with other client-systems and in gaining a new perspective of themselves as change-agents (subsystem) in a helping system.

System Feedback

General systems theory includes concepts of developmental change and goal-directedness that are congruent with traditional casework treatment. General systems theory also includes notions of feedback--feedback loops, deviation-amplifying and deviation-counteracting feedback processes that lend theoretical and empirical support to structured behavior therapy.   Some principles guiding the manipulation of elements in a loop are:

1.   A feedback system, or loop, is composed of elements which do not have, and do not need to have, any hierarchical or causal order.   The feedback loop is entered wherever possible.

2.   Within a feedback circuit, it is often advantageous, for the sake of control, to enter the loop as close as possible to the point of desired change.   Thus in bed-wetting, it might be more economical--but not because it is causally prior or historically more significant--to seek change nearest the point where the problem occurs, by use of an alerting system.

3.   Within a loop, one selects the unit of factor most closely related theoretically to the output one wishes to alter.   Thus the "habit of voiding when one's bladder is full is more vitally connected with the practice of bed-wetting than is either the effort to keep the bladder empty through limiting fluid intake or the attempt to discover a "basic" personality configuration to change (37, p. 96).

Behavior problems are often the result of the deviation-amplifying feedback process.   It is the deviation-amplifying process that determines whether the initial event leads to later problem behavior--not simply the initial event itself. The practitioner therefore introduces deviation-counteracting loops to interfere with ongoing self-defeating processes.   The goal is to eliminate unwanted behavior and reinforce desired responses--"to restore larger order in the organism's behavioral economy or to restructure behavior to achieve some desired end" (37, p. 105).   Thus, treatment would not be concerned with understanding solely the initial event or the connections between the initial event and later behavior. The therapist rather is concerned with alternatives to present unwanted behavior.   "How can these alternatives be set up, who should set them up, what means can be used?" (37, p. 104).

Structured behavior therapy, using the feedback model, seeks certain kinds of information from the client-system.

Phillips and Wiener state that "the information needed to
undertake and predict adult behavior should be derived from
the amount of information in the feedback process at each
crucial juncture in the development of the organism" (37,
p. 103-104). In other words, the information supplied at
the point of interaction of parts and processes is the information that is needed to accomplish change. It is necessary
therefore to gain relevant units of information at decision
points. The choice made at these junctures "can seldom be
predicted from general developmental facts or from remote
causes" (37, p. 104).

In sum, feedback loops and deviation-amplifying systems
may yield new insights into causality (whereby similar conditions may result in dissimilar products) that support the
use of behavior therapies currently viewed as incompatible
with casework theory and practice. It is believed by some
that structured behavior approaches, including operant conditioning, are antagonistic to the casework values of self-
determination and respect for the uniqueness and worth of
the individual. Typically, casework practice seeks to influence the client's behavior by strengthening the client's
motivation for self-change rather than by the caseworker's
directive interventions. It has been suggested that the positive results achieved by behavior therapy may be attributed
to the relationship between the client and therapist and not
to the therapist's directive interventions (23).

Criticisms of behavior therapy imply also that it is incompatible with general systems theory which looks at the
system as a whole (not simply the summation of its parts)
and places emphasis upon systems in the environment.
Focusing on the removal of symptoms or unwanted behaviors
without regard to the system of which it is a part and the
whole system-environment complex is incompatible with the
general systems approach. On the other hand, when
structured behavior therapy clarifies system goal and purpose, when it is a differential approach based on systems
analysis (especially the effects of feedback on the inter-
connections between system parts-whole and system-environment), and when it is one of a number of methods employed
in a series of systems interventions it may well have utility
for casework practice and enlarge its modalities. Values
per se are not inherent in a scientific theory--we draw upon
values to guide the ways in which we utilize theoretical
models but we also place values on the theoretical models
we use. The feedback (cybernetic) model must be evaluated

and utilized appropriately; that is, it must be viewed as part of or complementary to the open system model.

System Tension and Conflict

The utilization of general systems theory directs the practitioner to give particular consideration to the client-system's efforts on its own behalf and the client-system's opposition to the helping system. The notion that clients should be assisted in effecting changes in the helping system, in the larger environment, as well as in themselves, and the notion that clients need much more help in coping with societal institutions than in individual treatment alone indicates a much broader perspective of treatment than is currently accepted in casework practice (38, p. 14). Casework clients are commonly perceived as needing help to effect changes in themselves but the caseworker's horizon does not include the client's participation in the helping organization or his role in changing the helping organization. Nevertheless this notion of change strategy, derived from experience with institutional treatment, may have positive implications for other types of helping organizations (e. g., public welfare) and for casework practitioners in general. Moreover, this notion may not appear as foreign to caseworkers when placed in the context of some assumptions underpinning their practice. For example, caseworkers usually assume: 1) that there is transfer of learned behavior-- the client's active change role in the helping system will have carry-over effect thus enabling the client to assume more responsible, adequate roles outside the helping system; 2) that there are developmental changes in the treatment relationship--the worker and client "undergo successive stages of role evolution" in the change (treatment) process (38, p. 15).

Another aspect of this suggested change strategy has implications for caseworkers. Inducing change in the client implies that the client in the helping system is viewed as a participating subsystem and that the caseworker joins the client in his opposition as a means of achieving constructive change in both client and the organization. "It implies a view of clients not so much as passive dependent objects, but as active participating decision-makers" (38, p. 21-22). This conception of intervention may pose problems for the caseworker who has traditionally viewed the client's opposition to the helping process or the helping system as resistance to change.   Opposition is not ordinarily conceived as a constructive force, and the caseworker is likely to interpret it as part of the client's personality problem and as something to be "resolved" so that the client may better adjust to his environmental systems--family, work, as well as the helping system.   In other words, caseworkers are required to examine the helping systems, their role in helping systems, as well as the client's role in helping systems.   This intervention strategy is based upon systems theory notions of the system-environment complex, system stress and strain, and the active (in contrast to reactive) organism.   It emphasizes the positive functions of conflict and change and requires new conceptions of the roles of caseworker and client and the caseworker-client relationship.

Although the application of general systems theory to casework is a task for the future, discussion of a case in systems terms may provide some insights or clues to the practitioner.   The following analysis draws upon the systems formulations presented above; while these may be utilized selectively, there is overlapping and interrelatedness.   That is, one formulation may focus on the transmission process, another on stress and conflict, another on the steady state, another on the distribution of entropy, another on feedback, another on the process of communication of information and decision-making--but all these formulations are but different foci within the framework of systems theory.

CASE MATERIAL: THE RICCI FAMILY

Frank's parents were referred to a private family agency by a child psychiatric clinic for help with their personal and marital problems, which were reflected in Frank's emotional disturbance.   Shortly after they began treatment they asked for Frank to be seen; during the past year, two caseworkers, one for Frank's parents and one for Frank, have collaborated in the ongoing treatment plans.

The Ricci family consists of the father and mother, ages 29 and 26, and three children, Frank, age 11, Jean, age 9, and Patty, age 1.   Mr. Ricci is a butcher and the Riccis are financially self-sufficient, with Mrs. Ricci sometimes earning additional income by providing day care for a neighborhood boy about Frank's age.   Mr. Ricci's family is Italian; he is third generation American.   Mrs. Ricci's father is

Greek; Mrs. Ricci's mother, divorced from her father when
Mrs. Ricci was very young, was adopted and her nationality
unknown. Both Mr. and Mrs. Ricci have maintained close
ties to their families of orientation and there is much interaction in the extended family network. Despite Mrs. Ricci's
antagonism to the paternal grandmother, the latter is frequently present in the Ricci home and she took care of
Frank and Jean during an earlier period when Mrs. Ricci
worked as a waitress. Mrs. Ricci has always idealized
her father and is still attached to him; currently the maternal
great-grandmother is living with the Riccis.

The Ricci marriage has been fraught with conflict and
the parental interaction is characterized by frequent argu-
ments with much yelling and shouting. Mrs. Ricci de-
valuates Mr. Ricci; Mr. Ricci is nonsupportive of Mrs.
Ricci's emotional needs. Frank was conceived prior to the
Ricci's marriage. Mr. Ricci felt burdened by the responsibility of a wife and child and although Mrs. Ricci has always "loved babies" she was guilty about Frank's premarital
conception because she had failed to live up to her father's
expectations. Frank is viewed by both parents as having
qualities and traits like those of family relatives who are in
mental institutions (Mr. Ricci's sister and Mrs. Ricci's
cousin). Frank's caseworker noted, when visiting the home,
that the parents acted as though Frank were not present and
excluded him from conversations about himself. While the
parents have verbalized concern about their own part in
Frank's emotional disturbance, they tend to think that the
cause lay in his heredity.

Frank is in good physical health (although now over-
weight) but he continues to manifest the same symptoms
that he did when first referred to a child psychiatric clinic
at age 3. He is hyperactive (in constant motion) and easily
distractible, he has daydreams, fantasies, and night fears,
he has infantile ways of thinking and behaving (including
"bizarre" behavior, helplessness and manipulation of adults).
Reports of the onset of Frank's difficulties are conflicting.
At one time Mrs. Ricci stated that Frank was a "wonderful
baby, " at another she stated that "he showed problems since
birth. " When he was 19 months old, Frank's first sister
was born; when 26 months old he had a hernia operation.
The long trek through clinics began when Frank was 18
months old and Mrs. Ricci, pregnant with the second of her
three children, sought help for herself and continued in
therapy for three years. However, Frank's problem behavior

was pinpointed by the nursery school, and later by the
kindergarten, the grammar school, and the Catholic school
where he was placed by his parents when transfer to a
special class, for individual attention was recommended.
Despite some improvement (he is now doing fourth grade
work), Frank continues to need the "protection" of E. H.
(Emotionally Handicapped) class in public school to which he
was transferred at age 8.

Reports of medical and neurological tests (when Frank
was 6) were negative. A psychiatric consultant (1969) believed that Frank "might be borderline between neurosis and
psychosis." Psychological tests administered in August 1965
and in 1969 indicated normal intelligence and no evidence of
brain damage or "organicity." Frank's failure to function
at the age-appropriate level was attributed to neurotic trends
--his high degree of generalized anxiety, his separation and
castration anxiety, and his immature personality, including
his "difficulty in handling his instinctual needs" (psychiatric
interview, 1963). The source of Frank's problems, however,
was implicitly and/or explicitly identified as the parent's
personal needs, their inability to fulfill desirable parental
roles, and their disturbed marital relationship. It is significant that therapists who have worked with the Ricci family
continue to cite the parents' improvement while Frank is not
reported to have progressed demonstrably and continues to
be a "sick" child.

The treatment goals and interventions of the caseworkers
(past and present) reflected their explanatory formulations of
the case problem (not always made explicit) and their methodological knowledge and skills. While Frank's serious
problem behavior was identified as the target for change,
the underlying assumption guiding treatment was that the
parents had to be helped to change themselves and thereby
enabled to fulfill parental and marital roles more responsibly
and meaningfully. Frank's difficulties were "treated" separately; that is, Frank was to be helped, through the relationship with a caseworker, to express his feelings, to develop
inner controls, and to gain understanding of and security in
himself and his place in the family. The goal, stated
generally, was to improve the psycho-social functioning of
Frank and his father and his mother. As noted, no substantial improvement has been observed in Frank, although
Mr. and Mrs. Ricci are believed to have profited from
treatment for themselves and their marital relationship.
Finally, it should be remembered that Frank and his parents,

especially Mrs. Ricci, have been seen by a number of helping organizations in the community over the past eight years.
The Ricci case has been transferred from one clinic to another, and most recently, when Frank was ten, from a child
psychiatric clinic to a private family agency. It appears
likely that this pattern, namely the involvement of the Ricci
family with helping organizations, will continue in the future.

Systems Analysis of the Ricci Case

   Explanatory formulations about the emotional disturbance
of a child may focus on the disturbance in the marital
relationship (for example, schism or skew), [26] on the role
of the child in maintaining the family equilibrium, or on a
still broader perspective, the patterning of family roles
and interrelations, including the marital relationship and the
nature of the child's role in the family (29, 30, 48, 51).
Wynne's conceptualization regarding pseudo-mutuality appears
to be congruent with systems theory concepts and principles. [27]   This idea, therefore, may be fruitfully explored
particularly as a springboard for the application of systems
concepts to the Ricci case. Assumptions underlying the
notion of pseudo-mutuality may be recast in systems terms;
that is, that humans are essentially proactive--innately
striving to relate to their environment, and that the human
system is self-regulation and goal-directed--striving to
achieve a characteristic state such as "personal identity. "
These two notions are inextricably related to the growth
and development of the human system which involves the
processes of differentiation, centralization, progressive segregation and mechanization.

   Assumptions regarding the nature and development of
human systems may be best examined in the context of the
family system.   That is, the interrelations of the parts of
the family system as a whole must be the focus of attention
rather than the parts in isolation or the parts and their
summation. This interrelation, specifically here the psuedo-
mutuality, may be studied in terms of the steady state of the
system, the principles of stability, transactional process,
and the process of communication of information.   The key
system problem in pseudo-mutuality is the failure to permit
development and change in the family structure which results
in restrictions placed upon the system as a whole, its subsystems and components.   The patterned family relations
cannot be given up or "allowed to develop or expand" (51,

p. 631). Pseudo-mutuality involves certain characteristics of family structure and process:

1. A persistent sameness of the role structure of the family . . .

2. An insistence on the desirability and appropriateness of this role structure.

3. Evidence of intense concern over the possible divergence or independence from this role structure.

4. An absence of spontaneity, novelty, humor, and zest in participation together (51, p. 633).

Pseudo-mutuality may maintain family equilibrium but it does not maintain a changing steady state of the family which results from the dynamic interplay of the subsystems operating as functional processes. As noted earlier, the homeostasis model, characterized by reflex-type feedbacks is not appropriate for living, open, negentropic systems. It does not apply to proactive, self-regulating, goal-directed systems. When homeostatic mechanisms prevail there is evidence that the system is preoccupied with tension-reduction, with survival, rather than with growth and change. Stated differently, the feedback process in the pseudo-mutual family system is characterized by static homeostasis wherein the system must return to its former level of equilibrium and does not permit the dynamic interplay of system-environment and system-subsystem processes, or the use of higher order symbol-actuated feedbacks. Shared family mechanisms for maintaining pseudo-mutuality have a homeostatic function that imposes the self-reinforcing of the pathology of the individual family members. This rigid family role structure is perpetuated by communication processes that facilitate a failure in selection of meaning. The shared family mechanisms developed to maintain pseudo-mutuality "serve to mitigate the full impact of chaotic, empty, and frightening experience by providing a role structure in which the person can pseudo-mutually exist without having developed a valued and meaningful sense of identity or its age-appropriate precursors. . . . The difficulty . . . in articulating a differentiation of himself from the family role structure means that the family role structure is experienced as all-encompassing" (51, p. 635).

The notion that human organizations are hierarchically arranged open systems implies that the family system is a differentiated subsystem of a society.   In cases of intense, pervasive pseudo-mutual family relations, however, the family is viewed as a self-sufficient, encapsulated social system with a completely encircling boundary.

> The unstable but continuous boundary with no recognizable openings, surrounding the . . . family system, stretches to include that which can be interpreted as complementary and contracts to extrude that which is interpreted as non-complementary.   This continuous but elastic boundary we have called the rubber fence. This metaphor is a way of summarizing the effects of family pseudo-mutuality and the reinforcing shared family mechanisms in establishing a situation in which the person feels that he cannot trust his own perceptions and from which there seems no escape (51, p. 635).

The system boundary was identified earlier as a key concept to be applied by the practitioner; locating the primary system for intervention and investigating boundary characteristics, especially since it is at and through boundaries that there is system-environment and system-subsystem interchange.   In the Ricci case it might be hypothesized that the Ricci nuclear family was never differentiated as a system and its boundaries are continous with those of the families of orientation.   Lidz points out the significance of the parental coalition in maintaining generation boundaries: "Spouses cannot remain primarily in a dependent position to their parents to the exclusion of an interdependent marital relationship; nor can one [spouse] behave primarily as the other's child; nor as a rival with one's own children for the spouse's attention, nor reject a parental role completely" (30, p. 653).

The boundaries of the family may not only extend to encircle the families of orientation--but may also encircle intermediaries located in helping organizations.   "For a specific purpose the elastic boundaries have been stretched to include such persons, who are then not related to as separate identities" (51, p. 640).   When intermediaries, such as the caseworkers in the Ricci case, assume the role of communicating reciprocal expectations to family members, they assist in blurring the direct expectations within the family and thereby allow themselves to perpetuate the pseudo-mutual relations.   One of the shared mechanisms in maintain-

ing family pseudo-mutuality is the extrusion or threat of
extrusion from the family system. This may be applied to
intermediaries who are temporarily incorporated in the
family system. As might be expected from the disturbed
marital relationship of the Ricci spouse subsystem, threats
of extrusion were frequent between the parents, but were
primarily centered on the "sick" or "crazy" child, namely
Frank.[28]

The family role that Frank was assigned and "learned"
might well be termed "scapegoat. " However this term is
not used here in the sense that the child is simply the passive
victim of his family environment, since he has an active
investment in helping to establish and maintain the rigid
family structure characterized by pseudo-mutual relations.
The child is then the focus of family non-complementarity
and has internalized[29] the negative valuation of himself and
his role in the family. The scapegoated child thus takes an
important covert family role in supporting the pseudo-mutuality of the rest of the family. This shared family mechanism
in the Ricci case appears to be part of a more general type
of mechanism, namely, the creation and utilization of a
family legend or myth. Indeed, the fact that Frank was
selected as the scapegoat was "overdetermined. " He was
not only the carrier of the family mental illness; as the first
child and son, Frank was expected to fulfill Mrs. Ricci's
idealized relationship to the paternal grandfather--the role
expectations that she could not transfer to Mr. Ricci. At
the same time, since he could not realistically fulfill these
expectations (the idealized father-husband), and because being the recipient of such expectations threatened the existing
family role structure and created overwhelming nonutilizable
input for Frank, he internalized the overall family role
structure and specifically the scapegoat role of the "crazy"
child. As the eldest child in the family, Frank was the
first available appropriate object for the displacement of the
marital tensions. At times, Frank was threatened with extrusion because in filling the helpless, dependent, crazy,
scapegoat role he developed mechanisms for punishing his
parents, because his relationships with external systems
such as the school became problematic and troublesome
for the family, and because his problems fed back into the
Ricci's personal and marital difficulties. Nevertheless,
Frank's scapegoat role was necessary for the family "equilibrium. " The family legend of mental illness encompassed
this scapegoat role: it also prevented the extrusion of the
child since it was the mental illness not the child that was

the intruder causing the child's problem behavior and family difficulties. In other words, it could be rationalized that Frank really "meant to be good" but his behavior was determined by his mental illness.

The Ricci family, by failing to maintain essential generation boundaries--boundaries between family of orientation and nuclear family and boundaries between parents and child --led to the disorganization of Frank's personality system. The disorganized state of the child-system (in contrast to the expected state of organization and order characteristic of complex adaptive systems) suggests that entropic forces were at work. That is, instead of being characterized by negative entropy, the child-system was unable to import and convert matter-energy and information so as to counteract entropic processes and thereby lead to order and complexity in the system. The entropy distribution between parent (especially the mother) and child was distorted;[30] because of failure to differentiate between the parent's own needs and anxieties, the child-system was unable to become discrete, with ego boundaries of its own. "A parent's dependency upon a child occupies the child prematurely with completing the life of another rather than with developing his own ego structure defined by clear boundaries" (29, p. 585).

Although Frank's scapegoat role was integrated into his personality system it was not under the control of an actively perceiving and discriminating ego--the role thus governed his behavior in an automatic "reflex" manner. There is evidence that Frank was flooded with anxiety when he attempted "to articulate a meaningful indication of his individuality in the same way that pseudo-mutual family relations became flooded with anxiety when non-complementarity threatened to emerge into shared recognition" (51, p. 643). Because Frank had not mastered developmental tasks appropriate to his age his ego did not develop a differentiated identity of its own. The failure to establish an ego boundary made it impossible to distinguish between inner feelings and outer experiences, "to attach clear meanings to his own intrapsychic states" (such as anger at his mother), or to integrate new "learning" input. Using Lathrope's paradigm it might be hypothesized that the nature and form of the family system input, and Frank's selective use of this input, did not permit internal processing of primary developmental tasks and thus resulted in output such as his anxiety, hyperactivity, learning difficulties and so forth. Feedback processes played a very

important part in the direction and perpetuation of Frank's
problem-behavior. It would appear that deviation-amplifying
processes--the ongoing interpersonal transactions between
parents and child--were of greater significance in Frank's
deviant role than the "initial event" or the "anlage" of the
deficient very early mother-child relationship.[31] In other
words, to carry out his role as a problem child "the problem
behavior must be reinforced strongly enough so that it will
continue in spite of the hostility and anxiety it produces in
the child" (48, p. 420).

To maintain this delicate balance within the child and
family, the parents, who have superior sanction power over
the child, must utilize large amounts of inconsistency in the
ways they handle the child. Vogel and Bell cite several
types of commonly used inconsistencies: between the implicit and explicit expectations, between the expectations of
the two parents, and the changes in each parent's expectations
(48, p. 420-422). Information regarding these types of
parental behaviors and the feedback processes were not
explicitly identified in the Ricci case.[32] However, notations
regarding Frank's bed-wetting and weight-control diet suggested that these parental inconsistencies were utilized, especially
the alternation between critical or restrictive behavior and
supportive or indulgent behavior. Mrs. Ricci verbalized the
two conflicting desires of wanting Frank to behave properly
and yet not being "too hard on him." It may be speculated
that when the latter type of behavior predominated Frank's
previously disapproved actions were reinforced, and when
the former predominated Mr. and/or Mrs. Ricci were enabled to express their anxieties and anger.

The internalization of conflicting messages, continued
over a long period of time, involved circular feedback reactions in one direction--the vicious cycle of a positive
deviation-amplifying process. Viewed in the context of entropy distribution it is apparent that the deviation-amplifying
process in the family system and the child's symptom-output
may limit or injure the whole personality system of the
child. To effect change, then, removal of external pressures
alone will not suffice; it may be necessary to intervene at
selected appropriate points so as to "steer" the system into
different directions, to insert deviation-counteracting change
into the feedback loops. Stated in terms of system purposiveness, it is necessary to introduce feedbacks that will
facilitate the attainment of "actual external goals--not simply
the reduction of goal-drive" (11, p. 57). And stated in terms

of information theory, the personality system of Frank and the Ricci family system should be helped "to be organized so as to match the current state of affairs . . . to bring it up to date" (11, p. 47). The practitioner's role, conveyed through the communication process, must be focused on updating the state of orientation of the child system and the family system--to change the fit between system and environment.

The disorganization of Frank's personality system, his brittle and impoverished ego development, may result in acute identity diffusion as he approaches chronological adolescense and adulthood. It is possible that this will lead to temporary or chronic mental illness, or that his conflicts will find expression in a "negative identity":

> Perversely based on all those identifications and roles, which at critical stages of development had been presented to the individual as most undesirable or dangerous, and yet also as most real . . . the parents' weaknesses and unexpressed wishes are recognized by the child with catastrophic clarity.

> Such vindictive choices of a negative identity represent, of course, a desperate attempt at regaining some mastery in a situation in which the available positive identity elements cancel each other out. The history of such a choice reveals a set of conditions in which it is easier to derive a sense of identity out of a total identification with that which one is least supposed to be, than to struggle for a feeling of reality in acceptable roles which are unattainable with the patient's inner means . . . . The word total is not accidental in this connection . . . [it describes] a human proclivity to a "totalistic" reorientation when, at critical stages of development, reintegration into a relative "wholeness" seems impossible (16, p. 131-132).

Finally, since Frank's disorganized personality system and his covert family role may be the means whereby other family members can vicariously achieve some sense of their own personal identity, change strategy should be geared to the whole family system as well as to its subsystems and components. Interventions that alter feedback processes might be incorporated in a broader treatment approach that facilitates the family's relation to social institutions, including

the helping system.   There is the danger, however, that the
helping systems may themselves be "pseudo-mutual" organizations (38).   That is, the helping system may be absorbed
in projecting an image that does not permit altered expectations, divergence, growth or change.   In such a situation,
information and communications are directed so as to maintain the static equilibrium of the helping system and thus are
not "functional to the client-system's dysfunctioning" (38).

As noted earlier, Polsky's thesis that the client-system
will be helped to change as the helping system changes--and
that the client-system should participate in changes of the
helping system has important implications for the practitioner.[33] In perpetuating the professional role structure of
helping systems, practitioners may also be perpetuating dysfunctional family role structure and pseudo-mutual relations;
by serving as mechanisms whereby scapegoats and deviants
are labeled and treated, the stability of social systems
(family, work, school) may be supported and reinforced at
the cost of client-system change and development.   Clients
thus should be helped to negotiate other environmental
systems, as well as the helping system.   For example, Mrs.
Ricci's concern about Frank's school performance and school
placement could be the springboard for developing her own
skills--perhaps working jointly with other parents and with
Mr. Ricci--in negotiating the school system.   Assisting the
client-system to engage itself with the social institutions in
its field of transaction may enable the client-system itself
to change.   Indeed, this kind of practitioner and client
engagement may lead to change in the environment systems
as well as the client and helping systems.   It may require
a different treatment orientation involving a variety of innovative methods and skills.   The point here is that change
strategy must be rooted in the system-environment complex
and must be developed in terms of transactions that lead to
flexibility rather than rigidity and stereotypy, and growth
rather than fixed equilibrium.

Limitations and Dangers

Various parts of this presentation of systems theory
and its implications for social casework have included references to some limitations of the theory-model and some
possible dangers in its application.   Pointing up limitations
may well be fruitful in highlighting assets as well as dangers.
That is, the notion of limitation is not conceived as a nega-

tive value judgment but rather as a guide to understanding
the nature and aim of the theory-model (in contrast to the
nature and aims of other theories and models); the state of
development of the theory-model; the relationship between
the model and specified aspects of reality; the clarity and
synthesis of the conceptual notions encompassed by the theory-
model; the methodology of the theory-model. The determination of a limitation also depends upon the observer's
position with respect to the theory-model and with respect
to a concrete case, and upon assumptions and values with
regard to the practitioner's role. Thus, a limitation may
be interpreted by some as a barrier to utilization whereas
others may view the limitation as a challenge to theory
building and the advancement of practice.

One of the major limitations noted earlier is the highly
abstract level of general systems theory. This high degree
of abstraction makes it difficult to apply the theory-model
directly to the empirical events that confront the practitioner.
In other words, there is a large gap between the theory-
model and the concrete case. However, systems theory is
a frame of reference that enables the practitioner to widen
his range of observations and organize discrete phenomena
into coherent relationships. It is not technique-oriented in
the sense that it will "tell" the practitioner what to do. As
a framework that encompasses and synthesizes many conceptual ideas it offers a comprehensive base from which to
select and create methods and techniques for intervention.
General systems theory is also a holistic theory which,
while not immediately operational, embodies an interdisciplinary approach and incorporates middle-range sub-theories
that more closely reflect different aspects of reality. Because systems theory is highly abstract and broad in its
scope, it is difficult to obtain total understanding of the
theory-model in its entirety.

One misconception is frequently associated with these
characteristics and limitations of general systems theory;
that is, there is the danger of assuming that it is a unified
theory of behavior rather than a theory-model that provides
a framework for a number of theories. Moreover, general
systems theory does not purport to provide a model of the
"whole of reality"; it is pertinent to only certain aspects of
reality. There is need for further synthesis of its various
sub-theories but "it is an open question whether much progress can be made by attempts to construct a 'unified theory
of systems' on some rigorous axiomatic base." Given the

vastness of developing science, perhaps the emphasis should
be on synthesizing directions and the emergence of a "col-
lective scientific mind" (39, p. xxi). Bertalanffy states that
although effort must be expended to further develop general
systems theory it does not pretend to be "exhaustive, exclusive or final . . . . The danger . . . is to consider too
early the theoretical model as being closed and definitive--a
danger particularly important in a field like general systems
which is still groping to find its correct foundation" (8,
p. 17, 21).

Another danger connected with systems theory--as well
as with other theories--is "the seductive potential" of its
concepts. Rapaport points out that new systems concepts
have "triggered an avalanche of speculations which, upon
closer examination, reveal only a lack of understanding of
what is involved" (39, p. xxii). He refers here to extra-
polations that are unwarranted and detract from the full
understanding and proper use of systems theory. Failure
to comprehend clearly the actual content as well as breadth
of systems notions can lead to confusion and distortion which
hinders the development of the theory and its application to
practice. The writer has commented upon tendencies to
focus upon one system concept without reference to or to the
exclusion of other systems concepts, to give different interpretations to the same concept (or model), to use selected
systems theory concepts to support existing beliefs and
practices--that is, to use systems theory as a vehicle to
maintain the status quo.

A second major limitation, similar to the first, is the
inevitable discrepancy between the model and reality. Chin
believes that models do not fit the practitioner's diagnostic
ideas and interventions and that the practitioner does "what
works" without regard to any theory-model. He concludes,
therefore, that models are not and need not be utilized by
the change-agent (13). This position seems questionable to
say the least. The "do what works" approach may be a
rote form of practice that does not lend itself to systematic
examination, and indeed, may preclude the use of additional
and perhaps more effective approaches. Moreover, the
assumption that the practitioner is solely concerned with
doing, in isolation from a theory-model, seems unjustified.
Whether or not they intervene before diagnosing (see Chin),
practitioners use some theory-model even if unconsciously.
Perhaps the lack of fit between a theory-model and empirical
events (if the theory-model is made explicit) may enable the

practitioner to identify the discrepancies, incongruities, and gaps, and thereby facilitate modifications in the theory-model or the development of a new theory-model. It is exactly because we cannot be satisfied with the simplistic notion that if what we do works we need not be concerned with models. Practice does not require "the suspension of acceptance of such available models" (13, p. 214); rather, it requires that we make explicit the nature and degree of the fit between the model and the concrete case situation; it is only by such investigation and testing that we contribute to theory building and only in this way that we move forward in our helping work. As Bertalanffy points out, "new horizons have been opened up but the relations to empirical facts often remain tenuous...." Whereas there is danger of the domination of empiricism, there is also the danger of "'model-building' as a purpose in itself and often without regard to empirical fact" (8, p. 21-22).

A third major limitation, already cited in this chapter, concerns the state of development of general systems theory and the criticism of its "lack of methodology"--that is, the rules to establish and to apply system principles (8, p. 20-21). The testing, synthesis, and application of this interdisciplinary holistic theory cannot be quickly or easily accomplished. Hearn, in 1958, identified the types of studies required to fulfill these tasks (21); and we will make a few points in this connection. One is the identification and clarification of the characteristic states toward which the system tends to move. Erikson's formulation of eight life stages was one important contribution in this direction and has led to a number of significant studies of the psychology of the life cycle (16). [34] Two is the determination of the kind of system structure and process that is most desirable. This involves criteria for distinguishing better (or functional) from poorer (or dysfunctional) system-environment conditions and relations. [35] There is the empirical testing of cross-level hypotheses. Miller has formulated 165 hypotheses (some original with him and some proposed by other writers) that "if supported by empirical evidence, can be very powerful in generating general theory of living systems, so long as differences among the various levels, types and individual cases are taken into account" (35, p. 380). To date, interdisciplinary investigations covering two or three system levels have been carried out; the only complete five cross-level study is the information overload research. Subsequent investigations should confirm certain of these hypotheses and disprove or qualify others. Although some writers have pointed up the dangers of the use of isomorphisms and models in science, it has been demonstrated that this method enables us to "restore meaning (in terms of intuitively grasped understanding of wholes) while adhering to the principles of disciplined generalizations and rigorous deduction" (39, p. xxii). In short, the limitations noted here should serve as a challenge--for systems theory holds out great promise for the advancement of social casework theory and practice.

Notes

1. The terms systems theory and general systems theory are used interchangeably in this chapter.

2. The environment may be considered as proximal--of which the system is aware, or distal--that which affects the system but is beyond its awareness (22). Miller states that the next higher system in which the system is a component or subsystem is the suprasystem. That is, the immediate environment of the system is the suprasystem minus the system itself (34).

3. Abraham Kaplan points out that the term model should be applied only to those theories which explicitly direct attention to certain resemblances between the theoretical entities and the real subject matter (24). Meadows similarly states that "each model stipulates some correspondence with reality and some verifiability between model and reality" (32, p. 4).

4. Miller has defined the boundary of a system as "that region where greater energy is required for transmission across it than for transmission immediately outside that region or immediately inside it" (33, p. 516-517).

5. Hearn views subsystems as "comprising all of those functional processes upon which the life and continued existence of the organism depends" [e. g. , the circulatory and motivational systems of the individual]. Structural components of the individual refer to the various organs of the body, the psychological processes and their arrangement in relation to one another; structural components of groups refer to statuses and roles (22, p. 59-62).

Miller believes that Hearn confuses structure and function (34, p. 211). He defines subsystem as "the totality of all the structures in a system which carry out a particular process. A subsystem, thus, is identified by the process it carries out. It exists in one or more identifiable structural units of the system. These specific, local, distinguishable structural units are called components or members or parts . . . .There is no one-to-one relationship between process and structure. . . . The concept of subsystem process is related to the concept of role used in social science" (34, p. 218-219).

6. Katz and Kahn present nine characteristics of open systems: importation of energy; through-put, output; systems as cycles of events (see discussion here of deviation-amplifying processes); negative entropy, information input, negative feedback, and the coding process; steady state and dynamic homeostatis; differentiation; equifinality (25).

7. See The Functions of Conflict by Lewis Coser, in which it is pointed out that conflict may help to establish unity or to re-establish unity and cohesion (14).

8. Selye made a major contribution in his application of the concept of stress to living systems at the organism level (41).

9. Cybernetics as the study of methods of feedback control may be viewed as an important part of systems theory.

10. If prior events are proximal to the event being explained, we refer to "efficient causes"; if more distant, we refer to "historical causes. "

11. Defenders of the Parsonian structural-functional model state that it does allow for changes among the internal elements in the system.

12. Polsky (utilizing the Parsonian model) states that the helping social system serves "a function in society and with respect to clients and that the two functions are often not complementary. " He argues that "social work must constantly evaluate the functioning of a system in both directions, such an analytic operation being equivalent to classifying systems as normal or pathological"

(38, p. 16-17).

13.   Helen Perotti, a member of the 1957 Berkeley research
      group, under the faculty supervision of Gordon Hearn,
      applied general systems theory (and the organismic
      model) to the case of a 74-year-old client in a hospital
      setting (12).   Hearn states that her systems analysis
      led to new insights and to substantial improvement in
      the case (22, p. 76).

14.   The same final state may be reached from different
      initial conditions and in different ways.

15.   Studt has described an experimental unit in a correction-
      al institution which helped client inmates to cope with
      their current environment (21, p. 65).

16.   Self-awareness, another basic concept of casework, is
      also given new meaning by the general systems approach.
      Systems concepts will clarify much of what is happening
      to the worker and around him--it reveals facts about
      himself as well as clients and other parts of the social
      work system (43).

17.   The system model described here is based largely upon
      the writings of Miller, Bertalanffy, Grinker, and in-
      corporates change and development over time.   Thus,
      this system model would encompass the developmental
      model as well as the intersystem model presented by
      Chin.

18.   The terms conceptual and analytic model are used here
      interchangeably.   Miller distinguishes between con-
      ceptual, concrete, and abstracted models; Chin distin-
      guishes between analytic and concrete models; Lathrope
      distinguishes between the expository, the research, the
      perscriptive, and the practitioner models.   The latter
      may be master models for practice or working models
      for concrete cases (both the master models for practice
      and working models for concrete cases utilize the other
      three types of models; that is, they are expository,
      prescriptive and research-like).   Lathrope's master
      model for practice is similar to the conceptual or
      analytic model and his working model for practice is
      similar to Chin's concrete model (13, 27, 34).

19. For the behavioral scientist and change-agent "it is no
     mean task to pick out the essential variables from the
     non-essential; that is specification of the universe and
     subsequent dichotomization into system and environment
     is in itself, apart from analysis of the interrelationship,
     a problem of fundamental complexity" (20, p. 84).

20. A presenting problem, as perceived and formulated by
     the system itself, could from the practitioner's per-
     spective, fall into any of the four areas of input, pro-
     cessing, output, and feedback. Frequently the present-
     ing problem falls into the output area (27).

21. Polsky, using the Parsonian structural-functional model,
     distinguishes between production and maintenance types
     of outputs into social systems (38).

22. Samperi, in her discussion of Lutz' structural-functional
     system theory for case study, diagnosis and treatment,
     compares the treatment of two "family cases." She
     suggests that in the treatment of the personality systems
     of family members in one case the worker was the
     instrument of change whereas the worker in the other
     case treated the family system and was the source of
     change (40).

23. Shafer cites three such propositions. It is noted that
     slight stress improves the performance of individuals
     and groups. Data regarding continuously increasing
     stress could suggest the point at which system collapse
     is imminent and intervention seems indicated. The way
     in which the system best handles stress and strain, for
     example, using the least expansive defenses first and
     the reduction of the stronger strains before the weaker
     strains, also has implications for intervention strategies
     (42, p. 34-35).

24. The structural-functional approach has been largely
     utilized in practice with family, small group, and
     community client-systems. It has provided a different
     perspective for family diagnosis and treatment from the
     "traditional" casework which focuses on family members
     (and thereby affects the family system) rather than the
     family as a social system.

25. Subsequent discussion of other issues also concerns the
     utility of system concepts in causal analysis and change

strategy.

26.   See Lidz et al., "Schism and Skew in the Families of Schizophrenics" (30).

27.   Pseudo-mutuality refers to a quality of relatedness in which there is "a predominant absorption in fitting together at the expense of the differentiation of the identities of the persons in the relation" (51, p. 630).

28.   The Riccis have discussed placement of Frank many times during the course of their contacts with helping systems.

29.   Wynne uses the term internalization "to refer in a generalized way to the organized pattern of the meanings which external objects, events, and relations have acquired" (51, p. 642).

30.   To quote Gordon: "For growth and development to occur the transaction intersystem at the organism-environment interface must accomplish a substantial redistribution of entropy between the organism and environment systems. On the organism side, entropy must be rather continuously reduced or be extracted. For the environment to be preserved or ameliorated, the extracted entropy from the organism side must be deployed in such a way that the entropy level of the impinging environment is not itself increased" (17, p. 11).

31.   Lidz et al., "hypothesize that the ego weakness of the schizophrenic may be related to the introjection of parental weakness noted in the mother's dependency upon the child for fulfillment; to the introjection of parental rejection of the child in the process of early identification with a parent; and to the depreciated images for identification presented by the devaluation of one parent by the other" (30, p. 651).

32.   One type of inconsistency pressure noted in the Ricci case was the difference between the expectation that Frank achieve and be "perfect" like the idealized maternal grandfather and the expectation that Frank fail and be "crazy" like family relatives.

33. Polsky states that "a balance is struck whereby in-
     dividuals change by the system's changing its rules,
     procedures, policies, and structure. Clients in
     helping systems need assistance in overcoming the
     rules that lock them into patient roles so that they can
     eventually become ex-clients within the service system"
     (38, p. 19).

34. See for example Personality in Middle and Later Life
     and Middle Age and Aging, edited by Bernice L. Neu-
     garten.

35. See the discussion earlier regarding the possible
     utility of the concept of entropy in providing the basis
     for such distinction.

References

1. Allport, F. H. , "Self-Regulation and Self-Direction in
    Psychological Systems," in F. H. Allport, Theories
    of Perception and the Concept of Structure (New York:
    Wiley, 1955).

2. Allport, Gordon W. , "The Open System in Personality
    Theory," in Walter Buckley, Modern Systems Re-
    search for the Behavioral Scientist (Chicago: Aldine
    Publishing Company, 1968).

3. _____, Pattern and Growth in Personality (New
    York: Holt, Rinehart and Winston, Inc. , 1961).

4. Bell, Norman W. and Ezra P. Vogel (eds.), A Modern
    Introduction to the Family, (rev. ed.) (New York: The
    Free Press, 1968).

5. Bertalanffy, Ludwig von, "General System Theory and
    Psychiatry," in S. Arieti (ed.), American Handbook
    of Psychiatry, Vol. 3 (New York: Basic Books, 1964).

6. _____, "An Outline of General System Theory,"
    British Journal of the Philosophy of Science, Vol. 1,
    1950.

7. _____, "General System Theory," General Systems
    Yearbook, Vol. 1, No. 3, 1956.

8. _____ , "General System Theory: A Critical Review," General Systems Yearbook, Vol. 7, 1962.

9. _____ , Problems of Life (New York: Wiley, 1952).

10. Boulding, Kenneth E. , "General Systems Theory: The Skeleton of Science," Management Science, Vol. 2, No. 3, April 1956.

11. Buckley, Walter, Sociology and Modern Systems Theory, (New York: Prentice-Hall, 1967).

12. Carlson, Virginia, et al. , "Social Work and General Systems Theory," Group Research Project Under the Faculty Supervision of Gordon Hearn, University of California, Berkeley, School of Social Welfare, 1957.

13. Chin, Robert, "The Utility of Systems Models and Developmental Models for Practitioners," in Warren G. Bennis (ed.), et al. , The Planning of Change: Readings in the Applied Behavioral Sciences (New York: Holt, Rinehart and Winston, Inc. , 1961).

14. Coser, Lewis, "The Functions of Conflict, " in N. J. Demerath and Richard A. Peterson, System, Change, and Conflict (New York: The Free Press, 1967).

15. Ellis, David O. and Fred J. Ludwig, Systems Philosophy (Englewood Cliffs: Prentice-Hall, 1962).

16. Erikson, Erik, "Identity and the Life Cycle," Psychological Issues, (New York: International Universities Press, Inc. , Vol. 1, No. 1, 1959).

17. Gordon, William E. , "Basic Constructs for an Integrative and Generative Conception of Social Work, " in Gordon Hearn (ed.), The General Systems Approach: Contributions Toward an Holistic Conception of Social Work (New York: Council on Social Work Education, 1969).

18. Grinker, Roy R. (ed.), Toward A Unified Theory of Behavior 2d ed. (New York: Basic Books, 1967).

19. Gross, Bertram, "The Coming of General Systems Models of Social Systems, " Human Relations, Vol. 20, No. 4, 1967.

20. Hall, A. D. and R. E. Fagen, "Definition of System," in
    W. Buckley (ed.), Modern Systems Research for the
    Behavioral Scientist (New York: Aldine Publishing
    Company, 1968).

21. Hearn, Gordon (ed.), The General Systems Approach:
    Contributions Toward An Holistic Conception of Social
    Work (New York: Council on Social Work Education,
    1969).

22. _____, Theory Building in Social Work (Toronto:
    Toronto University Press, 1958).

23. Hollis, Florence, "And What Shall We Teach," Smith
    College Studies for Social Work, Vol. 42, No. 2,
    June 1968.

24. Kaplan, Abraham, The Conduct of Inquiry (San Fran-
    cisco: Chandler Publishing Company, 1964).

25. Katz, Daniel and Robert L. Kahn, The Social Psycho-
    logy of Organizations (New York: John Wiley and
    Sons, Inc., 1966).

26. Klein, Alan F., "The Application of Social System
    Theory to Social Work," Paper Presented at Annual
    Program Meeting of the Council on Social Work
    Education, New York, January 1966.

27. Lathrope, Donald E., "The General Systems Approach
    in Social Work Practice," in Gordon Hearn (ed.),
    The General Systems Approach: Contributions Toward
    an Holistic Conception of Social Work, 1969.

28. _____. "The Use of Social Science in Social Work
    Practice: Social Systems," Paper Presented at the
    National Association of Social Workers' Tenth anni-
    versary Symposium, Atlantic City, New Jersey, May
    1965.

29. Lidz, Theodore, "Family Organization and Personality
    Structure," in N. Bell and E. Vogel (eds.), A Modern
    Introduction to the Family, (rev. ed.) (New York:
    The Free Press, 1968).

30. _____, et al., "Schism and Skew in the Families
    of Schizophrenics," in N. Bell and E. Vogel (eds.),

A Modern Introduction to the Family, (rev. ed.)
(New York: The Free Press, 1968).

31. Lutz, Werner A., "Concepts and Principles Underlying
     Social Casework Practice," National Association of
     Social Workers, May 1956.

32. Meadows, Paul "Models, Systems and Sciences,"
     American Sociological Review, Vol. 22, No. 1,
     February 1957.

33. Miller, James G., "Toward a General Theory for the
     Behavioral Sciences," American Psychologist, Vol. 10,
     1955.

34. _____, "Living Systems: Basic Concepts," Be-
     havioral Science, Vol. 10, No. 3, July 1965.

35. _____, "Living Systems: Cross-Level Hypotheses,"
     Behavioral Science, Vol. 10, No. 4, October 1965.

36. _____, "Living Systems: Structure and Process,"
     Behavioral Science, Vol. 10, No. 4, October 1965.

37. Phillips, Lakin E. and Daniel N. Wiener, Short-Term
     Psychotherapy and Structural Behavior Change (New
     York: McGraw-Hill, 1966).

38. Polsky, Howard, "System as Patient: Client Needs and
     System Function," in G. Hearn (ed.), The General
     Systems Approach: Toward an Holistic Conception of
     Social Work (New York: Council on Social Work
     Education, 1969).

39. Rapaport, Anatol, Forward, in Walter Buckley (ed.),
     Modern Systems Research for the Behavioral Scientist
     (Chicago: Aldine Publishing Company, 1968).

40. Samperi, Florence, "Impressions and Reflections of
     Werner Lutz' System Theory for Case Study, Diagnosis
     and Treatment," Paper Presented at the Annual Pro-
     gram Meeting of the Council on Social Work Education,
     New York, January 1966.

41. Selye, Hans, "The Stress of Life (New York: McGraw-
     Hill, 1956).

42. Shafer, Carl M., "Teaching Social Work Practice in
     an Integrated Course: A General Systems Approach,"
     in G. Hearn (ed.), The General Systems Approach:
     Toward an Holistic Conception of Social Work (New
     York: Council on Social Work Education, 1969).

43. Shulman, Lawrence, "Social Systems Theory in Field
     Instruction: A Case Example," in G. Hearn, The
     General Systems Approach: Toward an Holistic Con-
     ception of Social Work (New York: Council on Social
     Work Education, 1969).

44. Sister Mary Paul Janchill, R. G. S., "Systems Concepts
     in Casework Theory and Practice," Social Casework,
     Vol. 15, No. 2, February 1969.

45. Stein, Irma L., "The Application of System Theory to
     Social Work Practice and Education," Paper Presented
     at the Annual Program Meeting of CSWE, New York,
     January 1966.

46. Strean, Herbert, "An Introduction to Theory in Case-
     work," Social Casework: Theories in Action (Metuchen,
     N. J.: Scarecrow Press, 1971).

47. Vickers, Gerald, "Is Adaptability Enough?", Behavioral
     Science, Vol. 4, No. 3, July 1959.

48. Vogel, Ezra and Norman Bell, "The Emotionally Dis-
     turbed Child as the Family Scapegoat," in N. Bell
     and E. Vogel (eds.), A Modern Introduction to the
     Family, (rev. ed.) (New York: The Free Press,
     1968).

49. Watzlawick, Paul, et al., Pragmatics of Human Com-
     munication (New York: W. W. Norton and Company,
     Inc., 1967).

50. Wiener, Norbert, The Human Use of Human Beings
     (New York: Doubleday Anchor Books, 1954).

51. Wynne, Lyman C., et al., "Pseudo-Mutuality in the
     Family Relations of Schizophrenics," in N. Bell and
     E. Vogel (eds.), A Modern Introduction to the Family,
     (rev. ed.) (New York: The Free Press, 1968).

Chapter 4

The Application of Role Theory to Social Casework

by Herbert S. Strean

Definition of "Role"

The construct "role" has been variously defined within and outside of casework. Its implications have been many and "role, " particularly "social role, " has been applied to a vast array of social and interpersonal situations. However, the dominant convention utilizes "role" to denote "the behavioral enactment of that part of the status which prescribes how the status occupant should act toward one of the persons with whom his status rights and obligations put him in contact" (12, p. 244).

"Role, " then, is a construct deriving from a concept, "status. " Every individual occupies positions or statuses within a number of status systems. A status system may be thought of as a multidimensional map that locates different statuses in relation to one another and shows how they are interconnected. A person's status is represented by his location on such a map (12). Status is a relational concept; it characterizes a person in terms of a set of rights and obligations that regulate his interaction with persons of other statuses. In American society, for example, the status of "father" implies, vis-à-vis his children, certain obligations such as the provision of food and shelter and certain rights, namely, the receiving of respect and obedience.

A specific status involves interaction with many others-- a foreman in a factory may interact with subordinates, supervisors and union officials, and with each his status rights and obligations differ. By virtue of occupying a particular social status, the individual is inevitably confronted with a complement of role relationships, often referred to as his "role set" (35). When the terms "role set" or "role" are utilized, they are usually applied to situations in which the

196

prescriptions for interaction are culturally defined and are
independent of the particular personal relationships that may
otherwise exist between persons occupying the positions or
statuses, as between a person appearing in court and judge
(44).

Those scholars and practitioners who have utilized the
"role" construct in casework have emphasized features of
the definition (or definitions) which focus on the social determinants of patterned behavior of individuals and the social
positions of which they are members. Paralleling its utilization in other disciplines, "role" carries a considerable
freight of meaning in casework (45) because as a construct,
it implies a means of individual expression as well as a
dimension of social behavior. As Ackerman has illustrated,
there are both social and individual determinants of role
and both must be taken into consideration; it can be conceived as a bridge between psychological and social processes (1).

Perlman, in her definition of "role" for caseworkers,
viewed the construct as "a person's organized pattern or
modes of behaving, fashioned by the status or functions he
carries in relation to one or more other persons. Such a
behavior pattern is selected, shaped, and colored by several
dynamic factors: 1) the person's needs and drives--what he
wants, consciously and unconsciously; 2) the person's ideas
of the mutual obligations and expectations that have been in-
vested (by custom, tradition, convention) in the particular
status and functions he undertakes; 3) the compatibility or
conflict between the person's conceptions of obligations and
expectations and those held by the other person(s) with whom
he is in reciprocation" (45, p. 167).

Perlman's definition seems to parallel the one used most
frequently in professional parlance and will be the definition
used in this chapter in discussing the concepts and constructs
of role theory and the application of the latter to the casework process.

Concepts and Constructs of Role Theory

Deutsch has stated: "Of all the scientific theories, role
theory is farthest from the ideal scientific theory.... It
consists mainly of a set of constructs with little in the way
of an interrelational calculus or rules of correspondence.

It is often difficult to find consensus on the nature of the
concepts themselves.   On the other hand, the constructs of
role theory are exceptionally rich in their empirical referents and provide an approach to the analysis of social behavior which is missing from many other theories" (12,
p. 244).

Role theory, while still a relatively new field of study
and far from the ideal scientific theory, already possesses
an identifiable domain of study, perspective, and language.
Role analysts have chosen as their domain of study, real-
life behavior as it is displayed in genuine ongoing social
situations.   Role theorists and role analysts have examined
such problems as the processes of socialization, inter-
dependencies among individuals, the organization and characteristics of social positions, processes of conformity and
sanctioning, specialization of performance and the division
of labor, and others (6).

A major tenet of role theory is that the real-life behavior which it studies is determined socially--much, although not all of the variance of behavior is ascribed to the
operation of immediate or past external influences. Such influences include the demands and prescriptions of others,
the behavior of others as it rewards or punishes the person,
and the individual's understanding of these factors.   As such,
role behavior is in large measure learned behavior.   What
is known about the learning of role behavior derives largely
from the concept called "socialization," which is concerned
particularly with the learning of socially relevant behavior
at various stages of the life cycle (6).

George Herbert Mead was the first writer to focus on
the learning of socially relevant roles.   He delineated two
stages in the development of the self-play and games (32).
In play, the child takes on a set of dual roles, his own and
that of some other person, e. g. , teacher, mother, grocer.
Such activity affords the child an opportunity to explore the
attitudes held by others toward himself.   By taking the role
of the other, the child learns to regard himself from an external point of view.   At this early stage of development a
person's self is constituted by an organization of the specific
attitudes held by other persons toward himself and toward one
another in the contexts of those social acts he has explored
in his play.   It is through this process that the child eventually learns the generalized attitudes of the community of which
he is part.   In the fullest sense, according to Mead, the

development of the self requires that the person also take on the group's attitudes toward its own organized social activity. In effect, he experiences his social group as an organized community of attitudes, norms, values, and goals that regulate his behavior and the behavior of others. The attitudes of the group become incorporated into the structure of the self, just as did the attitudes of individuals important to him.

By Mead's formulation, a means of evaluating the individual's capacity for interpersonal relations is provided. A limited capacity or ability to extend the range of introjected roles implies an inability to "put oneself in the other guy's place" and therefore limits the range of possibilities in interpersonal interaction. Asch, for example, has demonstrated that tension in interpersonal relationships may be ascribed to an inability or resistance to introjecting appropriate roles (2).

The more rigorously roles are defined, the more stringently are their prescriptions enforced and the more difficult it is for a person to resolve conflict by deviating from them. "Role rigor," as developed by Getzels and Guba, refers to the amount of deviation that is permitted from the role's prescriptions (18). In contrast to our rural society in America, where roles were clearly demarcated and little deviance from them was permitted, our contemporary social structure permits a great deal of role rigor. Consequently, many individuals are uncertain about which roles to enact and have experienced doubt concerning the ingredients of many role-sets. As a result, contemporary man has been described as searching for identity. In his essay, The Quest for Identity, Wheelis concluded that the quest for an identity is a search for meaningful social roles (63).

Newcomb's investigations have illustrated the many different roles most individuals enact (41). Implicit in the fact that one's status set involves a wide variety of role relations is the possibility that one will find oneself occupying positions with incompatible role requirements. For example, a frequent client of the family agency and child guidance clinic is the mother who feels pressure to nurture her children to the exclusion of other interests but who wishes simultaneously to maintain a role in communal or professional activity (57).

The personality assumes various types of roles with sundry people at various times for variegated purposes.

Therefore, role theory provides a means to study and describe the interaction of two members of a social group as they adjust to each other within a social system. Spiegel has stated: "A role is a goal-directed pattern or sequence of acts tailored by the cultural process for the transactions a person may carry out in a social group or situation" (52). Any small social group, such as the nuclear family, achieves some level of stability or equilibrium. Each actor (or person) in the group has his allocated roles in relation to each other member of the group. Complementarity, or the fit of the roles of ego and alter, is desirable. For every speaker there should be a listener, for every writer a reader, for every parent a child and for every teacher a pupil (22). Complementarity exists when the reciprocal role of a role partner is carried out automatically without difficulty, and in the expected way. Strains in the equilibrium of the system may occur because of an unstable role structure, ambiguous role definitions and expectations, or the failure of role complementarity between role partners (52).

Spiegel has specified five main causes for failure in role complementarity. The first is a "cognitive discrepancy" in which one or both parties are not familiar with the roles which they are expected to assume and thus miss their cues. The second cause for failure is a discrepancy of roles-- when ego or alter require roles that the other does not possess. Third, there is an "allocative discrepancy" which indicates that roles are not accepted by at least one of the role partners. The fourth reason for failure of role complementarity is the absence of "instrumental means." For example, a person who is expected to be generous may be unable to be so because of the lack of money. A teacher may not be able to satisfy a student's expectations because he does not possess the necessary knowledge, or a caseworker may not have the knowledge or ability to handle a particular situation or problem. A fifth reason for failure in role complementarity offered by Spiegel is "a discrepancy in cultural value orientations," as in mixed marriages (52).

Roles are allocated in a variety of ways. They may be "ascribed" automatically by age, sex, etc. They may be "achieved" by virtue of occupation or they may be "adopted" because they satisfy some need of the individual. Finally, roles may be "assumed" in a playful, "let's pretend" attitude (31).

As mentioned, when there is an allocative discrepancy in roles, there is a failure of complementarity or disequilibrium. After disequilibrium has occurred, there is usually an effort to establish equilibrium again which is called "requiliberation." Requilibration may be established by ego who attempts to "induce" alter into an appropriate role such as by coercing, coaxing, evaluating, masking, and postponing. Alter has a series of defenses that he can utilize in order to avoid being inducted into the role which ego desires. Thus, he may defy, refuse, deny, unmask the pretensiveness or provoke ego. Another means of requilibration may be established through "mutual modification" of roles. The two participants may resort to joking, referring the matter to a third party, exploring or re-exploring the issue, compromising, and consolidating their positions in their transactions (52).

Roles may be "explicit" or "implicit." Explicit roles are conscious, exposed to observation, and both participants in a transacting system are aware of them. An individual who comes to a social agency as a client and states that he is a client and enacts the role of client is enacting an "explicit" role. Implicit roles are those of which the person may not be aware and of which he is usually unconscious (52). Therefore, the client, by virtue of his explicit role, may enter the agency in order to understand and cope with his situation better but may implicitly enact the role of a dependent child who is not really interested in self or situational understanding but in having the caseworker indulge his infantile demands (22).

The most comprehensive examination of role theory has been performed by Biddle and Thomas. They found that the basic concepts and constructs for behavior used by most role analysts could be classified as prescription, description, sanction, action, and evaluation. For each of these "partitions" there is a "descriptive similarity among the behaviors falling within a classification, and this is apparently what distinguishes basic behavioral concepts from one another (6).

Prescription. Many of the terms used in role theory apply to prescriptive behavior. The term "role" itself is often used prescriptively as referring to behaviors that "should" or "ought to" be performed; "expectations, "standards" and "norms" are others. Much of social behavior is affected by prescriptions and many social situations are dominated by the expression of overt demands. Demands appear, for example, in parent-child communications, work, politics, and education (6).

Because prescriptions are ubiquitous and salient in their various forms, they appear to be among the most significant guides and standards by which men live. By defining the rights and obligations of individuals, prescriptions appear to be among the most potent factors in the control of human behavior, either by "directly triggering conformity behavior or through a system of positive and negative sanctions that accompany them" (6, p. 103). Prescriptions are important also because they emerge from the interaction of individuals and groups and thus, to some extent, are themselves controlled by some of the same behavior which they are presumed to govern. Prescriptions may be formal and informal, expressed and implicit, individual and shared. They may vary in permissiveness, completeness, complexity, and in the degree to which they are universal.

The notion of role prescription has been utilized in social casework treatment by Strean. In "Role Theory, Role Models, and Casework: Review of the Literature and Practice Applications, " the writer suggested that every client in casework treatment is induced by the worker to enact a specific role in order to receive casework help. If the role prescribed is not congruent with the client's expectations, strain occurs between the two actors (57). In another paper, the writer suggested that rather than prescribe roles for clients, particularly for those who resist enacting standard client roles, the client should be treated as a consultant who prescribes what roles the two actors would take (58). This type of role reversal has been followed by Schwitzgebel in Street Corner Research where delinquents were not only utilized as consultants in treatment but were paid for doing so (50). In casework with the poor, many writers have felt that impoverished clients have not responded successfully to treatment because the workers involved have prescribed roles incompatible with the clients' customary ones (47).

Gouldner has referred to a prescription or "norm" of reciprocity. The concept demonstrates that A is functional for B which helps to account for A's persistence and stability but only on two related assumptions: 1) that B reciprocates A's services; and 2) that B's service to A is contingent upon A's performance of positive functions for B.   Unless B's services to A are contingent upon the services provided by A, it is pointless to examine the latter if one wishes to account for the persistence of A (20).

Psychoanalysts Meerloo and Nelson in their book, Transference and Trial Adaptation, contend that if analysts wish
to take into fuller account the concepts of transference and
counter-transference, certain problems of role reciprocity
that permeate the therapeutic relationship must be considered.
One example given by them is that the patient's resistances
overtly manifest themselves as a sequence of presented roles
which he mobilizes to influence or compel the analyst to
modify his role.   By implication, the fundamental tenet of
analytic neutrality is questioned by the authors' assertion
that the patient's efforts to induce the analyst to abandon
his therapeutic role and actualize a different role (e. g.,
parent, sibling, lover) are matched by the analyst's efforts
to induce the patient to enact a prescribed role despite the
latter's resistances.   Thus, analyst and patient alike engage
in efforts to induce one another to enact the role or roles
which each deems necessary to maintain the interpersonal
situation (33).

Description.   Behavior in which persons represent events,
processes, and phenomena without affective or evaluative
accompaniment is designated as descriptive.   In role theory
literature one encounters many different terms that refer
to descriptions.   "Concept, " "anticipation, " "expectation, "
are among the most frequent.   Descriptions may be overt
or covert, distorted or nondistorted; they are the individual's
representation of aspects of the real world as he experiences
it and are shaped by the individual's experience--by the
positions to which he belongs, by the role behavior engaged
in, while a member of positions and by the ways in which
he is interdependent with others (6).

Descriptive role expectations have been researched in
psychotherapy and casework.   In The Anatomy of Psychotherapy, Lennard and Bernstein studied role expectations in
the therapeutic situation.   They viewed therapy as a social
system involving two sub-systems, those of role expectations
and communication.   Their research documented the hypothesis that asymmetry in the system of role expectations is
reflected in asymmetry in the system of communication.   If
therapist and patient differ in the expectations each holds for
the other, strains will appear and the participants will attempt certain strategies to resolve the strains (29).   Overall
and Aronson demonstrated that when patients of lower socio-
economic groups hold expectations for treatment at variance

with the actual behaviors of the therapist, a higher dropout
rate follows than with patients holding more accurate expectations (42).   Further research by the same authors revealed differential treatment expectations of patients in different socio-economic classes (3).   Treatment expectations for
casework as a function of reference group expectations has
been well documented by Rosenblatt (48).   The incongruity
of expectations between caseworker and client, particularly
in the intake situation, has received attention from Perlman.
Like Rosenblatt, she attributed client dropout to the di-
vergency of role expectations between client and worker (45).
The relationship between role expectations and performance
was the subject of a study by Dinitz et. al., who reported
on the relationship between the role expectations of family
members and the performance of female mental patients
following their discharge from a mental hospital.   Their
findings demonstrated a direct relationship between the expectations held for the patient's role performance, that is,
the higher the expectations held for the patient's role performance, the higher the level of the patient's actual performance (13).

Sanctioning.   Sanctioning is behavior engaged in by individuals with the intent of achieving a modification in another's behavior; this modification is usually toward greater
conformity.   Sanctions may or may not be effective in a-
chieving an actual alteration of the behavior in question and
conformity may occur without any sanctioning whatsoever (6).
Goode has pointed out that conformity is necessary for the
smooth operation of institutions and that, generally, individuals conform because of their motivation to do so.
Sanctioning is not only necessary to enforce role conformity
but acts of sanctioning become the obligations, and hence,
the role of others (19).

A friend's sanction may be different from that of some
representative of society and, therefore, the concept of consensus is very much inherent in role theory, particularly in
the "partition" of sanctioning.   The degree of consensus can
vary from near maximum disagreement, through polarization
or conflict, to unanimous agreement or consensus (6).

Jacobson's research related to consensus and conflict of
marital partners.   The study indicated that divorced couples
exhibited greater disparities than did married couples in
their attitudes towards the roles of husband and wife in
marriage (27).   Considering the same phenomenon, Ingersoll

has stated: "Each young man who marries brings with him
his idea of the part to be played by himself as husband and
the part to be played by his wife as wife.   Similarly,   the
young woman enters marriage with a preconceived notion of
the roles of husband and wife. ... If the conceptions of both
are reasonably fulfilled, we can expect a satisfactory adjustment.   We should remember, however, that we enter marriage with definite expectations, and if reality falls short of
them, dissatisfaction follows" (26, p. 316).

    Action.   Action is behavior distinguished on the basis of
its having been learned previously, its goal directedness and
its apparent voluntariness.   Much of the behavior of the
child at play, the employee at work, and the individual at
home is "performance."   Role analysts are concerned with
such aspects of performance as its complexity, uniformity,
adequacy, the bias with which it is presented, and the extent
to which individuals are organismically engaged (6, p. 193).

    Most persons are interdependent with others in their
performance and, as a consequence, an individual may incur
rewards and costs and have his performance facilitated or
hindered by the performance of others.   Performance is also
related to the personality characteristics of those perform-
ing, to the positions of which they are members, to the prescriptions for their behavior, among many other factors.
Sarbin's notion of "role enactment" (49) impinges on the concept of action or performance.   Elaborating on several of
the dimensions of his notion, Sarbin, like Newcomb (41), has
referred to the number of roles simultaneously enacted by
the individual which is associated with the individual's social
adjustment.

    Role enactment has received attention in the therapeutic
area.   In "Paradigmatic Psychotherapy in Borderline Treatment," Coleman and Nelson have taken the position that each
individual is a group with a blend of introjected and internalized roles.   In aiding the patient to strengthen his equipment and function at a greater capacity in his life situations,
the writers advised that comprehensive treatment necessitates
the adoption of multiple roles by the therapist.   These roles
vary according to the dynamic unfolding of each individual
case.   The therapist, therefore, acts as a paradigm of the
world in which the patient must learn to move (9).   Enacting
the role of the helpless and naive child can help self-destructive clients verbalize aggression (54).   Enacting the
narcissistic self-indulgent role can involve rebellious ado-

lescents in treatment (56) and enacting a role which is a
mirror image of the highly defended client can prevent
further acting out and the compounding of resistances (59).

Evaluation. Behavior is partitioned as evaluative as it
relates primarily to approval or disapproval. "Preference, "
"value, " "affect, " and "esteem" are terms which generally
pertain to evaluative behavior. . . . Evaluations are pervasive
in social life. The mother who rejoices over her child's
performance, the audience member who claps or boos, the
teacher who grades a paper are expressing overt assessments of the performance of others (6, p. 27).

Closely linked to evaluation is a role concept, namely
"position. " In no society are the members entirely alike or
are the individual differences among members random and
unordered. Leader, follower, dwarf, Negro, client, caseworker, neurotic, relief-recipient, are among a host of
positions in American society, and each position is evaluated
by the social system of which the position is a part. "Dwarf, "
"Negro, " "client, " "relief-recipient, " "mental patient, " all
contain an evaluative implication so that we prefer, value,
and esteem some positions and not others. An important
dimension in evaluating any social system is the status or
heirarchal factor with its implications for communication
patterns and relationships (6).

The Application of Role Theory to the Casework Process

Social Study

Role theory may be applied in the two essential parts of
the study phase in casework, namely, inducing the person to
move from readiness to ask for help to a readiness to use
it, and in understanding the person who has the problem as
well as the problem itself (48, 24). We shall consider first
how role theory may aid in helping the person eventually to
enact the role of client.

Several writers have alluded to client dropout, i. e. , the
client leaves the casework relationship prematurely (53, 51,
45). One of the underlying reasons that has been proposed
is that the applicant's understanding and expectations of the
agency were not clear to the caseworker, and the caseworker's
understanding and expectations of the applicant were not clear
to the applicant (45). Therefore, the barriers that can be

created between client and caseworker in the study phase may
be considered within a role theory context--the two actors
can be viewed as having incongruent expectations regarding
their respective roles.   For example, if the client views
his role as an actor who will receive financial help as soon
as possible, while the caseworker perceives the situation as
one in which he will slowly help the applicant understand the
etiology of his joblessness, we have a failure in complementarity of roles and the client may very well withdraw
from the agency (45).

The study phase usually creates role strains.   Most
frequently, the worker expects the applicant to provide data
(tell the story of his life, get to the root causes behind his
requests, etc.), while the client frequently expects initially
to receive rather than to provide.   This role incongruency
has been cited as one of the failures of casework, particularly in work with clients from lower socio-economic groups.
Many such individuals do not view the putting into words of
feelings, thoughts, memories, and facts as a legitimate or
prescribed part of any role-set.   Consequently, to the more
action-oriented client who wants the worker "to act rather
than talk, " the caseworker's reluctance to act and provide
materially and tangibly for him, is baffling and he may interpret the worker's behavior as disinterest or rejection.   The
middle class, verbally oriented caseworker can be equally
baffled by the applicant's "reluctance to verbalize" and may
interpret his client's behavior as pathological acting out or
resistance.   The social situation just described may end by
the applicant asking, "When are you going to start helping
me?" and the worker inquiring of the client, "When are you
going to get involved with me and the agency?" (47, 3, 42).

The role theorist, therefore, would advise the caseworker
that one of his fundamental tasks during the study phase of
the casework process would be to clarify the respective role
expectations of the two actors, client and worker, so that
they both may attain some consensus regarding their respective positions and tasks.   As Perlman has stated, "The aim
of the beginning phase of casework is to help an 'applicant'
to undertake the role of 'client. '"   Thus, certain understandings must evolve between caseworker and applicant before the latter becomes a client.   What an applicant will do
in the study phase is conditioned by his conception of what
is expected of him and what he may expect in return from
the caseworker and the agency--in short "by his conception
of his and the caseworker's roles in relation to the problem

he brings" (45).   It may be confidently hypothesized that if
the applicant wishes to discuss his physical aches and pains
while the worker wishes to discuss the clients psychological
dynamics, dropouts will occur (3).   Until the caseworker
and applicant have come to some tentative or rudimentary
agreements about their present and future transactions, the
caseworker does not have a client (45).

It is further suggested that where role expectations
differ, as between the middle class worker and lower class
client, the latter must be provided some form of gratification
of his expectations.   If the lower class client's expressions
of aches and pains are empatically heard and his request for
tangible assistance receives some priority in the study
phase, the client will be less inclined to drop out.

The role and status set of client, as prescribed by
many caseworkers for the study phase, is probably acceptable to only a very small percentage of casework's clientele.
The worker expects that his future client should attempt to
"involve himself in a relationship, " attend "regularly sched-
uled appointments, " "take some responsibility for his role in
the psychosocial difficulty, " "reveal secrets from his present and past, " and listen to the "worker's supportive and
clarifying remarks. "   However, a client may not be able to
form the relationship that the worker may demand (57) because of all of the causes we have alluded to for failure in
role complementarity--cognitive discrepancy (the applicant is
not familiar with the role he is expected to assume); discrepancy of roles (he may not possess the necessary ingredients for the role he is required to enact); he may refuse to
accept the role because the caseworker's prescribed role
clashes with his subjective role as he sees himself with the
caseworker (allocative discrepancy); there may be an absence
of "instrumental means" (the applicant does not have the
verbal facility or motivation to "involve himself"); and there
may be a discrepancy in the cultural value orientations between worker and client (52).

Becoming a client can interfere with an existing status
or role set when the applicant adds the status of client to
it and a host of conflicts may then be generated (48).   In
addition to the potential discomfort of enacting a dependent
role in a culture which champions independence, many members of the client's current role network may not sanction
his receiving of casework help.   As several writers have
reiterated, it appears quite conclusive that for the casework

relationship to be sustained, the applicant's reference groups
must support the idea. An unsupportive social environment
does not foster the client's continuance with a social agency
(48, 51, 45).

In attempting to understand the person and his situation--
the other objective of a social study--how role theory can
contribute is quite clear. By studying the client's role-set
and status-set, the worker may be able to note a wider
ramification of the presented problems of the client. As his
reciprocal role relationships are studied, different members
of his family or his job situation may emerge as more strategic, i. e. , where is there role complementarity and where
is ther complementarity failure in the family, job, etc. ?
The utilization of role theory in the study phase would inevitably induce the worker to investigate what demands for
social performance are being made on the client, by whom
and in what social contexts. The worker would be more
sensitized to the client's subjective view of his psychosocial
difficulties as he focused on the client's and his reference
groups' social standards with their prescriptions, sanctions,
evaluations, etc. (7).

Each social role is composed of a number of activities,
a few of which seem to be so essential for the role that impaired performance or failure to perform them is an indication of social dysfunctioning. For example, a husband
is expected to work for a living and to provide economic
support--alone or together with a wife. He is expected to
share in family decisions and other activities, and his wife
is expected to engage in reciprocal activities in many of
the same areas. The role concept makes it possible to
identify crucial tasks which, if not performed or inadequately
performed, may make for individual or family stress and
may lead to specific types of social dysfunctioning. As the
role concept is utilized in the study phase, the specific
stresses of the client may emerge as his role expectations
are investigated. Frequently, there may be a lack of consensus on these expectations between him and significant
others. There may be differences in definition of the same
role on the part of different members of the family or job,
differences in perception of the role performances, or of
disagreement about the role rigor (degree of freedom) each
member of the family has to perform his roles (7).

Because the social study is a psychosocial process in
which the worker must achieve a social level of perception,

210   Social Casework

as he correlates socio-economic, cultural, and psychological
data (24), the role concept can facilitate an understanding of
these phenomena in light of the interaction of psychic, social,
somatic, and cultural factors as they impinge on the client's
role and status set (7).

     In gathering information during the social study phase,
a role analysis is an efficient means for locating the person-
situation strengths as well as deficiencies because as the
worker focuses on role expectations, role reciprocity, and
role complementarity, he avoids the danger of an exclusive
concern with clinical pathology. In studying the role interaction of two people, e. g. , a marital pair, he learns that
a "good" marriage with congruent reciprocal role expectations
may very well be two neurotic individuals who meet many of
each other's needs and wishes.   The dominant wife-passive
husband constellation has been offered as a prime etiological
factor in virtually every psychosocial disturbance, but it also
consists of two role partners who are enacting implicit roles
that each partner implicitly prescribes and sanctions.   The
constellation may not be congruent with the worker's role
prescriptions for husband and wife but this is not sufficient
to label it "a sick relationship" and throw it into disequilibrium by questioning it (1).

Diagnosis

     As the caseworker attempts to draw inferences from the
facts gathered during the social study and organize these
inferences in a systematic manner so that a comprehensive
psychosocial diagnosis may evolve, role theory and role
analysis may enrich the diagnostic formulations. As the
worker attempts to understand the client's subjective interpretation of the latter's expectations of his various roles
and role relationships, and as the worker sensitizes himself
to the way individuals in the client's role network view the
client's and their own role obligations, a more individualized
diagnosis may be the result.   The utilization of role theory,
with its emphasis on interaction and transaction and its respect for the client's and "significant others'" own definitions
of appropriate role behavior, truly meets the client where
he is and accepts him as he is.   The worker's own biases
may be exposed and need not interfere with his diagnostic
objectivity as he compares and contrasts his own role expectations with those of his client's and his client's "significant others. "

The utilization of role theory will require the worker to draw inferences from the facts gathered concerning the "norms" that impinge on the client. The diagnostic interpretation will take into consideration the way the client's ethnic group, religion, and social class view certain behavior and what the role prescriptions are for the client. What the worker may view as pathological might very well be "normal" for a specific role network and, therefore, might yield a different treatment prescription, once cultural and subcultural norms are considered.

Hellenbrand has advised that values are the major agent in a client's role commitments and therefore are a necessary part of the data that go to make up a diagnosis. The cultural norms or values determine to a large extent parent-child, marital, school, and work relationships. Therefore, in formulating a diagnosis, the worker must ask, "What has priority--the individual's wishes or cultural imperatives?" A conflict between them pinpoints in part the locus for therapeutic intervention (25).

The application of role theory for purposes of organizing data enlarges the diagnostic picture in another way. As the worker diagnoses a mother, he will take into consideration that the latter is not only a mother but a wife, daughter, daughter-in-law and possibly a wage earner. These roles may or may not be in conflict with each other and may conflict with some and may not conflict with others in the role-set (36).

Boehm has utilized role theory for the purposes of a comprehensive diagnostic classification. By classifying role performances and viewing all clients as role carriers, diagnosis can be more comprehensive and point to a clearer direction for intervention according to Boehm. He classifies role performance at four levels:

Level I--Role performance violates minimum societal standards and may cause stress to individuals and groups in the client's role network.

Level II--Role performance meets minimum societal standards but causes stress to individuals and groups in the role network.

Level III--Role performance meets minimum societal standards for members of the role network, but is not commensurate with role performance potential.

Level IV--Role performance meets minimum societal standards and is commensurate with role performance potential.

Clients classified at the first level (Level I) would come to caseworkers from courts and similar institutions. At Level II, the impetus for casework help comes from the person whose role performance is impaired. Public health measures are required for clients at Level III and no casework services seem to be required for clients at the last level.

The usefulness of Boehm's classification is that it provides a clearer picture of the role of society in the provision of casework and social services. It clarifies the social control aspect of casework in that at Level I, it is deemed essential for society to provide social resources; at Level II, social services are essential for full effectiveness but not for the existence of society, and at Level III, the provision of social services is deemed desirable. Boehm's scheme views role performance against certain norms when assessing role performance. For diagnostic purposes, the scheme helps locate areas of dysfunction. Because the client is viewed almost exclusively as a role carrier in this classification, it points a diagnostic direction in helping the worker assess what aspects of the role-set the client accepts or rejects (8, pp. 118-124).

Treatment

No formula has yet been devised for determining the specific weight of factors in the etiology or resolution of emotional disorders and social dysfunctioning and no single theory or a priori resolve can make the decision about the appropriateness for any particular client or different sorts of treatment plans and settings (9). An approach predicated on the assumption that psychosocial factors are inherent in both the etiology and treatment of these disorders and that utilizes role theory in casework treatment would proceed from a number of linked postulates: 1) the roles that individuals in the client's environment assume (past and present) play a critical influence in his past and present socialization; 2) faulty learning and dysfunctional role habituation are critical, if not the only sources of emotional and

social disorder; and 3) the caseworker-client relationship
constitutes an opportunity for new learning (9, 55, 57).

In considering the relationship of caseworker and client
as a system of interaction and transaction between ego and
alter, we may apply what has been learned from role theory.
Casework treatment can be visualized as a system consisting
of the behavior of a client in terms of his role in transaction
with the caseworker as a role partner. When established,
complementarity of roles represents stability and harmony
and is conducive to the worker's obtaining the data that he
needs to understand the client and to the client in incorporating the worker's suggestions and other prescriptions.
Disequilibrium, because of noncomplementarity, eventually
resulting in re-equilibrium, represents the disruption of an
old repetitive process and the establishment of a new system.
This can produce learning, change, and a therapeutic result
(22).

In order to feel comfortable in any interpersonal situation, the individual attempts to induce his role partner to
enact roles which will maintain the feeling of comfort (52).
In the casework treatment relationship, this phenomenon
occurs as well. Consequently, the client will mobilize changing role patterns of cooperation and resistance that will be
designed to influence the worker to modify his role. The
caseworker is also minimally obliged to induce the client to
enact a role because the cooperative effort required of the
client may be felt by the latter as purely formal and ego-
dystonic. Therefore, it can be postulated that worker and
client will try to induce one another to enact the role or
roles which each deems necessary to maintain and promote
the interpersonal situation (40, 55, 57, 33).

It would appear that the psychoanalytic concepts "transference," "counter-transference," and "resistance" can be
fused into one role construct, "role induction," and in adapting these concepts for role theory, their meaning may be
enriched. Transference may be seen as the client's efforts
to induce the worker to abandon his chosen role of either
helper, explorer, or environmental manipulator and instead
project roles of parent, sibling, etc.; resistance may be
viewed as the client's non-compliance with the worker's role
prescription for either himself or the client (57, 29, 33, 40).
Because the client's efforts at role induction are paralleled
by those of the worker, we may consider as counter-transference those efforts of the worker to persuade the client to

enact prescribed roles when the latter resists them (33).

Any person who has been engaged in the practice of casework or psychotherapy has recognized that in the face of all logic and reason, the client can often behave in a most obstinate and uncomprehending manner.   To try to convince a suspicious client that his spouse is well-meaning, or a self-hating client that he is competent in certain areas, usually intensifies the client's self doubts.   Consequently, caseworkers have long held that no client is so completely rational and no worker so sufficiently wise that a dialogue could ensue in which the worker could interpret the client's problems so that the client, having arrived at a reasonable understanding, would embark on a new course of action based on the new insights he has acquired from the worker (5, 40).

Recognizing the above, it was Freud who first considered the application of role theory (although not labelling it as such) when he was faced with the "negative therapeutic reaction" (16).   Realizing that certain patients repudiated every interpretation and suggestion that he had made, in "The Outline of Psychoanalysis, " Freud virtually suggested role-playing or role enactment (17).   In this essay, the founder of psychoanalysis advocated that presenting role prescriptions to the patient should be part of the role-set of the psychoanalyst.   He stated that in every individual case of analysis, the psychoanalyst is obliged to use a mixed panel of authorities to back up his direct or indirect therapeutic demands. Depending on the factors that decide what will influence the patient at the moment, he shifts from one to the other. Freud stated that the analyst has to enact many different roles--the analyst will be a teacher, a parental figure; he will instruct, give guidance, and impose rules of conduct; he will praise or condemn depending on the degree of narcissism of the patient.

The statements of Freud referred to above could be interpreted as a suggestion to the analyst that by his enacting roles of teacher, parent, etc. , he may enable the patient through role induction to cooperate with his analyst and eventually assimilate the latter's interpretations.   Other analysts and therapists have utilized role theory in relating to similar therapeutic problems.   Greenson has referred to "re-education" in which the therapist offers himself as a role model for introjection and identification, enabling the client to emulate the therapist's more mature role behavior (21). Coleman and Nelson have utilized "paradigmatic treatment" in which the treatment situation "becomes a model of the world, a stage on which all possible dramas and roles may be played out" (9). The consistent theme in all of the literature in which role theory has been applied to treatment situations has been that for an individual with defective ego functioning to learn again is similar to problems of learning in children. To be effective in the treatment situation, it has been suggested, the worker must realize that comprehensive treatment necessitates throughout, the adoption of multiple stances and roles determined by the dynamic unfolding of each individual case. As many writers have advised (54, 55, 40, 5), to be truly helpful, the worker must demonstrate love and hate, reason and unreason, sickness and health, acceptance and rejection, confidence and insecurity, and a whole gamut of roles. To quote Coleman and Nelson, who state that by adopting various roles the therapist serves a complex of functions:

> He helps correct faulty perceptions of reality and demonstrates to the patient those ego functions which the latter does not have or misuses; he assists in giving the patient needed practice in coping with life situations. The therapist thus acts as a paradigm of the world in which the patient must learn to move (9, p. 41).

Equilibrium and Disequilibrium in Casework Treatment

In applying the concepts and constructs of role theory to the treatment process, one may view the treatment decisions that the worker has to make as always involving a choice in either promoting equilibrium of disequilibrium in the interaction. It has already been suggested that during the study phase, when the worker is gathering information and attempting to induce the client to move from the applicant role to the client role, some role complementarity is necessary; otherwise, there is the danger of the client leaving the situation prematurely. Therefore, for the action-oriented client, some form of worker action (home visit, relating to the employer, material assistance) would probably be indicated; and for the verbal client, some form of verbal interaction would appear to be the procedure of choice. Therefore, as Varley has stated in "The Use of Role Theory in the Treatment of Disturbed Adolescents" (62), the caseworker in the early interviews should first state how he views his own role and how he and the client can work together.

Second, he should discuss with the client what is expected
of him during treatment--the client's role.   Also, the client's
involvement in the evaluation process is considered crucial
so that early discomfort and confusion can be avoided.

While role complementarity and equilibrium will preserve
the casework interaction, most caseworkers would concur
that the old, repetitive, self-defeating processes that the
client will inevitably bring to the casework encounter cannot
be eternally unattended to by the worker.   It would appear,
therefore, that certain role prescriptions that the client
offers must be frustrated, otherwise, learning of new and
healthier roles by him will not be achieved.   For example,
to gratify the wishes of a demanding, self-destructive client
and obey his role prescriptions is, in effect, to join him in
his self-destructiveness.   Although this client may enact an
explicit role which seems logical to the worker, such as
consistently asking for advice and guidance from the casework
expert, acquiescence to the induced role by the worker may,
in fact, further weaken the client's sense of self and autonomy.
If the role of the caseworker is that of frequent giver, the
frustration tolerance of the client will be limited instead of
his being able to sustain a sense of conflict, so important
for the socialization process (38, 11).   The client will find
it difficult to express disagreement or deal with external
reality, since his learning experience with the caseworker
will at best result in an egocentric identification (38, 57).

The following case illustration is presented in order to
demonstrate how the caseworker's refusal to be induced into
enacting the role the client prescribed, promoted a disequilibrium in the casework interaction and resulted in the client's
eventual assumption of more mature social roles.

> Miss A was a twenty-eight year old divorced woman
> who sought a casework agency's help because of in-
> decisiveness, depressed feelings, sexual inhibition,
> somatic symptoms (migraine, hives, and insomnia)
> and job failure.   She had left two previous casework
> contacts abruptly and prematurely because she "couldn't
> establish contact" with her workers.   In the casework
> encounter, as she did in life situations, Miss A pre-
> sented herself as sweet, docile, naive, and helpless.
> In all of her interactions, she tended to idealize the
> other person, ascribe omnipotence to him, and when
> she felt an absence of 'appropriate love,' she would
> eventually become discouraged and withdraw.   She

usually blamed herself for her 'failures,' calling herself on frequent occasions, 'a good for nothing.'
When her first two caseworkers interpreted her wish
for infantile love and for an omnipotent mother, she
acknowledged these interpretations as valid, but no
modification in her interpersonal behavior followed.
She would tell her caseworkers that she guessed that
she, Miss A, was a failure and then made appeals to
the caseworkers to get her jobs, boyfriends, better
apartments, etc.   When the caseworkers attempted to
do the latter for her, Miss A always found that she
was 'a failure' in these areas, as well, since she
couldn't "cope with a better apartment or job. "

In her third encounter she pleaded with her worker
again to be an idealized mother, but the worker refused.   On entering treatment with him, she early
reported that she was about to be fired from her
current job and needed some 'help and direction.'
'Help and direction' meant getting a new job for her.
When the worker responded by saying that he couldn't
do this very well, Miss A responded that she didn't
'know which way to turn' and needed 'a suggestion.'
When the worker suggested that maybe she would just
have to remain jobless because she was a failure,
Miss A told the worker that he was so unlike her
previous caseworkers 'who always tried to help and
be nice.'   Other similar types of frustrations by the
caseworker gradually began to release feelings of resentment against the worker.   When Miss A com-
plained about her fiancé, saying that he wasn't con-
siderate and she needed advice to 'make him be
kind,' the worker suggested that maybe he was in-
corrigible.   Eventually the client began to express
surprise and shock at the caseworker's attitude which
she thought was 'sadistic.'   She accused him of being
too pessimistic and began to find solutions for problems which the worker appeared to consider in-
soluble.

While the client expressed rage at the caseworker for
being unkind, concomitantly she found by herself a
'better' apartment, a 'better' job, and a new and
'better' boyfriend.   Eventually she recalled how her
'mother spoiled me and indulged me and never left
me on my own to grow up.'   She further likened her
first two caseworkers to her mother, 'who never had

faith in my abilities and therefore, I couldn't either.'
Near the end of her casework contact, she thanked
the worker for 'putting me on my own so I could
have faith in myself.'

The above case illustrates how the explicit role of the
client (a helpless little girl who seeks advice) was frustrated
by the worker.   This induced a failure in role complementarity and disequilibrium.   However, the disequilibrium induced in the patient a wish to mobilize her own capacities
which resulted in the acquisition of healthier social roles
(40).

In contrast to the above situation in which the client's
third caseworker was helpful by not submitting to the prescribed role, there are certain situations where the client's
prescription can be complied with and a disequilibrium can
result to the client's eventual benefit.   These are situations
in which the client's prescribed roles have never been complied with by previous workers or other significant people in
authority, and no amount of persuasion or appeal to the
client's logic on their part seems to have distracted the
client from his pleas.   The clients are usually individuals
who have suffered a great deal of deprivation--either psychological deprivation, social, or economic.   In many ways they
are trying to prove that "no one cares" and they are convinced of this when the worker refuses to consider their
prescriptions which frequently can appear, on the surface,
as absurd.   The following case illustration of Jack is an
example of the worker's explicit compliance with the client's
attempts at role induction which created the necessary disequilibrium to help the client eventually enact more mature
social roles.

Jack, a young man of seventeen, has successfully defeated two previous caseworkers.   The product of two
overly-intellectualized parents, Jack rebelled against
the idea of accepting his worker's diagnostic apprais-
als as he did his parents' over-promotion of intellectual accomplishments and school teachers' directives.
Jack had his own ideas of how things should be done.

With his third caseworker, Jack said, 'The other
ones (referring to his previous social workers) didn't
let me have a big say about the way things should be
done.'   When Jack's third casework activity enlisted
his directions on how the casework treatment should

proceed, Jack gave many prescriptions. 'First of all,
I am not interested in your opinions--you should just
listen. I have a lot to say. Also, I'm not calling
you by your real name. I'm calling you "String Bean."
You look like one!'

The worker complied with his client's instructions and
for many interviews maintained his silence, interrupted
only very occasionally with a 'Right, Mr. Jack.'
Jack made the casework office a lecture hall where
he presented his ideas on philosophy, sociology, sex
and religion, without a challenge or question from the
worker.

With strong anger after several interviews, Jack ad-
monished the worker for being so lazy and for not
doing his job. He asked, 'Aren't you tired of listening to me by now?' The worker responded, 'I'm only
obeying your orders.' Jack spent several more interviews castigating the worker for listening to a person
younger than himself, urged him to get to work, and
then offered many items for a realistic casework
agenda.

Jack later told the worker that he guessed he had
'never felt important' but wanted to feel as if I
amounted to something.' He also told the worker that
he wanted 'to lecture at least once instead of always
being in the audience.'

In the above case, the worker not only permitted his
client to receive the gratification his parents did not allow
but also demonstrated by his role behavior that intellectualized speeches do not necessarily have to ruffle the listener.
As Jack's prescriptions were seriously complied with by the
worker, disequilibrium in the transaction slowly evolved.
The disequilibrium mobilized the client's capacities to see
reality more clearly and use the help that the caseworker
could realistically offer.

Jack had been a "casework dropout" because his previous
workers would only enact roles that were prescribed by themselves and refused to be induced even to consider Jack's requests. Only when Jack received the gratification of having
his prescriptions adhered to could he accept the client role
(55, 56, 40).

The two cases that we have described are seeming contrasts. In the first illustration, the worker refused to com-
ply with the client's prescriptions and in the second he complied completely. The one feature that the two cases do
have in common, however, is that the clients received responses from the caseworker which were different from the
responses of the clients' previous role partners. This may
offer a clue to what the treatment needs of many clients
should be. It would behoove the worker to study the unsuccessful role transactions in which the client has parti-
cipated and to note the responses of alter (of previous caseworkers' and significant others) which did not promote the
client's socialization processes. Then, the worker may
select treatment procedures which seem most to differ from
those utilized by previously frustrating role partners. This
could only be determined by a comprehensive psychosocial
diagnosis which would have contained a thorough analysis of
the client's role relationship.

The above treatment procedures have been criticized because they appear insincere--i. e. , the worker doesn't present his "true self, " he is behaving unrealistically, he is
being unethical, etc. (22). In response, it may be said that
the role of corrector and interpreter may be more demeaning to the client than one which allows him to maintain de-
rogatory fantasies toward the worker. Secondly, the role
theorist would have to respond to the imperative, "Act yourself!" with the query, "Which self? The self that wishes
to keep the client in treatment? The rational self ? The
irrational self?" Those workers who would utilize the concepts of role theory in the casework interaction would see
both client and worker as an aggregate of selves. The treatment encounter, therefore, would consist of two groups
interacting on the basis of many "selves. " The caseworker,
like a loving parent with sufficient mastery over his impulses, attempts to ascertain the maturational needs of his
child and without contaminating the interpersonal situation
with his own preferences, attempts to meet the needs of his
child by demonstrating appropriate behavior that will stimulate his child's socialization processes. He uses his many
"selves" in the treatment situation, choosing that "self" or
role which will help his client grow (57, 40, 55, 9).

Limitations of Role Theory in Its Application to Casework

As noted throughout this chapter, the construct "role"

has referred to the individual's social status and the behavior accompanying this status.   While the construct embodies psychological, biological, and social considerations,
its major emphasis is on the task oriented aspects of social
functioning.   Consequently, one of the weaknesses of "role"
for casework is that it does not always bring into full focus
the special qualities of the individual involved in adaptation
to society.   While the term "social functioning" is compatible with the "role" construct, when we study, diagnose,
and treat the unique individual and his situation, we still
have to ascertain how an externally induced conflict leads
to idiosyncratic and specific forms of behavior in a designated role.

A common observation of caseworkers is that the same
external stimulus can activate a host of different behaviors
in different individuals.   The "role" construct can contribute
towards an understanding of the individual's response, but
it may only partially explain the particular individual's very
specific motives behind his behavior.   If the "role" construct
is utilized exclusively in diagnosis and treatment, there is
the inherent danger of what Fraiberg has called attention to,
namely, we can be led into the position of manipulators of
social roles which call for a wisdom beyond the scope of
anybody (15).   Although there is nothing in role theory which
negates psychoanalytic theory or other orientations, by focusing exclusively on the client's role, one might unwittingly
fail to individualize the client as completely as possible.

While the role theorist would envision all casework
intervention as the enactment of various roles, we alluded
earlier to the criticism that the conscious assumption of
various stances by the worker has a certain connotation of
insincerity.   Certainly, if the worker is uncomfortable in
utilizing any treatment procedure because he feels it is inappropriate or unethical, the client will sense this and an
unnecessary type of disequilibrium will eventuate in the casework transactions.

As with other incomplete scientific theories, role theory
has to be used together with other orientations and with the
practice wisdom which is part of every caseworker's role
set.

References

1. Ackerman, Nathan, The Psychodynamics of Family Life
   (New York, Basic Books, 1954).

2. Asch, Solomon E., "Forming Impressions of Personality," Journal of Abnormal and Social Psychology,
   Vol. 38, No. 1, January 1943, pp. 225-249.

3. Aronson, Harriet and Betty Overall, "Treatment Expectations of Patients in Two Social Classes," Social Work,
   Vol. 11, No. 1, 1966, pp. 35-42.

4. Benedict, Ruth, "Continuities and Discontinuities in
   Cultural Conditioning," Psychiatry, Vol. 1, May, 1938,
   pp. 161-167.

5. Bernstein, Arnold, On the Nature of Psychotherapy
   (New York, Random House, 1954).

6. Biddle, Bruce J. and Edwin Thomas, Role Theory (New
   York, John Wiley & Sons, 1966).

7. Boehm, Werner W., "The Social Work Curriculum
   Study and Its Implications for Family Casework,"
   Social Casework, Vol. 40, No. 8, October 1959,
   pp. 428-436.

8. _____, "The Social Casework Method in Social Work
   Education," New York, Council on Social Work Education, Vol. 10, 1959.

9. Coleman, Marie and Benjamin Nelson, "Paradigmatic
   Psychotherapy in Borderline Cases," Psychoanalysis,
   Vol. 5, No. 3, Fall, 1957, pp. 28-44.

10. Cottrell, Leonard S., "Roles and Marital Adjustment,"
    Publications of the American Sociological Society,
    Vol. 27, May 1933, pp. 107-112.

11. Davis, Kingsley, "Adolescence and the Social Structures,"
    Annals of the American Academy of Political and
    Social Science, Vol. 26, No. 5, November 1944,
    pp. 11-12.

12. Deutsch, Morton and R. H. Krauss, Theories in Social Psychology (New York, Basic Books, 1965).

13. Dinitz, Simon, Shirley Angrist, Mark Lefton, and Benjamin Pasaminick, "Instrumental Role Expectations and Posthospital Performance of Female Mental Patients," Social Forces, Vol. 40, 1962, pp. 248-254.

14. Faris, Ellsworth, "The Social Psychology of George Mead," American Journal of Social Psychology, Vol. 43, November 1937, pp. 391-403.

15. Fraiberg, Selma, "Psychoanalysis and the Education of Caseworkers," in Ego-Oriented Casework: Problems & Perspectives, (eds.) Howard J. Parad & Roger R. Miller (New York, Family Service Association of America, 1963), pp. 236-258.

16. Freud, Sigmund, "Freud's Psychoanalytic Method" in Collected Papers, Vol. 1 (London, England, Hogarth Press, 1953), pp. 264-271.

17. _____, "On Psychotherapy," ibid., pp. 249-263.

18. Getzels, J. W. and E. G. Guba, "Role, Role Conflict & Effectiveness," American Sociological Review, Vol. 19, No. 1, February 1054, pp. 164-175.

19. Goode, William J., "Norm Commitment & Conformity to Role-Status Obligations," American Journal of Sociology, Vol. 61, 1960, pp. 246-258.

20. Gouldner, Alvin W., "The Norm of Reciprocity: A Preliminary Statement," American Sociological Review, Vol. 25, 1960, pp. 161-178.

21. Greenson, Ralph, "The Borderline Case," Journal of the American Psychoanalytic Association, Vol. 3, No. 2, April 1955, pp. 295-297.

22. Grinker, Roy, Helen MacGregor, Kate Selan, Annette Klein, and Janet Kohrman, Psychiatric Social Work: A Transactional Case Book (New York, Basic Books, 1961).

23. Gross, Neal, Ward S. Mason, and Alexander W. McEachern, Explorations in Role Analysis (New York,

John Wiley & Sons, 1958).

24. Hamilton, Gordon, Theory and Practice of Social Case-
     work (New York, Columbia University Press, 1951).

25. Hellenbrand, Shirley, "Client Value Orientations: Impli-
     cations for Diagnosis and Treatment," Social Case-
     work, Vol. 42, April 1961, pp. 163-169.

26. Ingersoll, Hazel L., "Transmission in Authority
     Patterns in the Family," Marriage and Family Living,
     Vol. 10, 1948, p. 316.

27. Jacobson, Allvar Hilding, "Conflict of Attitudes Toward
     the Roles of the Husband and Wife in Marriage,"
     American Sociological Review, Vol. 17, 1952,
     pp. 146-150.

28. Komarovsky, Mirra, "Cultural Contradictions & Sex
     Roles," American Journal of Sociology, Vol. 52,
     November, 1946, pp. 193-203.

29. Lennard, Henry L. and Arnold Bernstein, The Anatomy
     of Psychotherapy (New York, Columbia University
     Press, 1960).

30. Linton, Ralph, "Culture, Society, and the Individual,"
     Journal of Abnormal and Social Psychology, Vol. 33,
     October 1938, pp. 425-436.

31. _____, The Study of Man (New York, Appleton-
     Century, 1936).

32. Mead, George Herbert, Mind, Self & Society, Charles
     W. Morris, ed. (Chicago, University of Chicago
     Press, 1934).

33. Meerloo, Joost A.M. & Marie Coleman Nelson, Trans-
     ference and Trial Adaptation (Springfield, Illinois,
     Charles Thomas, 1965).

34. Merton, Robert K., George Reader, and Patricia
     Kendall L., The Student Physician (Cambridge,
     Massachusetts, Harvard University Press, 1957).

35. _____, Social Theory & Social Structure (Glencoe,
     Illinois, Free Press, 1957).

36. Meyer, Carol, "Quest for a Broader Base for Family
     Diagnosis," Social Casework, Vol. 40, July 1959,
     pp. 370-376.

37. Moreno, Joseph L., Who Shall Survive? (Washington,
     D. C., Beacon Hill, 1934).

38. Nagelberg, Leo, "The Meaning of Help in Psychotherapy,"
     Psychoanalysis and the Psychoanalytic Review, Vol.
     46, No. 4, 1959, pp. 50-63.

39. Neiman, Lionel J. and James W. Hughes, "The Pro-
     blem of the Concept of Role--A Resurvey of the
     Literature," Social Forces, December 1951, pp. 141-
     149.

40. Nelson, Marie, Benjamin Nelson, Murray Sherman,
     and Herbert S. Strean, Roles and & Paradigms in
     Psychotherapy (New York, Gruen and Stratton, 1968).

41. Newcomb, Theodore and E. L. Hartlay, Readings in
     Social Psychology (New York, Holt, 1967).

42. Overall, Betty and Harriet Aronson, "Expectations of
     Psychotherapy in Patients of Lower Socioeconomic
     Class," American Journal of Orthopsychiatry, Vol.
     31, pp. 421-430.

43. Park, Robert E. and Ernest W. Burgess, An Intro-
     duction to the Science of Sociology (Chicago, Uni-
     versity of Chicago Press, 1921), pp. 114-117.

44. Parsons, Talcott, The Social System (Glencoe, Illinois,
     Free Press, 1951).

45. Perlman, Helen Harris, "Intake & Some Role Con-
     siderations" in Social Casework in the Fifties, ed.,
     Cora Kassius (Family Service Association of America,
     New York, 1962), pp. 163-174.

46. Reuter, Edward B., "Sociological Research in Ado-
     lescence," American Journal of Sociology, Vol. 42,
     July 1936, pp. 81-94.

47. Riessmann, Frank, Jerome Cohen, and Arthur Pearl,
     Mental Health of the Poor (New York, The Free
     Press, 1964).

48. Rosenblatt, Aaron, "Application of Role Concepts to the
     Intake Process," Social Casework, Vol. 43, 1962,
     pp. 8-14.

49. Sarbin, Theodore, "Role Theory" in G. Lindzey (ed.)
     Handbook of Social Psychology, Vol. 1 (Cambridge,
     Massachusetts, Addison-Wesley, 1954), pp. 223-258.

50. Schwitzgebel, Ralph, Street Corner Research (Cam-
     bridge, Massachusetts, Harvard University Press,
     1964).

51. Shyne, Ann W., "What Research Tells Us About Short-
     Term Cases in Family Agencies," Social Casework,
     Vol. 38, No. 5, pp. 223-231, 1957.

52. Spiegel, John P., "The Resolution of Role Conflict
     Within the Family," The Family, (eds.) Norman W.
     Bell and Ezra F. Vogel (Glencoe, Illinois, The Free
     Press, 1960), pp. 361-380.

53. Stark, Frances B., "Barriers to Client-Worker Com-
     munication at Intake," Social Casework, Vol. 40,
     No. 4, 1959, pp. 177-183.

54. Sternbach, Oscar and Leo Nagelberg, "On the Patient-
     Therapist Relationship in Some Untreatable Cases,"
     Psychoanalysis and the Psychoanalytic Review, Vol.
     5, 1957, pp. 63-71.

55. Strean, Herbert S., "The Contribution of Paradigmatic
     Psychotherapy to Psychoanalysis," Psychoanalytic
     Review, Vol. 51, No. 3, Fall, 1964, pp. 29-45.

56. _____, "Some Difficulties Met in the Treatment of
     Adolescents," Psychoanalytic Review, Vol. 18, 1961,
     pp. 69-80.

57. _____, "Role Theory, Role Models, and Casework:
     Review of the Literature & Practice Applications,"
     Social Work, Vol. 12, No. 2, April 1967, pp. 77-88.

58. _____, "The Use of the Patient as Consultant,"
     Psychoanalysis & the Psychoanalytic Review, Vol. 45,
     1959, pp. 36-44.

59. _____, "Treatment of Mothers & Sons in the Absence of the Father," _Social Work_, Vol. 6, 1961, pp. 29-35.

60. Sullivan, Harry Stack, "A Note on Formulating the Relationship of the Individual & the Group," _American Journal of Sociology_, Vol. 44, May 1939, pp. 922-937.

61. Sutherland, Robert L. and Julian L. Woodward, _Introductory Sociology_ (New York, Lippincott, 1940), pp. 250-253.

62. Varley, Barbara K., "The Use of Role Theory in the Treatment of Disturbed Adolescents," _Social Casework_, Vol. 49, No. 6, June 1968, pp. 362-368.

63. Wheelis, Allen, _The Quest for Identity_ (New York, W. W. Norton & Company, 1958).

64. Znaniecki, Florian, "Social Groups as Products of Participating Individuals," _American Journal of Sociology,_ Vol. 44, May 1939, pp. 799-812.

Chapter 5

The Application of Organization Theory
to Social Casework

by Sherman Merle

Introduction

   Social casework has had a long history of borrowing
relevant theories, concepts and constructs from the domains
of medicine, psychiatry, and psychology, most particularly
dynamic psychology, and from the various social sciences.
A review of the history of these borrowings establishes
fairly consistently that these concepts are mainly related
to the individual (actor) in the role of client (patient) either
as an individual or as a member of small affective groups
(e. g. , the family or other small face-to-face groups).
Writings about social casework also are replete with considerations of the social case worker in his individual role
as purveyor or deliverer of a service, but again for the
most part the unit of analysis in these writings has been the
case worker and client, or at best "a client system" frame
of reference, e. g. , the family or other small treatment
groups.

   It is only recently that some writers have begun to give
attention to the impact of the case worker's work environment upon casework service delivery (1).   The impact of
"the organization" and the work context within which casework services are performed upon social casework practice
is real and the concepts of organizational theory can increase
understanding of the conduct of social casework practice.

   Social casework practice is almost exclusively conducted
under the aegis of socially and legally sanctioned formal
organizations.   Although the private practice of social casework exists, the amount of social casework conducted within
the context of organizations easily represents the bulk of
such services now offered by the social work profession.

Casework is practiced in a very large variety of formal organizations. These differ in size, mission (or function), legitimation (their source of power), auspice (public-private, sectarian - non-sectarian), location (urban, suburban, rural), staffing patterns (professional - nonprofessional and inter-actions with other disciplines), source of clientele (voluntary non-voluntary, socio-economic class) etc. Some have begun to examine the impact of these variables upon the function-ing of formal organizations (2).

Since casework is conducted within an organization framework certain identifiable organizational factors, both explicit and implicit, affect the delivery of social casework services. Despite overlap between such agencies (e. g. , family services, mental hygiene clinics, school social work, child guidance clinics, public child welfare and voluntary child welfare agencies, etc.) it can be generally agreed that these agencies have organizational contexts that differ, and which materially influence the casework services they offer.

An historic concept within social casework practice is that of the importance of the function of the agency. The function or purposes of an agency immediately suggest agency (organizational) goal(s) that clearly express its area of concern and interest. Within the context of organizational theory, the notion of purpose is viewed as one of the organ-izational boundaries or constraints that infringe upon the ser-vice that the organization is prepared (sanctioned) to give. It can be observed that specific agency function has signifi-cant impact upon the structures of the agency and what the agency does, and that this has impact upon the activities any given social caseworker may be engaged in within a specific agency.

Organizational Theory: A Discussion of Relevant Concepts Applicable to Casework Practice

It is a commonly accepted fact that man and his work are increasingly being found in the context of large organ-izations. Social theorists have noted repeatedly that more and more of man's experiences take place within large scale impersonal organizations. This fact and social arrangement have had considerable impact upon how man works, what work he performs and how such work is accomplished. Ever since Max Weber presented a systematic theory of bureaucratic

organization, more and more attention has been given to
both the empirical and theoretical investigation or organizations. Weber's theories and the concepts they involve
have had a profound influence upon social scientists who
found them the touchstone for further investigation of the increasing phenomenon of formal organizations and its impact
upon man and his work (3).

Organizational theory may be defined as a series of conceptual constructs that attempt to describe, explain, and predict various aspects of events found to occur within formal
organizations. These formal organizations may be said to
be man's response to the high value that modern civilization
has placed upon rationality, effectiveness and efficiency.
The modern formal organization can also be seen as a social
invention required by the Industrial Revolution. The profession of social work and the development of social casework can also be seen as products of the forces that produced the formal organization. Modern organizations co-
ordinate large quantities of diverse human activities. The
organization can be regarded as a powerful social tool invented by man and society to get its work done. One of its
major purposes is to combine a large quantity of resources
(material, as well as human) in a rational and systematic
fashion so that the achievement of organizational goals may
be enhanced. Theoretically, all formal organizations can be
examined as deliberate and purposeful groupings of human
beings which are constructed rationally and by design to
achieve specific goals (4). Thus it can be seen that schools,
hospitals, social welfare agencies, as well as corporations,
armies and churches, are defined as organizations.

It should be noted, and needs continual re-emphasis, that
organizational theory is presently conceived at a very high
level of abstraction. In the main, the theory deals with
general propositions which can be applied with equally good
or bad fit to all organizations. Since the differences among
organizations are considerable, the "theory of organizations"
must be highly abstract to be applicable and useful in the
study of these varied organizations. This caution should be
continually kept in mind in the discussion of concepts that
follows. More particularly the reader is advised to apply
these constructs--which, as indicated, are exceedingly ab-
stract--with caution to the real life social casework practice
situations.

Organizational theorists have hypothesized and empirical

research has found that all formal organizations have the following characteristics in common in some measure:

1) a division of: a) labor; b) responsibilities; c) power; d) lines of communication. These divisions are consciously planned to enhance the achievement of specified organizational goals. 2) A formal personnel employment system which provides for the recruitment, retention and substitution of personnel in keeping with the achievement of organizational goals. 3) The clear delineation of authority in a hierarchical structure which has designated responsibility for controlling organizational resources and directing these resources toward organizational goal achievement. 4) A formally established system of rules and regulations which govern official decisions and actions. These regulations insure the uniformity of organizational operations and, in concert with the authority structure, make possible the continuity and coordination of organizational activities. 5) Officials are expected to assume an impersonal orientation to other officials and to clients (customers). Personal considerations are to be disregarded in contact with clients and emotional detachment is to be maintained. This impersonal detachment is intended to prevent the personal feelings of officials from distorting their rational judgement in carrying out their duties.

It was stated earlier in this chapter that social casework services are typically provided within the context of organizations, formally organized and sanctioned to deal with human problem situations by bringing a casework service and a client together. Social casework as a method of helping people has been practiced in a formal agency context in the United States since the early days of the Charity Organization Societies (5). Thus the social casework method and practice had their very genesis in an organizational context. It was in fact a tool developed for the "rational" administration of 19th century charity. The charity organizations themselves were social inventions created and developed to meet societal imperatives for a "rational," "formally established system of rules and regulations" to govern the "impersonal application" of these rules and regulations governing the dispensation of charity. Social casework first emerged as a discernible discipline with the advent of Mary Richmond's Social Diagnosis (6) in 1917; and the movement of what had been essentially an apprenticeship training program conducted by agencies for its employees began to move to a university-

based professional education (7).   Vinter has stated that
"Bureaucracies and the professional are consequences of
similar forces in Western society.   Both are expressions of
general trends toward division of labor and specialization
that characterize complex and highly technological societies"
(8).

Social caseworkers typically are educated and trained to
work within organizations, i. e. agencies.   Early in their
educational socialization process they learn that the bureaucratic and formal organizational imperatives of division of
labor, responsibility, power and communication will affect
how they offer their services.   Thus the selection of clientele
is influenced, if not dictated, by an "impersonal" organizational structure that limits the caseworker's power to
select his clientele.   This can be conceived of as a potential
strain for the social casework professional as he compares
himself to some other professional helpers.   The model of
other helping professionals, characteristically used by the
social caseworker as reference groups (psychologists, psychiatrists, doctors), suggests to the caseworker that his
practice is constrained by organizational imperatives not
faced by other professionals.   On the other hand, professional
nurses and teachers also have the same constraints.   What
becomes obvious is that the more the professional (of whatever discipline) is organization-bound, the more obvious becomes the constraint on client choice.   Secondly, the caseworker's responsibility is in no small measure regulated by
the organizational structure.   It is only recently that social
casework agencies have attempted to arrange their adminis-
trative and hierarchal structures to permit for the "independent practice of casework" in which a social caseworker is
not closely guided by a supervisor (9).   But even with these
suggested changes in organizational structure, the caseworker's
responsibility is clearly circumscribed by the agency, and it
is really the agency that assumes the full responsibility for
what happens to the client.

Similarly, the distribution of power and means of communication clearly show that working within organizational
contexts places some quite obvious constraints upon the social
caseworker.   The caseworker's power to give or withhold
services is largely dictated by the organization, and his
access to communications and responsibility for communication
(e. g. , record keeping) is also regulated by the organization.
These factors must have consequences on casework practice.

That these organizational constraints produce stresses
and strains for the caseworker and consequences for his
practice receives support in the literature (10).   Social casework agencies, as organizations, may be modifying the day-
to-day application of organizational imperatives of division
of labor, responsibility, power and communication, in order
to accomodate to changing professional norms and values.
Vinter suggests that "One approach to reduction of this type
of conflict has been to re-define the situation so that the
agency and professional value systems may be perceived as
congruent" (11).   A possible recent example of an attempt
to redefine a practice situation in the above terms is the
anticipated changes in the administration of public welfare.
It is and has been urged that the service functions of public
welfare departments be separated from the fiscal functions.
If this organizational change were to take place we would
anticipate a redefinition of the division of labor responsibility,
power and communication of the caseworkers in public welfare departments.

It has been suggested that such a redefinition would enable the social caseworkers in public welfare to concentrate
on the provision of casework services, and would free them
from fiscal eligibility and clerical tasks which now take up
so much of their time.

Organizational Goals

Organizations are formed for the achievement of specific
goals.   These goals may be as varied as the production and
sale of automobiles, the defense of the country, or the care
and treatment of the ill.   This ". . . primacy of orientation
to the attainment of a specific goal . . . " is, according to
Parsons, ". . . the defining characteristic of an organization
which distinguishes it from other types of social systems, "
and ". . . has implications for both the external relations
and the internal structure of the system referred to . . .
as an organization" (12).   Goal setting and goal achievement
are important in any examination and understanding of the
concepts related to organizations.

The stated goals of an organization chart a course or a
direction that it has decided at some time to pursue; they
are precursors to organizational policy and program.   Usually
stated at a fairly abstract level, organizational goals become
operational and therefore observable only in the organization's

policy and in its procedures.   Frequently, an examination of
the stated goals compared to specific policy and activity at
the programmatic level reveals gross discrepancies between
stated goals and organizational program and outcome.   In
general, however, organizational goals serve to orient the
system to desired directions; to provide guidelines for the
development of policy and program; and to determine organizational resource allocation and activity.   Organization goals
frequently serve as a source of legitimation.   This legitimation comes from many sources--legal, quasi-legal or
social--but is always granted on the basis of the organization's
explicated goals, be they a corporation prospectus or a
social agency's charter.   The organization's approximation
of these goals is most often the measurement used to evaluate its effectiveness, and gross deviation from its explicated
goals can cause severe sanctions to be leveled against the
organization.   Organizational analysts note, however, that
organizational goals should not be viewed as a static element
in organizations but rather as a dynamic.   Thompson and
McEwen state that "Because the setting of goals is essentially
a problem of defining desired relationships between an organization and its environment, change in either requires review and perhaps alteration of goals.   Even where the most
abstract statement of goals remains constant, application requires re-definition or interpretation as changes occur in the
organization, the environment, or both" (13).   Additionally,
Etzioni notes that "organizations are social units which pursue specific goals; their very raison d'etre is the service of
these goals.   But once formed, organizations acquire their
own needs, these sometimes becoming the masters of the
organization" (14).

The processes of goal setting and goal maintenance within organizations are purposive, and careful study can in most
cases reveal the intent of a goal.   To say, however, that a
goal has purpose is not to say that goal setting or goal
maintenance within organizations is necessarily rational.
Organizational goals may have their genesis in accidents and
chance combinations of factors.   On the other hand, the most
rational and carefully conceived goals of an organization may
be negated, sabotaged or brought to naught by happenstance
and events outside the control of the organization.   Organizational goals also fall or are sustained to the degree that
a society or a sub-sector of that society is willing to support
them.   Often, this support or lack of it is not entirely the
result of a rational process.   The familiar fluctuations of
the market-place force corporations to shift, alter and at

times abandon previously developed organizational goals. In
like manner, other organizations--universities, hospitals,
and social welfare agencies (e. g. , child-caring institutions,
public welfare departments, etc.), --their particular mandates
notwithstanding, are continuously reviewing and readjusting
their goals. In most instances these reviews and readjust-
ments of organizational goals are responses to new techniques,
new definitions of the situation, and new arrangements within
society.

        This can be seen in even a cursory examination of the
history of American welfare agencies. Thus orphanages became residential treatment centers as the phenomenon of
orphanage shrank and society made other institutional arrangements for the care of orphaned children or children in one-
parent homes; the social problem of the emotionally disturbed
child became identified and services were developed to deal
with this "new situation. " Some of the present-day attacks
upon our public assistance programs derive from dramatic
changes that have taken place in society and in the population
of the public assistance programs which have necessitated re-
examination of organizational goals. These examples can
easily be multiplied as one looks across the network of social
agencies in which social casework is practiced.

        The necessity for organizations to review their goals
is related to the activity in which they are engaged. In most
instances, organizations engaged in the production and sale
of goods and services are more responsive to the feedback
they receive from the market-place regarding their goals.
Such an organization fails to heed this feedback at the peril
of its existence. On the other hand, it can readily be seen
that organizations like those engaged in social work, in which
goals are not subject to the same rapid kind of market
economy regulation, and in which the end results of the goals
are services, intangible and difficult to measure, the press
for goal re-evaluation is less immediate and it is thus more
possible for the organization to resist changes in its goals.
This observation has important implications in the analysis
and understanding of how organizations engaged in social welfare fulfill the goal setting and goal re-evaluation functions.
It is even more relevant in the case of social work organizations in which the major function is the provision of social
casework services. Vinter has noted that the very development of "treatment agencies" (social casework agencies) has
been in tandem with the emergence of the "service professions" (social work) and that these treatment organizations

rely on the service professionals to ". . . compose their
elite cadres and to implement their goals. " But he goes on
to note that this reliance upon the professionals poses a
problem for the organization in that the organization ". . .
may become primarily a context for professional practice,
which is something different from being a goal oriented
enterprise" (15).

Organizational goals by definition reflect directions, aims,
future states and desires that come from many sectors in
the organization.   In fact, even initial organizational goals
are seldom the goals of one person, or even of one sector
of an organization (i. e. , Board of Directors); eventually
they are the goals of the entire collectivity that comprises
the organization.   Organizational goals are the amalgam of
the goals of individuals--executive, Board, staff, clients
(customers, or consumers of service)--as well as of the
organization's outside environment.   They are determined
in a variety of ways, from those which are explicated by a
charismatic personality, to others that derive from consul-
tations, coalitions, competition, negotiation, and co-optation
among the various parts of an organization, and its environment.

Goal setting within organizations may be viewed as a
complicated power play which brings into contention various
individuals and/or coalitions of individuals, organizational
structures such as divisions and units, and environmental
forces with which the organization is at any time interacting.
Thus the establishment of a goal in, let us say, a hospital
social service department will involve a whole complex of
personalities and hospital structures at least, and may also
involve organizations and personalities outside of the hospital
complex itself.   It is usually at the level of goal setting that
constraints upon the organization are most obvious.   Even
the large scale organizations which are monopolies (i. e. , the
public utilities) find that particularly in the setting of goals
the environment is most sensitive to the organization's goal
setting procedures.   The point of this brief discussion is
that organizational theory continually notes that, far from
being a simple "rational" process, goal setting within organizations is a complex process, in which a whole variety of
forces set limits and constraints on the goals of the organization.

One very fruitful and revealing way to study organizations
is to compare the organization's announced goals with its

actions. This can be done in a variety of ways. For example, various individuals, representing different sectors of
an organization, can be asked about their perceptions and
understanding of organizational goals. Organizational directives, memoranda, minutes and other documents are other
sources in which organizational goals may be stated. But
more dynamic and revealing is an analysis of specific organizational processes. For example, an analysis of the organization's budget; division of labor--and even more important,
the statuses (explicit and implied) accorded to various divisions of labor within the organization; and allocation or
resources (material and manpower) reflect more convincingly
the goals to which the organization is really committed and
to which its efforts are being directed.

Frequently an examination of the dynamic elements noted
above will reveal (sometimes with amazing and embarrassing
clarity) a commitment to goals that differ considerably from
the stated organizational goals. Examining the allocation
and distribution of manpower resources in service organizations, particularly social welfare and other service organizations, can be particularly revealing. Thus an agency with
a stated goal of rehabilitation and restoration which is seen
to expend significant man-hours in investigatory and eligibility
procedures seems to manifest a serious difference between
the organization's expressed and actual goals. Or again, a
psychiatric hospital which has stated goals of therapy and
rehabilitation but has a very low doctor/patient ratio or
social caseworker/patient ratio, and has a very large staff
of hospital aides who have limited education and/or training,
suggests that the organization has goals quite different from
those it may proclaim publicly.

These examples can be multiplied, probably endlessly.
The important notion for understanding casework practice is
that the particular practice can be examined against the
stated function(s) of the organization. Congruence between
the agency's (organization's) goals and those of the casework
practitioner can easily be discerned, and such analysis can
afford both the organization and the casework practitioner a
means of more sharply identifying the "fit" of goals. By
identifying the degree of congruence or incongruence, the
potential stresses and strains for social caseworker, organization, and client or user of service can more readily be
noted, analyzed, and understood. Billingsley's findings are
particularly noteworthy here. When he compared two casework settings, his findings suggested that either the settings

seemingly exerted a distinctive influence upon the caseworker's
attitudes, behaviors and activities, or that caseworkers with
particular attitudes and behaviors found themselves in organizations that had goals which supported their particular casework activities (16).

   We have distinguished between an organization's stated
goals and its real goals.   The real goals can be defined as
those to which the organization actually commits a significant proportion of its resources and efforts.   Distribution
of resources is not to be conceived as having come about
accidentally, but rather because of very clear, intended and
widely accepted mandates within the organization, even when
the real goals may be quite different from the stated goals.
Billingsley's research indicates that "Relatively speaking,
both the clients and the community have less influence than
profession or agency in the orientation of these (case)
workers. "   And that despite ". . . the social (case) worker's
intellectual and emotional commitment to meeting the needs
of his client, it is apparent that these needs must be met
within the framework of structured approaches imposed by
the agency and the profession, even over the worker's own
estimation of the needs of the client" (17).

Goals and Effectiveness

   We noted that formal organizations could be conceived
of as social inventions made as a result of the Industrial
Revolution, a response to the high value society placed upon
effectiveness and efficiency.   An organization's effectiveness
is judged by how well it achieves its goals.   If an organization is being measured against its stated goal, which may
not in fact be the goal to which its resources are committed,
it may appear ineffective.   If, however, the effects of the
organization are related to its real goals, quite a different
estimate of effectiveness may emerge.

   There are yet other difficulties in measuring effectiveness.   To the extent that an organization has a concrete
goal, its effectiveness is simpler to measure.   To illustrate,
it is fairly easy to measure the effectiveness of an organization involved in constructing a road.   The goals are easily
measurable and encompass certain time dimensions (how long
will the job take?) and certain other criteria dimensions
(e. g. , depth of road bed, quality of materials to be used).
However, if the organizational goal to be measured is a

continuous one--for example, to enhance the social role performance of clients known to a public assistance agency--and
one in which the output is not physically measurable, it is
extremely difficult to validate any assessment of effectiveness.
This suggests another reason why social welfare and social
work service organizations are slow to change goals when
compared with other types of organizations, particularly
those involved in the manufacture of goods which lend themselves so much more easily to quantification and measure
of effectiveness.   Vinter has noted that "all treatment organ-
izations--indeed, all people-changing organizations--encounter
difficulties in evaluating their effectiveness" (18).

Since the formal organizations under discussion by definition attempt to be rational and to undertake tasks in an
efficient manner and to achieve goals effectively, a high
value is placed and considerable pressure exerted upon
organizations to measure the outcomes of their activities.
Some very interesting empirical studies have demonstrated
the effect of such measurement upon organizational goals (19).
It has been noted by these researchers and others that
measurement devices can have a profound effect upon the
organizational efforts and can be used wittingly or unwittingly
to distort organizational goals.   Etzioni has noted that "Frequent measuring tends to encourage overproduction of highly
measurable items and neglect of the less measureable ones"
(20).   These findings have particular importance to organizations whose goals and outcomes are difficult to quantify.
For example, it is infinitely easier for a public assistance
department to measure the number of clients who have moved
off the assistance payment roster than it is for the same
agency to measure the effectiveness of a program aimed at
helping mothers with young children to adopt a series of
health-promoting procedures in their daily child-rearing
practices.   The ease with which the agency can measure
the former and the difficulty of measuring the latter can
have profound effects upon the goals of the organization in
relation to its allocation of resources.   What can frequently
happen is that a serious shift of goals takes place.   This
shift of goals can be seen as a result of the organization's
over-concern with the measurement of certain aspects of the
organization's operation which begin materially to shape or
design the real goals of the organization.

Goal Displacement

When carried to an extreme, it can readily be seen that
the social work organization's concern with the measurement
of certain aspects of its overall operation may culminate in
what has been identified as goal displacement. Merton speaks
of this phenomon and notes that the bureaucracy (formal
organization) has inherent tendencies to goal displacement:

> Adherence to the rules, originally conceived as a
> means, becomes transformed into an end in itself;
> there occurs the familiar process of displacement of
> goals whereby an instrumental value becomes a termi-
> nal value . . . .Formalism, even ritualism, ensues
> with an unchallenged insistence upon punctilious ad-
> herence to formalized procedures. This may be
> exaggerated to the point where primary concern with
> conformity to the rules interferes with the achieve-
> ment of the purposes of organization. . . (21).

This tendency on the part of formal organizations has received
much attention. Goal displacement can be seen when, within
the day-to-day functioning of an organization, the original
goal(s) of the organization for which it is sanctioned and
legitimated becomes blurred and finally obliterated, and the
organization begins to allocate resources towards goals (ends)
which originally may only have been means. The serious
consequences of this in service organizations is amply documented by Merton and others (22). Thus caseworkers may
become more concerned with their interview count, that is,
the numbers of client contacts they have, rather than with
the quality of service being offered. The agency can become
overly concerned with units of service being offered in order
to demonstrate the heavy quantity of service it offers. Or
the public assistance agency may implicitly or explicitly give
the caseworker "high marks" for getting clients off the welfare roster, but give little accord to a worker's efforts
aimed at other service functions such as the enhancement of
the client's role performance, or taking an advocate's stance
with regard to clients' needs.

In the foregoing we have presented a view of the organization that has been characterized as the "rational model
of organizational analysis" (23). In this model the organization is seen as an "instrument" rationally planned to a-
chieve the ends for which it was originally created. Gouldner

notes that although this model takes into account departures from rationality, the tendency is to see these deviations as deriving from ". . . random mistakes due to ignorance or error in calculations" (24).

Gouldner suggests another pattern for thinking about organizations, the "natural-system model of organizational analysis. " In this conceptualization the organization is viewed as a system and "the realization of the goals of the system as a whole is but one of several important needs to which the organization is oriented" (25). According to this model, the organization, like any system, has a strong commitment to maintain its equilibrium and has, as a primary motive, its own survival. And it is this emphasis upon survival that may lead to the distortion or displacement of goals discussed above. According to this view, organizations inevitably become ends in themselves and "once established . . . generate new ends which constrain subsequent decisions and limit the manner in which nominal group goals can be pursued" (26).

Vinter applied this concept of organizational goal displacement to the practice of social casework services. He notes that in such organizations the displacement of goals is marked by two distinct symptoms. One is the over-concern with means that we have already noted. The other is an emphasis on "secondary objectives"; and the risk is " . . . that treatment organizations become essentially a context for professional practice rather than a goal-directed enterprise. Belief systems become self-validating, routines are not objectively assessed, and ideological commitment is pervasively inculcated. Charismatic leaders emerge since they offer coherence and guidance in otherwise ambiguous situations. Similarly, personnel in treatment organizations develop strong feelings that only insiders, immersed in the rhetoric and reality of the agency, can adequately appreciate its processes and accomplishments" (27).

The Application and Limitations of Organization Theory to Social Casework

Social casework practice has been described as both a science and an art. The mastery of either a science or an art is a difficult process. The mastery and sophisticated application of social casework as a method of help is difficult even under the most optimal conditions.

Organization theory can help the caseworker understand the unique organizational contexts in which he works. This understanding may not have direct applicability to his employment of this method of help, but it can help him better understand how he is using this method of help within the organization and how some organizational processes may be influencing his use of the casework method.

The major limitation of organization theory is that it is formulated at a high level of abstraction and is intended to capture generalizations about the organization rather than about the particular processes such as casework that the organization may use in fulfilling its mission. Further, it cannot provide a casework practitioner in one of these organizations with the nuances and subtleties of the application or utility of the casework method. Organization theory does not address itself to the study, diagnosis and treatment processes in casework practice. However, as indicated at the beginning of this essay, caseworkers for the most part find themselves carrying out their practice in the context of organizations. The context variables of these organizations-- size, function, value orientations, location, etc. --may have distinct influence upon the caseworker and his practice. These insights regarding organizational arrangements, though admittedly quite abstract, when studied carefully are suggestive of the subtle, and sometimes not so subtle, organizational factors that influence the application of the casework method.

References

1.   Peter M. Blau and W. Richard Scott, Formal Organizations (San Francisco: Chandler Publishing Co., 1962), esp. pp. 59-86; Robert D. Vinter, "The Social Structure of Service, " and "Analysis of Treatment Organizations, " in Behavioral Science For Social Workers, ed. Edwin J. Thomas (New York: The Free Press, 1967), pp. 193-207 and 207-221; Andrew Billingsley, "The Role of the Social Worker in a Child Protective Agency; A Comparative Analysis, " (doctoral dissertation, Brandeis University, 1964); and "Bureaucratic and Professional Orientation Patterns in Social Casework, " Social Service Review, Vol. XXXVIII, No. 4, (December 1964), pp. 400-407; Otto Pollock, "Contributions of Sociological and Psychological Theory to Casework Practice, " Journal of Education for Social

Work, Vol. 4, No. 1, (Spring 1968), pp. 49-54).

2. Ibid.

3. See Amitai Etzioni, (ed.) Complex Organizations: A
    Sociological Reader (New York: Holt Rinehart, 1964).

4. Talcott Parsons, Structure and Process in Modern
    Societies (Glencoe, Ill: The Free Press, 1960), p. 17.

5. N. A. S. W., Encyclopedia of Social Work, "History of
    American Social Work," p. 5.

6. Mary Richmond, Social Diagnosis (Russell Sage Foundation,
    1917).

7. N. A. S. W. Encyclopedia of Social Work, "Education for
    Social Work," p. 277.

8. Robert D. Vinter, "The Social Structure of Service,"
    Edwin J. Thomas, (ed.) Behavioral Science for Social
    Workers (New York: The Free Press), pp. 193-194.

9. See: discussions by Lucille N. Austin, "An Evaluation of
    Supervision," Social Casework, Vol. XXXVII, No. 8,
    (October 1956), pp. 375-82; Frances H. Scherz, "A
    Concept of Supervision Based on Definitions of Job
    Responsibility," Social Casework, Vol. XXIX, No. 8,
    (October, 1958), pp. 435-443; Ruth Fizdale, "Peer-
    Group Supervision," Social Casework, Vol. XXXIX,
    No. 8, (October 1958), pp. 443-450; "Editorial Notes,"
    Social Casework, Vol. XXXIX, No. 8, (October 1958),
    pp. 463-464; Evelyn Stiles, "Supervision in Perspective,"
    Social Casework, Vol. XLIV, No. 1, (January 1963),
    pp. 19-25.

10. See: Charlotte G. Babcock, M. D., "Social Work as
    Work," and Esther Shour, "Helping Social Workers
    Handle Work Stress," in Social Casework, Vol. XXXIV,
    No. 10, (December 1953), pp. 415-428; Lydia Rapaport,
    "In Defense of Social Work: An Examination of Stress
    in the Profession," The Social Service Review, Vol.
    XXXIV, No. 1, (March 1960), pp. 62-74.

11. R. Vinter, op. cit., p. 195.

12. Talcott Parsons, "Suggestions for a Sociological
     Approach to the Theory of Organizations" in Complex
     Organizations, A. Etzioni (ed.), p. 33.

13. James D. Thompson and Wm. J. McEwen, "Organ-
     izational Goals and Environment: Goal Setting as an
     Interactional Process," American Sociological Review,
     February, 1958, Vol. 23, No. 1, pp. 23-31.

14. A. Etzioni, Modern Organizations (New Jersey:
     Prentice Hall, 1964), p. 5, italics added.

15. Vinter, "Analysis of Treatment Organizations," op. cit.,
     p. 213-214.

16. A. Billingsley, "The Role of the Social Worker in a
     Child Protective Agency: A Comparative Analysis,"
     (doctoral dissertation, Brandeis, 1964).

17. A. Billingsley, "Bureaucratic and Professional Orienta-
     tion Patterns in Social Casework," Social Service Re-
     view, Vol. XXXVIII, No. 4, (Dec. 1964), p. 402-403.

18. Vinter, op. cit., "Analysis of Treatment Organization,"
     p. 219.

19. See Blau and Scott, op. cit.

20. A. Etzioni. Modern Organizations, p. 9.

21. Robert K. Merton, Social Theory and Social Structure,
     pp. 199 ff.

22. Philip Selznick, "A Theory of Organizational Commit-
     ments" in R. Merton (et. al.), Reader in Bureaucracy,
     (Free Press, 1961), pp. 194-202; Peter M. Blau,
     The Dynamics of Bureaucracy.

23. See Alvin W. Gouldner, "Organizational Analysis" in
     Robert K. Merton, et. al. (ed.) Sociology Today
     (New York: Basic Books, 1959), pp. 404 ff.

24. Ibid., p. 405.

25. Ibid., p. 405.

26.   Ibid., p. 405.

27.   Vinter, "Analysis of Treatment Organization, " in
      Thomas (Ed.) Behavioral Science for Social Workers,
      1967, pp. 220-22.

Chapter 6

Communication Theory and Social Casework

by William Neal Brown

Communication lies at the core of casework as a helping process. Despite this fact, inadequacies in communication skills continue to plague caseworkers, presenting obstacles to the attainment of their problem-solving goals and bringing them criticism from other professionals, particularly researchers, for the lack of clarity, rigor, and uniformity in their verbal and written presentations. One often advanced reason for this is the complexity of therapeutic communication, the weight of latent cues and messages, the importance of implication and innuendo, and the gestalt "total person" quality of what transpires between the caseworker and the client. If anything, this reason underscores and increases the need to conceptualize the communication phenomenon and spell out the ways that good communication helps or defective communication hinders the casework process.

The Nature of Communication

It seems appropriate here to try to define what we mean by the term "communication." This might best be done by explicating the essence of communication theory. Communication theory posits an open-ended system through which "messages," "receptions," and "responses" constantly flow from sender to receiver and back. The theoretical formulation of this system makes use of such descriptive terms as input, output, encoding, decoding, interpretation, feedback, and signal. (It is obvious that these terms are drawn from what could be described as the technology of communication. Thus, the terms themselves may seem somewhat out of place in a discussion of human communication, but the meanings they represent are no less applicable.) "Encoding," for example, refers to all those activities employed by the communicator to formulate the message or "signal" that is to be transmitted. "Interpretation" and "decoding" refer to those activities required to "make sense" out of the message on

the part of the recipient.   All these factors are conditioned
by the life experience of the recipient, in terms of readiness
to receive or understand the signals sent.   Wilbur Schramm
notes that "messages are made up of signs, " and a sign is
a signal that stands for something in experience (1).

The communication process requires at least three elements: a source, a message, and a destination.   The
source does the encoding and transmitting.   The message is
the image or sign that is transmitted.   Destination designates
the recipient of the message; at the destination the message
must be decoded and interpreted.   The following diagram is
a graphic exposition of the process:

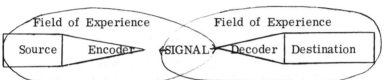

Schramm comments further: "It is obvious that each
person in the communication process is both an encoder and
a decoder.   He receives and transmits.   He must be able
to write readable shorthand, and to read other people's
shorthand. "   Earlier, the communication process was described as an openended system.   The diagram illustrates
this by the overlapping areas designated "Field of Experience. "   But for this element, the transactions between the
sender and the receiver would constitute a "closed system. "
However, these transactions cannot be assessed without also
assessing the input, the "cues" that enter the process from
the field of experience.

"Feedback" is another of the technical terms often used
in describing the communication process.   Feedback refers
to both the manifest and latent responses to the signal received.   The combined processes of transmittal and feedback
are reflected in the following eliptical diagram:

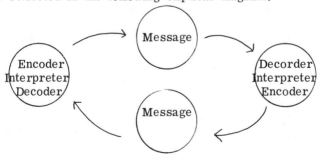

This is the process in which individuals are constantly engaged.   They are constantly decoding signs from the environment, interpreting these signs, and encoding something as a
result.   "In fact, it is misleading to think of the communication process as starting somewhere and ending somewhere.
It is really endless.   We are little switchboard centers
handling and rerouting the great endless current of communication.   We can accurately think of communication as passing through us--changed, to be sure, by our interpretations,
our habits, our abilities and capabilities, but the input still
being reflected in the output. "

Communication theory postulates certain conditions for
success in communication.   Most basic of these are:

1.   The message must be so designed and delivered
as to gain the attention of the intended destination.

2.   The message must employ signs which refer to
experience common to source and destination, so as to
'get the meaning across. '

3.   The message must arouse personality needs in the
destination and suggest some ways to meet those needs.

4.   The message must suggest a way to meet those
needs which is appropriate to the group situation in
which the destination finds himself at the time when he
is moved to make the desired response.

A dictionary definition states: "An interchange of
thoughts and opinions by words, letters, or messages. "   In
a more refined attempt at definition, Theodore M. Newcomb
states that "Every communicative act is viewed as a transmission of information, consisting of discriminative stimuli,
from a source to a recipient.... Thus, in the simplest
possible communicative act one person, A, transmits information to another person, B, about something, X" (2).
George M. Mead discusses empathic responses in relation
to good communication, making the point that clarity of
communication is enhanced when people like one another (3).

Berelson describes communication as that body of meanings through symbols (verbal, musical, pictorial, plastic,
gestural) which makes up the message itself.   He gives what
he describes as "the classic sentence identifying the process
of communication --- Who says what to whom, how, with
what effect" (4).   Ward Hunt Goodenough, writing of the pro-

blems of practice of the change agent in underdeveloped
countries, emphasizes the central role of communication in
success or failure. He comments:

> When people communicate they do more than exchange
> mutually intelligible words. An important purpose of
> communication is to share experience, or to enlarge
> the area of mutual understanding between persons
> whose experiences differ. When the degree of such
> difference is slight and the desire to share is strong,
> as with well-adjusted married couples, communication
> is almost automatic, requiring little conscious at-
> tention. The words and gestures of each partner are
> familiar to the other, immediately revealing to each
> the changing moods of the other. Basic areas of
> agreement (or sometimes disagreement) are known and
> taken for granted, and we frequently observe between
> such persons the signs of their accord in the way
> either one is able to finish the unfinished thoughts of
> the other. But communication is never completely
> effective even under optimum conditions. There are
> always some areas of experience, even for the most
> compatible spouses, that remain resistant to com-
> munication. ... If lack of communication and the
> mutual understanding resulting from it sometimes
> creates crises in the lives of well-adjusted spouses,
> it is clear that where differences between people in-
> clude differences in every aspect of experience, in
> social and cultural background, and even in language
> itself, communication becomes a major problem (5).

All these writers emphasize the dimensional nature of
communication, the fact that the messages conveyed from
one person to another are much more than the sum of the
words spoken between them. This communication gestalt is
best portrayed by Berelson in his "who, what, to whom, how,
with what effect" categories.

In the literature on social casework, Feldman (6),
Hollis (7), May Irvine (8), Perlman (9), Frances B. Stark
(10), and Strean (11), have commented on the centrality of
communication skills in the casework process. Jay Haley
(12) and Virginia Satir (13) describe communication as the
most important aspect of the method. Hollis comments:

> A significant aspect of interaction is communication--
> the extent to which two people are able to convey their

feelings and opinions to each other, either verbally
or non-verbally. Such defenses as repression, suppression, and inhibition may interfere with the communication. Attitudes expressed verbally may be
contradicted by non-verbal behavior (which is often
unconscious or ego-dystonic preconscious). Words,
tone of voice, gestures, and bodily behavior may be
misinterpreted because of the internal needs of the
'alter.' Defenses of projection, denial, and turning
against the self are particularly likely to 'distort
reception.' Even differences in the literal meanings
of words exchanged between individuals using the same
basic language will cause misunderstanding. Not only
different classes and geographical regions but even
individual families give special meaning to words (14).

Perlman and Strean speak of communication difficulties
occasioned by discrepancies of perception and acceptance of
role. In this view it is postulated that every client in casework treatment is induced by the worker to enact a specific
role in order to receive help. If the role suggested is not
congruent with the client's expectations, strain occurs between caseworker and client (9, 11). This strain and the
distorted perceptions within the relationship result in difficulties in communication. Approaching the same aspect of
treatment from a different point of view, May Irvin sees
effective communication as an integral part of relationship.
Thus, she sees it as the worker's responsibility to deal with
problems of communication; since, as long as such problems
exist, no viable relationship can develop. She states:

Communication is the word that sums up an entire
process that is fundamental in the practice of casework. The process has two aspects, neither of which
can be separated from the other: first, the rapport
between worker and client which can occur without
any words being spoken and which is a matter of
feeling; second, an ordering, structuring process that
must operate at some level if the experience of one
person is to be conveyed to another in words.
Language is social and serves to communicate needs;
it is also symbolic and has an organizing function (15).

The sum of these considerations of the communications
process is that it involves much more than the spoken word.
They note the impact of personal needs, perception, and
motivation on communication. The essence of this thinking

is that what any person--worker or client--puts into a communications process is largely conditioned by what he brings to the process from other reference points in his surroundings--family, kind and amount of education, exposure to social institutions, and nature of life experiences.   The existence of these reference points is indicated by the term "levels of communication." Such expressions as "affective-cognitive," "latent-manifest," or Newcomb's "cathectic-cognitive" or "inner forces-induced forces" are used to denote differing levels or degrees of communication.   Other writers have spoken of "the hidden agenda" which any person brings into group participation (16).

In the casework process it is anticipated that the worker's input to the communication process is conditioned and controlled by the development of self-awareness which enables the worker to view objectively the verbal and behavioral productions of both participants.

The Importance of Effective Communication

It is a truism of casework practice that no significant change occurs in the client's situation until he is "engaged" in the problem-solving process.   This engagement involves a meeting of the minds and a congruence of goals between the helper and the helped.   Some writers have referred to this phase of the process as the establishment of a "contract" for the ongoing work together (17).   If the perceptions of either communicant are out of focus relative to the other's, the difficulty of arriving at viable agreement is obvious.   If the caseworker's manner indicates condescension or some negative value judgment of an aspect of client life style or behavior, this manner will inhibit the free expression of important dimensions of the problem situation.   Even when the caseworker's manner is most objective, initial fear of condemnation or disapproval may inhibit client expression. When any of these conditions exist, it is difficult for either communicant to really "understand" what the other is trying to convey.

In discussing how the worker's manner can inhibit client production, Yonata Feldman states:

> As the worker becomes more rigid and more guarded during the interviews, the client often senses the worker's anxiety and becomes less frank in his state-

ments. ... The breakthrough of the worker's anxiety
because of his inability to accept the meaning of the
client's communication may lead to the closing of a
case. One beginning male social worker, when discussing his work with the mother of a difficult child,
was told by the supervisor that his client was trying
to tell him she was in love with him and craved his
response. It was obvious, even during the conference,
that this statement made him very uncomfortable.
Very soon he reported that the case had taken such
a turn that it had to be closed. Even though the case
had started successfully, the worker had created a
situation where treatment had to be broken off because of the anxiety aroused in him (18).

This is also an excellent example of "levels of communication." The worker was able to talk with this client
about the "manifest" content in her communication about her
problems, but he was unable to understand or accept the
"latent" message. For this situation to move to a point of
effective problem solution, the worker would have to recognize and deal with both levels of communication as appropriate goals were set for joint work on the problem
situation. It points up, too, the tremendous need for self-
awareness on the part of the worker. In this instance the
worker would have to answer for himself the question: Why
his latent response to the client's latent message? It re-
calls Berelson's "classic sentence"--"Who says what to whom,
how, with what effect." In this communication process the
worker needs to recognize both the "what" and the "what
effect," and his input to the process must deal with both if
they are to move together toward problem solution.

The caseworker's problem is to understand what it is
the person in a variety of ways is trying to express
and to find ways that will facilitate communication.
Each individual as well as each family is unique in
patterns of communication. At the same time, we do
know that people of different personality types, in
different psychiatric classifications, from different
cultural groups, and at various stages of development,
tend to use patterns of communication that offer a
broad guide to understanding the meaning of the communication. The verboseness of the compulsive
talker, the particular distortions of the hysteric, the
exaggerations of the adolescent, the reticence or
volubility of people from different cultural backgrounds,

can be understood in the context of specific individual
dynamics. Similarly, patterns of communication within a family must be understood in cultural and dynamic psychological terms. The unique flavor of each
family requires that the caseworker make no pre-
judgements about values, strengths, and problems
until he understands the prevailing mode of family
communication, its strengths and interferences in
family operation (19).

This is more easily said than done. The complexity of
the methods of communication and their rapid shifts, the
different levels of communication, as well as the difficulty
of complete self-awareness, all contribute to difficulties in
understanding the communication process. Scherz has observed that it may be "somewhat uncomfortable for us to
face the fact that caseworkers also communicate on different
levels; that people often sense, quite accurately, the meaning
of our non-verbal communications and that these may conflict
with what we are saying" (20).

However, it does require at least two communicants to
establish a communication process; and, while the caseworker
has a professional responsibility to maintain disciplined control of his own attitudes and behavior, he has an equal responsibility to use his own unique modes of communication
freely and spontaneously and to learn his particular strengths
and limitations with different people. Caseworkers do influence people by attitudes that are the result of their own
life experience, including professional development. Sometimes, in an effort to be "objective," they try to suppress
personal, cultural, and professional attitudes that might
better be expressed and dealt with. As in the case of the
young worker and mother alluded to earlier, there are times
when it is better for the caseworker to express his feelings
and then deal with the consequences, rather than attempting
to suppress and handle them by "running away" or by labeling the client as resistive to treatment.

In the spin-off from the knowledge explosion of the
fifties, the helping professions learned much from social
scientists about how communication theory could make their
helping efforts more rigorous, more systematic, and fruitful.
Such conceptual notions as input, output, storage, feedback
and correction were helpful to the professional whose goal
was to help others. These considerations gave the helper
a broader, more systematic view of the person needing help;

no longer could the client be considered in isolation or perceived as having a problem that existed in a vacuum.   He
must be considered within the matrix of his family and social
relationships, and communication patterns give new insights
into the ties that bind these relationships together.   When
deviance in individual behavior or breakdown in social relationships occurs, it is always accompanied by distortion
or rupture in communication.   It has been noted earlier that
there are theorists who view all psychopathology and social
pathology as disturbances in communication (12, 13).
Reusch states: "While the organ or the individual may be
analyzed in terms of neurophysiology or psychoanalysis, the
relationship of one part to another can be explained better
in terms of communication theory than by any other theory
(21).

> Reginald C. is a 7-year old Negro child referred to
> a family agency by the school social worker.   He was
> described as a 'problem child,' restless and emotion-
> ally high-strung, a source of constant confusion in his
> classrooms.   He is alleged to have kicked another
> boy down a flight of stairs, and it is said that at
> times he screamed aloud in class, apparently without
> provocation; he has been described as 'talking to him-
> self,' giving answers completely unrelated to the
> question he was asked, and other unusual and peace
> disturbing behavior.   There had been difficulty with
> truanting and taking things that did not belong to him.
> School reports indicate that academically the child has
> little, if any, problem; he has an I. Q. of 110.

> Interviews with the parents revealed that Reginald was
> an only child.   The mother had completed high school;
> the father, the third year of high school.   This was
> the first marriage for both, and they had been
> married for nine years.   At the time of referral, the
> mother was pregnant and expecting the second child
> in about two months.   Both parents were evasive as
> to details about the child's early development.   They
> stated that the child had been kept by both its own
> mother and the maternal grandmother.   When the
> worker attempted to explore this arrangement in de-
> tail, both became evasive.   The mother was employed
> but asserted that she had remained at home with the
> child until he was old enough to attend nursery school.
> The father stated that he and the son had always had
> good relations.   (Subsequently, the worker learned

that the child barely knew the father; and, that from
a very early age he had been torn and pulled between
the varying authority relationships of a mother, an
aunt, and the maternal grandmother.)

From the beginning, it was clear that the child seemed
different from other seven-year-old children.   As
work with the family progressed, the impression was
strengthened that the child was quite disturbed and
much in need of help on an emotional level.   This was
difficult for the parents to discuss, and they were
never able to accept this need.   Both parents seemed
to be extremely protective of the child and defensive
about any criticism of him.

After several interviews at the agency, the worker
requested permission to make a home visit to see
how the child handled himself there.   The request was
granted and the home visit made.   The home was
located on the second floor of a barracks-type apartment house in the center of an already condemned
slum area.   Inside, the home was neatly furnished,
though not well cared for, and had a jumbled, confused
atmosphere.   There was tension and confusion in the
emotional tone of the household which seemed over-
crowded, though there was actually enough room for
the four people there.   There seemed to be an intangible grating or clash of personalities and a constant bickering, which seemed to be precipitated
mainly by the mother.   She was constantly correcting
the child on unimportant things, prompting him as to
what to say or not to say, and apparently 'putting on
airs' for the worker's benefit.   The child had a dog
four months old, a beautiful pedigreed German police
dog.   The dog was constantly confused by conflicting
demands or orders.   The father would tell him to go
in the bedroom and stay there.   The child would call
him out two minutes later.   Then the aunt would shout
at the child and drive the dog back with a strap.   A
few minutes later, the mother herself was calling the
dog, petting and playing with him.   Then someone
else would shout and drive him back into the bedroom.
The animal could not but be confused by this kind of
treatment; and, it was the worker's impression that
this must have been the pattern of the child's development.

Here were all of the seeds of distorted communication:
the fear of self-incrimination evidenced in the parent's e-
vasions with the worker, the unclear "signals" to the child
represented by the varied and differing authority figures who
may have conveyed the same "messages" but with differing
expectations, and the gaps that existed between verbal and
non-verbal transmissions.   Diagnostically, the child's erratic
behavior could be construed as his reaction to the lack of
clarity in the communication patterns that surrounded him.

Whether or not one chooses to accept this total view,
there is much in communication theory that can enhance the
caseworker's diagnostic and treatment skill.   Regardless of
theoretical base, the communication concepts of clarity,
specificity, awareness of personal needs, perception, motivation, and feedback could do much to sharpen and strengthen
practitioner skills.

Obstacles to Effective Communication

A number of factors can operate to hamper, blur, or
prohibit communication.   Most notable of these are such
things as culture barriers, differences in language systems,
marked differences in role and status, and defensiveness or
resistance.   It should be noted that the impact of any one or
a combination of these factors can be operative between the
client and his social matrix, his significant others, and, in
the interchange between worker and client.   Where there are
communication blocks in any of these areas, they will inevitably manifest themselves in the "charged" situation of
the casework relationship.

It is common knowledge among caseworkers that the
most difficult situation with which a worker has to deal is
that one in which the client comes in and places his (the
worker's) problem on the table before him.   Caseworkers,
too, live within a network of personal, social, and family
relationships; like all other human beings, they, too, experience problems in life adjustment.   The client's situation
may present a marital problem, or a parent-child problem,
or a problem in money management, or a problem with
time, or with authority.   Any one of these (and, obviously,
the list is not exhaustive) could be a problem with which the
caseworker has experienced or is currently experiencing
some difficulty.   Unresolved feelings about the problem are
likely to hamper the worker's freedom of communication in

significant areas essential to problem solution. To the degree that the caseworker can be aware of his problem and control it adequately for the objectivity of his involvement with this client, to that degree will communication remain unhampered. Naturally, it is the intent of advanced study, professional development, supervision, and the on-going development of self-awareness to control this aspect of practice. Such control, however, is rarely complete. Thus, the worker must be constantly alert to and aware of how his "input" affects the communication process.

Culture Barriers

The literature of the social sciences and of social casework is replete with reference to the impact of culture on communication (7, 19, 21, 22, 23). In this context, culture is defined as the composite of specific ways of thinking, feeling, and acting which differentiates one group from another. It includes such factors as mating patterns, modes of family organization and structure, ceremonial styles of marking the beginning and end of life, dietary peculiarities, religion, and language. While for most ethnic sub-groups such characteristics are essentially homogeneous, the concept of culture (for purposes of communication) also includes intra-group differences in life style (as occasioned for example by migration from one country to another) and the generational differences now commonly referred to as the "generation gap." For example, Brown, in discussing some of the causes of alienation among youth, comments that they have been unable to deal in any functional way with the generational conflict occasioned by the rapidity of change in the world and the loss of communication between them and their elders, because they are, in fact, talking about two different worlds, seen from completely different perspectives and evolving widely different sets of values (22).

Fantl and Reissman have written extensively about cultural barriers to communication, particularly as these are related to class differences or socio-economic status. Fantl, writing of casework practice in lower class districts, comments that "there is little status or challenge to work in our area and many ask for a transfer to a 'better' district as soon as they get here. They (caseworkers) have trouble understanding and communicating with the various ethnic groups and they feel that their efforts to help people are not appreciated. Some are inclined to consider our

clients 'lazy,' 'dumb,' 'people on relief,' 'bad,' and 'in-
different.' " Reissman, whose work has dealt primarily
with the lower class child, attacks the middle class perception of this child as lacking in verbal skills.   He feels
that deprived individuals are not necessarily restricted by
verbal forms of communication, but tend to allow language
to interact more with non-verbal means of communication,
such as gestures and pictures.   This interaction with other
kinds of communication gives them the potential for breaking
through the language barrier (23, 24).   Pollak has commented
significantly that people are usually able to recognize such
cultural differences with considerable ease but find it exceedingly difficult to relinquish their belief that their own
way of life is after all the best and the "most natural" one
(25).   He makes the added point that professional social
work is in itself a sub-culture with its own set of styles,
ceremonies, and values which become superimposed on the
culture of the individual practitioner.

    Within these social networks, values, expectations, and
patterns of communication become stabilized.   Social workers
have been often accused of holding or aspiring to the traditional "middle class" values.   Middle class values could
be loosely defined as the dominant values of this society.
They focus on the successful outcome of a self-reliant
struggle and include disapproval of drinking, gambling, and
other "vices," the adherence to thrift, industrious work and
tested worth by demonstration of material success, stability of family life and participation in self and community
supporting organizations.   Obviously, there is nothing wrong
with these values as goals for every individual in the society.
In actuality, these values are difficult of achievement for
many individuals who presume themselves to be "middle
class."   The wrongness which is the theme of the critics
of social work stems from the often inflexible attempts of
social caseworkers to impose these values on people who,
out of their life circumstances, have developed for themselves different kinds of values.

    Where such differences in values and expectations exist,
distortions in communication are inevitable.   The worker who
would open up viable channels of communication must find a
way to recognize and accredit the values of the client, without necessarily relinquishing or imposing his own.

Difference in Language Systems

    Since language is an integral part of culture, and, we have acknowledged that cultural difference is a major obstacle to effective communication, it follows logically that differences in language systems (the primary medium of communication) complicate the communicative task. This is one reason that social work as a profession has been accused of "catering" to the middle classes. Here there is essential congruence in language systems, while, when dealing with other classes, the social worker has to make an effort to adapt to or enter into a different language style (21, 24). For example, when working with the lower classes, the caseworker has to be sure that he understands the "linguistic shorthand" of the ghetto, the abbreviated style, and the lack of qualifying embellishment to speech patterns. He must be careful, too, not to mistake taciturnity for intellectual inadequacy. Jean Baratz states:

> The syntax of low-income Negro children differs from standard English in many ways, but it has its own internal consistency. Unfortunately, the psychologist, not knowing the rules of Negro non-standard English, has interpreted these differences not as the result of well-learned rules but as evidence of 'linguistic underdevelopment.' He has been handicapped by his assumption that to develop language is synonymous with the development of the psychologist's own form of standard English. Thus he has concluded that if black children do not speak like white children they are deficient. One of the most blatant errors has been a confusion between hypotheses concerning language and hypotheses concerning cognition (26).

    One of the first things that a professional social worker learns is that he must "start where the client is." Nowhere is this more true than in the area of language. Where language systems are different, the onus is on the caseworker to find a way to reduce or reconcile the differences so that he may enter into the client's "world" and find him "where he is." This is not a simple task; for this reason, differences in language systems remain a major hurdle to be surmounted in the achievement of effective communication.

Role and Status Obstacles

   The social roles of helper and helped (worker-client)
combine to form a situation in which supraordinate status
is imputed to the one and subordinate to the other. Regardless of the accustomed, the ordinary, or the desired status
of the client, in seeking help from a social agency, he is
placed in a position where he has to feel, in varying degrees, some dependence on the worker. Many people re-
sent the feeling of helplessness, of "lack of control," which
this situation engenders. Clients attempt to minimize this
feeling in many different ways. Some attempt to socialize
the relationship, to establish a climate of camaraderie which
is an effort to negate the role and status differentials in the
relationship. Others, once they are involved in the relationship and feel the impact of the role and status difference,
attempt to minimize the problem for which they actually
came, demeaning its importance or pretending to have arrived at a solution. Others react with diffuse hostility or
other forms of subtle resistance. Whatever the nature of
the client's response to this aspect of the relationship, it
must be recognized and dealt with by the worker for it is
sure to influence the kind and quality of communication between them.

   If, for example, the client is unable to accept the role
of "client" with its attendant feelings of dependency and subordinate status, then his productions are much more likely
to be superficial and to deal with manifest, cognitive material.
This is especially true when the latent feelings pricked in
the casework relationship are similar to those which contribute to or are a part of his problem situation.

   In terms of effective communication, role and status
differentials pose a danger to the caseworker, too. It is
all too easy for the insecure worker to "hide" behind them,
to assume a condescending manner, and "talk down" to the
client. This approach increases the client's anxiety about
his status and creates more defensiveness and resistance in
the communication process.

   By the very nature of their work together, as a result
of the kind of life circumstances that bring them together,
there is a difference in the role and status of the caseworker
and the client. This fact has to be recognized and accepted
by both. On the caseworker's part, in order to open up the

most free channels of communication between them, he must constantly work at reducing the gap caused by this difference, without allowing the relationship to deteriorate to one of "buddies" or of antagonist and protagonist.

Some Ways to Improve Communication

It has been suggested earlier that the onus is on the caseworker to insure that lines of communication are open between him and the client. The caseworker comes with a store of background knowledge about how people behave individually and in groups, he brings the knowledge obtained from work with many other individuals and families, he has some degree of advanced study, and he has the advantage of the supraordinate position in the relationship. While he does not know this particular individual, his background knowledge and his skills should enable him to come to know him quickly. This section is devoted to a discussion of some ways that the caseworker can improve communication within the casework relationship. Four approaches will be discussed; they are: 1) Questioning as opposed to telling; 2) Empathic Response; 3) "Cutting Through"; and 4) Reaching out to the language system. Obviously, these approaches may be used in combination rather than discretely.

Questioning

We are not quite sure of the dynamics of the phenomenon but caseworkers know that people who are troubled find release in discussing their troubles with a receptive listener. At the same time, there are caseworkers who spend disproportionate amounts of valuable interview time telling, admonishing, and directing the client. (One might hypothesize that they secure the same kind of release in this type of activity.) However, this is a sure way to dam up communication. The skillful caseworker will encourage the client to talk and give him ample opportunity to do so. To be sure, the flow of the client's production has some direction from the caseworker, but this direction takes the form of well placed and carefully worded questions. When the client has only to listen to the admonitions of the caseworker, we have little opportunity to assess his thought processes, his feelings, and his expectations. On the other hand, when the client has to respond to questions, he has to struggle to develop a response, he must order his thought processes, and

he is forced to an evaluation of his own situation. Quite
often, in the midst of such a process, the client will pause
to acknowledge feelings or relationships of which he had
been unaware before, because he had not had this type
of struggle to put his own situation in perspective. It is a
cliche of the profession that the skillful caseworker is a
"good listener. " I would add that he is also a good questioner.

Empathic Response

Empathy is often loosely and somewhat simply defined
as the capacity to put oneself "in the other fellow's boots. "
It is differentiated from sympathy, because that term implies pity or condescension. However it is defined, it is
much more easily described than actualized. In reality it
is extremely difficult to understand the other person's situation and to put oneself figuratively in his place. Much more
important, when such understanding is achieved, it rarely
lends itself to verbal communication. It is asking a lot to
ask a young, unmarried female caseworker to put herself
"in the boots" of an unmarried ADC mother; or, a young up-
wardly mobile, middle-class oriented probation officer to
understand "the boots" of a delinquent adolescent. Yet, this
is what is required for a truly empathic response.

Communication is enhanced when the caseworker does
understand the situation of the client and can convey verbally,
in manner, and in other non-verbal responses some understanding of the problems with which the client must cope.
When this occurs the client is freed to discuss his situation
in dimensions which would be avoided if he felt the worker
could not understand.

"Cutting Through"

Much of what occurs in the communication process between the worker and the client is non-verbal, or it is
tangential or circuitous to the expressed issue at hand. As
in the case of the wife and mother who come to the agency
asking for financial aid or for help with a non-conforming
child, when the story unfolds, it is clear to the worker
that neither of these is really the problem. Rather, a marital
problem about which she cannot talk is really the problem
that needs to be dealt with. For reasons of apprehension
or self-protection, clients frequently need to communicate at

a superficial level.   Communication is enhanced when the
worker is able to recognize unexpressed problems or concerns that have more bearing on the difficulty of the situation
than those which the client is expressing.   To "cut through"
to these latent levels is one of the surest ways of conveying
understanding of the situation.   Once this has happened--and
without catastrophe--the client's apprehension is diminished,
and he is freed to fully discuss his situation.

Reaching out to the Language System

When a person is burdened with problems and suffering
under the added pressure of a language barrier, nothing is
more likely to reduce tension and increase self-esteem than
an honest effort on the part of the caseworker to bridge this
barrier, without all of the "giving" being by the client.   At
a point where the caseworker does not understand the client's
expression, it would be appropriate to stop and acknowledge
and discuss the lack of understanding.   At this time similarities and differences in language style might also be discussed.   It should be noted that such a situation offers the
possibility of role reversal, for at this point in time, the
client is the teacher and the worker is the learner.   However, such a temporary shift in roles could be repaid by a
subsequently strengthened relationship.   Using the client's
"input" as a base, the caseworker would be well advised
to do some research to reduce the gaps in verbal production
and comprehension between him and the client.   Needless to
say, this is a non-verbal way of saying, "I care" and "I
want to help. "   The time and the temporary sacrifice of role
would be well spent, because it would result in the two
communicants being able to "understand" one another and
thus to arrive at the necessary congruence of goals.

Summary

Communication lies at the core of casework as a helping
process.   Despite this fact, inadequacies in communication
skills continue to plague caseworkers, presenting obstacles
to the attainment of their problem solving goals.   This
chapter has looked at the nature of communication in casework from the perspective of communication theory.   The
point has been made that this process is dimensional in
quality, meaning that the messages conveyed from one person to another are much more than the sum of the words

spoken between them.

An effort has been made to consider the "inputs" of
both worker and client in the communications process, and
the process itself has been viewed in terms of its importance,
the obstacles to effective communication, and some ways to
improve communication in the casework relationship.   Among
the modes suggested are: 1) Questioning; 2) Empathic Response; 3) "Cutting Through"; and 4) Reaching out to the
Language System of the Client.

Throughout, the onus for viable and effective communication has been placed on the caseworker.   For it is only
as the caseworker is able to recognize and appropriately relate to the communication patterns of the client that open and
clear communication will be achieved.

References

1.   Schramm, Wilbur (ed.), Process and Effects of Mass
        Communication (Urbana, Illinois, University of Illinois
        Press, 1954), p. 3.

2.   Newcomb, Theodore M., "An Approach to the Study of
        Communicative Acts," in Hare, P. A., Borgotta, E.
        F. and Bales, R. F., Small Groups (New York,
        Alfred A. Knopf, 1955), p. 149.

3.   Mead, George M., Mind, Self and Society (Chicago,
        University of Chicago Press), 1934.

4.   Berelson, Bernard, Content Analysis in Communication
        Research (Glencoe, Illinois, Free Press, 1952).

5.   Goodenough, Ward Hunt, Cooperation in Change (New
        York, Russell Sage Foundation, 1963), p. 387.

6.   Feldman, Yonata, "Understanding Ego Involvement in
        Casework Training," in Parad, H. J. and Miller,
        R. R., Ego-Oriented Casework (New York, FSAA,
        1963), p. 294.

7.   Hollis, Florence, Social Casework--A Psychosocial
        Therapy (New York, Random House, 1964), p. 190.

8. Irvine, May, "Communication and Relationship in Social
    Casework," Social Casework, Vol. 36, No. 1,
    January 1955, p. 13.

9. Perlman, Helen Harris, Social Casework--A Problem-
    Solving Process (Chicago, University of Chicago
    Press, 1957), p. 71.

10. Stark, Frances B., "Barriers to Client-Worker Com-
    munication at Intake," Social Casework, Vol. 40,
    No. 4, April 1959, p. 177.

11. Strean, Herbert S., "Role Theory, Role Models and
    Casework," Social Work, Vol. 12, No. 2, April 1967,
    pp. 77-88.

12. Haley, Jay, Strategies in Psychotherapy (New York,
    Grune and Stratton, 1963).

13. Satir, Virginia, Conjoint Family Therapy, A Guide to
    Theory and Technique (Palo Alto, Service and Be-
    havior Books, 1963).

14. Hollis, Florence, op. cit., p. 192.

15. Irvine, May, op. cit.

16. Bradford, Leland P., "The Case of the Hidden Agenda,"
    Adult Leadership, Vol. II, No. 7, December 1953;
    and Schutz, William C., "Interpersonal and Under-
    world" in Bennis, W. G., Benne, K. D. and R. Chin,
    The Planning of Change (New York, Holt, Rinehart,
    & Winston, 1961), p. 293.

17. Perlman, Helen H., op. cit., pp. 53-63.

18. Feldman, Yonata, op. cit., p. 299.

19. Scherz, Frances H., "Family Interaction: Some
    Problems and Implications for Casework," in Parad,
    H. J. and Miller, R. R. (eds.), Ego-Oriented Case-
    work (New York, FSAA, 1963), p. 129.

20. Ibid., p. 132.

21. Ruesch, Jurgen, Therapeutic Communication (New York,
    W. W. Norton & Company, 1961).

22. Brown, William Neal, "Alienated Youth," Mental Hygiene, Vol. 52, No. 3, July 1968.

23. Fantl, Berta, "Casework in Lower Class Districts," Mental Hygiene, Vol. 45, No. 3, July 1961.

24. Reissman, Frank, "Are the Deprived Non-Verbal?" in Reissman, F., Cohen, J., and Pearl A. (eds.) Mental Health of the Poor (New York, The Free Press, 1964), p. 188.

25. Pollak, Otto, "Cultural Dynamics in Casework," Social Casework, Vol. 34, No. 7, July 1953, p. 279.

26. Baratz, John C., "The Language of the Ghetto Child," The Center Magazine, Vol. 2, January 1969, p. 32.

Chapter 7

The Behavior Modification Model
and Social Casework

by Edwin J. Thomas

A revised version of the author's 'Selected Sociobehavioral Techniques and Principles: An Approach
to Interpersonal Helping,' reprinted from Social Work,
Vol. 13, No. 1 (January, 1968), pp. 12-26, with the
permission of the author and the National Association
of Social Workers.

The field of casework confronts at least two perplexing
problems. The first is the relatively rudimentary state of
the conceptualization of its techniques. Despite the articulate
efforts of such scholars as Hollis, there still have been too
few efforts to identify, codify, and conceptualize casework
techniques (1). Many new ones--and some old ones, too--
have not yet been adequately explicated. In addition, important knowledge about behavioral maintenance and change
that may have utility for casework exists in related behavioral science disciplines and helping professions and
certain areas of social work practice.

The second problem concerns whether the techniques are
actually effective. The results of evaluative studies of casework and other traditional forms of interpersonal helping
have been consistently disappointing (2). Despite occasional
methodological shortcomings, enough careful studies have
been done to sustain the conclusion that, in general, it has
not yet been demonstrated that casework and related forms of
conventional helping are effective. This is not to say that
research has proved such treatment to be ineffective--that
judgment has not been corroborated and probably never will
be. As for the comparative effectiveness of the various
conventional casework techniques themselves, even less is

known.   In fact, some of the inquiries done in related fields show that techniques such as insight therapy produce very modest results as compared with selected sociobehavioral techniques (3).

The infusion of selected sociobehavioral techniques into social work practice may help.   Many of these may directly augment the existing battery of conventional techniques in casework.   Despite their newness in the therapeutic market place, sociobehavioral techniques have already been utilized with uncommon success in a variety of settings (4).   Although virtually no evaluative studies have yet been conducted on them in social work, the techniques evaluated in related fields have generally involved behavioral problems similar to those regularly dealt with in casework.   Some sociobehavioral techniques may be readily adapted to the professional activities of caseworkers, as will be noted in the later discussion, and perhaps eventually we will find some use for all of them.

Furthermore, because some of the therapeutic activities in which caseworkers currently engage have sociobehavioral features, this review of selected techniques may serve to help crystallize and distinguish these sociobehavioral features of practice.   As will be noted later, when applied to the techniques of behavioral maintenance or modification in casework, the sociobehavioral approach suggests fruitful, alternative ways to analyze selected, existing casework techniques.

Elements of the Approach

The Sociobehavioral approach is a recent development. With the exception of a few pioneering efforts, many of the innovations in "behavioral practice" have occurred in the last twenty years, and most within the last ten years.   The body of knowledge (which has an even longer history than this) that forms the basis of sociobehavioral theory derives mainly from research on learning and behavioral modification in the field of psychology, although behaviorally oriented research in such areas as personality, social psychology, and sociology has been relevant too.   Practice, at present, consists largely of procedures and techniques from several emerging schools of behavioral therapy--the Pavlovian, the operant, the "personalistic, " and that of the specialized technique (e. g. , Wolpe's systematic desensitization).   Increasingly, however, the practice is becoming more eclectic.

Despite important differences, all the behavioral approaches to therapeutic problems are based on several
common assumptions. Only a few can be mentioned here.

First, most proponents agree about features of the
nature of human behavior. Without denying differences in
native endowment and the behavioral effects of organic and
chemical factors, behavioral approaches emphasize the
learned aspects of behavior. Learned behavior, including
problem and deviant behavior, has natural, empirical antecedents, according to its advocates, and the behavior may
be modified through application of the findings derived from
research on learning and behavioral modification. In this
sense, problem behavior is regarded as being no different
from normal behavior, despite differences in response reper-
toires and in labels for the behavior.

By this time the reader has undoubtedly observed from
the repeated use of the term "behavior" that behavior is
viewed generically. The observable responses of human
activity are behavior. All activity is pertinent--"thoughts, "
"affect, " as well as the more obvious motor action--pro-
vided only that it is denotable through the senses of the
observer. Real internal workings of mind occur, of course,
and some of these have been studied scientifically by means
of chemical and electrical indicators as well as through
overt response. Although dubious hypothetical inner psychic
states are not postulated, this view of behavior is much less
narrow than is sometimes alleged. A good rule of thumb
is that anything is fair game for behavior analysis--"ego
state, " "defense, " "habit, " or whatever it happens to be
called--if the behavior that controls the use of the verbal
labels can be pointed to and known to an observer's senses.

Second, various assumptions are made about treatment.
If a central assumption does indeed exist, it probably would
be that treatment consists of achieving behavioral maintenance
or modification. Modification, in turn, may be specified as
the acquisition, strengthening, weakening, or elimination of
behavior. In this context, treatment consists of the activities
of the helper and others that serve to bring about desired
modification or stabilization of the client's behavior. The
roles of the helper as a modifier and stabilizer of behavior
revolve mainly around producing direct behavioral change in
the client, around instruction of the client on how he may
alter the variables that control his behavior, or around behavioral "programming" of others so that they in turn may

modify or maintain the client's behavior.

Third, behavioral approaches are based on the conviction that knowledge used in practice should have empirical corroboration. Every major school of behavioral therapy rests upon what would be considered a strong research edifice, at least in comparison with the conventional methods. Every major type of behavioral technique--for example, the operant group to be discussed later--has scores, if not hundreds, of laboratory studies behind it and now numerous applied research studies buttress the principles being used. (The reader may not realize that the principles of classical, Pavlovian conditioning rest upon over six thousand laboratory studies conducted with humans and animals.) Although the basic and applied research on which behavioral approaches are based varies in volume and quality, it is generally much superior to research connected with conventional techniques of interpersonal helping.

In this brief introduction some of the common assumptions in behavioral approaches have been stated, but there are some important uncommon ones as well. Also, many other general characteristics of the knowledge and practice of sociobehavioral theory exist, to say nothing of the specific researches and practices themselves. For lack of space, the reader is necessarily referred elsewhere (5).

Overview of Assessment Procedures

Before examining the selected techniques of modification that constitute the major focus of this chapter, attention will be given briefly to the requisites of behavioral assessment. Like more conventional approaches to casework, the socio-behavioral approach has its own version of study and diagnosis. We shall refer to the study and diagnosis of socio-behavioral practice as the procedures of assessment. Such assessment should be undertaken and hopefully completed before modification is undertaken.

The objectives of sociobehavioral assessment are: 1) to determine the frequency (or magnitude) of the specific problem behavior (often called the "baseline"), prior to beginning modification; and 2) to stipulate the associated stimulus antecedents and consequences of the problem behavior. The determination of the pre-intervention baseline of problem behavior serves to indicate to the worker the seriousness and pervasiveness of the problem and to specify the initial level of behavior so that the post-intervention levels of behavior may be compared to calibrate whether or not the modification techniques have been successful.

The particular procedures of sociobehavioral assessment most suitable for social work are currently in the process of development and evolution. Nonetheless, several common features are now discernible in the procedures being employed in social work and in related fields. These may be conveniently arranged as steps, as follows:

1. The selection of a problem to work on. Where possible, a verbal agreement is reached concerning which one of the client's problems is to be worked on first. To this end, a contract in the form of a verbal or written agreement that this is the problem to be worked on is often obtained.

2. Specification of the behavioral referents of the problem. Starting from what is often little more than the client's label for a problem, the worker specifies the behaviors that occur and control the client's use of the verbal label. Typical and concrete instances of the concrete problem behaviors are sought. To achieve this objective, the worker solicits verbal examples from the client and others, endeavors to obtain observational specimens in the natural environment in which the behavior typically occurs, and seeks corroborative reports of others. Emerging from this specification are the particular behaviors that constitute the problematic behavioral events to be worked on.

3. Assessment of the frequency (or magnitude) of the problem behaviors. This consists of a pre-intervention measurement of the level of problem behavior. The client, the worker or others may serve as reporters or observers to collect such data.

4. Determination of the controlling antecedents and consequences. The particular stimuli that immediately antedate and follow the problem behavior are isolated in order to learn about the sustaining environmental causes of the problem behavior. Such information may be collected when a baseline is obtained or other, special assessment activities may have to be employed.

5. The formulation of an intervention plan. The foregoing information is appraised and an intervention plan formulated. This plan identifies the desired intermediate and
terminal behaviors and the particular modification techniques
to be employed. As the discussion below will endeavor to
indicate, each technique of modification is generally suitable
for only a particular class of problem behavior.

The Techniques

In contrast to most familiar techniques, sociobehavioral
techniques derive from knowledge about the modification and
maintenance of behavior, they are specific behaviorally in
their operations and consequences, and in their use they
bear an explicit relationship to behavior designated as
problem behavior, to the controlling conditions for such behavior, and to the treatment objectives. The basis for the
assertions will be more apparent to the reader as the paper
develops.

Although full agreement does not yet exist on what
specific techniques constitute a set that can be identified as
sociobehavioral, there is already concurrence on the essential
features of, and even the labels for, many of the techniques.
Still, no satisfactory taxonomy has been developed to date
(6). As a matter of fact, this paper grew out of the author's
efforts to find a way to order and systematize sociobehavioral
techniques. Apparently, the most sensible way to do this is
around two major axes. The first is the class of behavior
dealt with (to be explained shortly) and the second is the
specific concrete operations of the helper that will produce
known consequences. The objectives of sociobehavioral intervention correspond directly to the known behavioral consequences produced by using these techniques. These objectives
(and consequences) are the acquisition, strengthening, maintenance, weakening, or elimination of behavior (7).

The discussion of selected operant techniques will illustrate these observations. Seventeen sociobehavioral techniques
have been isolated and ordered through this framework by the
author, but because of space limitations only five will be
covered in this article.

Selected Operant Techniques and Principles

Operant behavior is one of at least two fundamental classes of behavior. The other class, respondent behavior, is discussed on page 286 (8). Operant behavior involves "voluntary" actions of the skeletal-muscular system. Here the striated muscles under the individual's "control" are implicated in the conditioning process. Walking, talking, writing, and many features of thinking are examples.

The main premise relating to the emergence and alteration of such behavior is that operant behavior is governed by its consequences (9). The first recognition of operant behavior came from Thorndike, after he observed that cats who had some experience with a puzzle box could subsequently solve puzzles with greater ease. From this initial observation he formulated the Law of Effect, which stated essentially that behavior was influenced by the effects of such behavior in the environment (10). Essentially, the operant techniques are names for specific "operations," or activities, that are known to produce identifiably different consequences for operant behavior.

Six operant techniques have been identified: positive reinforcement, extinction, differential reinforcement, response-shaping, punishment, and negative reinforcement. The first five are elaborated on in this article.

Positive Reinforcement

Let us begin with a case that derives from a demonstration project in which probation officers were trained to use various techniques of behavior modification.

> Claire is a bright, reasonably attractive 16-year-old who was referred to the project for truancy, poor grades, and incorrigibility at home. The referral came from the local high school where it was stated that Claire was about to be expelled for being delinquent. The project staff persuaded the school to hold up expulsion for several days, during which time they instituted a new regimen with Claire's mother, the only parent in the home. At the time the staff intervened, Claire had been staying home from school and was threatening to run away. All money, the use of

the telephone, and dating privileges had been withdrawn despite the fact that all these were potentially
very powerful reinforcers for Claire and her mother
had not provided any definite way for Claire to earn
them back.

The intervention plan, agreed to by the mother,
Claire, and a staff member, consisted of the following.
Telephone privileges and weekend dates were made
contingent on attending school all day. If Claire
attended all classes for a given day, the school
attendance officer would dispense a note to Claire at
the end of each day. Upon presenting the note to
the mother, Clarie would then earn telephone privileges that day (both receiving and calling out). If
four out of five notes were obtained during the week,
one weekend date was earned; two weekend dates were
earned if five out of five notes were sent home. The
use of the phone on the weekend was not included in
the plan. Although the mother had always been in-
consistent and ineffective in her relations with Claire,
she was surprised to discover that Claire accepted
the plan. Despite many family difficulties, Claire
attended school regularly from the first day of intervention. The plan was altered after a month so that
Claire would have to receive only two notes a week.
If classes were attended on Monday, Tuesday, and
Wednesday, one note was required to certify to this;
and this note earned the privilege of one weekend
night out. A second note, on Friday, certified to
the full attendance on Thursday and Friday, which
earned a second night out on the weekend. Telephone
privileges were removed from contingency. Notes
were stopped entirely about seven weeks later.

Claire's school attendance improved immediately.
Whereas during the period prior to intervention Claire
had missed thirty days of school out of the first
forty-six days, she was only absent illegally twice
during the three months that the project was involved.
What is more impressive, however, was that she was
never absent illegally again following termination of
the project, and this involved a period of the entire
second semester of school. The project staff was
thus successful in preventing Claire from being expelled from school and probably from running away from
home, and accomplished this with a very small invest-

ment of staff time (11).

This case illustrates various points: 1) Before the staff intervened, the indigenous and powerful reinforcers in the situation--money, telephone use, and dating--had been withdrawn, and Claire had no way of earning them back. Other behavioral controls had obviously not been effective either. 2) The treatment regimen consisted essentially of restoring these reinforcers, making their availabilty contingent on attending school. 3) There was a schedule of reinforcement--every desired set of responses was reinforced. Telephone privileges were provided each day and depended on whether Claire attended school that day. The number of weekend dates also depended on how many days she attended school. Later the schedule was altered so that, for example, telephone use was taken off "contingency. " 4) There were no other apparent elements in the contingency system. No punishment was provided for not going to school, only the absence of available indigenous reinforcers.

As for the concept of reinforcement itself, it should be observed that there are related concepts in social work practice. Notions such as "reassurance" and "support" often pertain to phenomena for which the concept of reinforcement would be appropriate. However, these practice concepts do not specify the behavior of the worker that produces given consequences and may not be considered synonymous with reinforcement. The fact that the reinforcement of client behavior occurs widely in social work under different names should not be confused with the fact that, in general, reinforcement is not often utilized as a technique in casework in the deliberate, conscious manner described here.

Positive reinforcement may be defined as the use of stimuli following a response in such a way that the future rate of responding is increased. Any stimulus that is used following a response and serves to increase the rate of responding may therefore be called a positive reinforcer.

Some reinforcers--called primary--function innately to increase the rate of responding. Food, sex, and water are examples, provided that the organism is in a state of deprivation ("need"). Shock, cold, and rest are additional primary reinforcers. Other reinforcers, commonly called secondary (or learned) reinforcers, have acquired their capacity to increase the rate of responding because of a learning history in which they have been paired together in time with various conditions of primary reinforcement. Money, approval, domination, submissiveness, and affection are generally, but not always, examples of such secondary reinforcers. These also illustrate a third type, namely, the the generalized secondary reinforcer, which is the reinforcer that has been learned on the basis of its relationship to primary reinforcers and whose effectiveness, in general, is presumed to be relatively independent of states of deprivation involving such primary reinforcers.

Both primary and generalized secondary reinforcers have been used frequently in intervention based on principles of behavior modification. Thus, institutionalized psychotic patients who had had a history of not feeding themselves were enabled to eat regularly and on time merely by making the availability of food contingent on eating behavior (12). Verbal behavior in interviews has been shown to be clearly affected through the use of such generalized secondary reinforcers as a smile, a nod, or "mmmhmm" (13). Through the use of diverse reinforcers that may be exchanged for "tokens" (e. g., poker chips or other substitutes for money), institutionalized mental patients have been enabled effectively to perform a variety of on- and off-ward jobs (14).

Positive reinforcement is widely applicable to problems that involve strengthening and maintaining behavior. However, it may also be used to weaken behavior, depending on the nature of the schedule of reinforcement used (15). In general, it is believed that reinforcement is not effective for acquiring new behavior. Rather, reinforcement has been found to affect the rate of behavior, once behavior has been acquired or has occurred. And, properly speaking, it may not be used to eliminate behavior (16).

Positive reinforcement is considered to be of primary use in strengthening behavior. Following are listed some of the conditions that relate to its effectiveness when used toward this end:

1.   The response to be reinforced must first be emitted, otherwise reinforcement is impossible.

2.   Reinforcement must not be delayed; in general, the more immediate the reinforcement, the better. (It has been found that, in general, reinforcement is most effective when given at . 5 of a second after the response.)

3. Reinforcement of every desired response emitted is most effective for establishing behavior (17).

4. Not reinforcing every desired response during response establishment, while less effective in achieving immediate high rates of responding, is generally more effective in producing responses that endure after reinforcement is terminated.

5. The stimuli suitable to reinforce one individual's behavior may not be the most appropriate for another. In general, each individual has his own profile of reinforcers (18). Recent research suggests that one important clue to what the reinforcing conditions are in the profile is simply the rank order of activities in which a person engages in his free time (19).

Extinction

Extinction has two features. Its operation consists of withholding the reinforcer when a response, previously reinforced by that reinforcer, is emitted. The consequence of this operation, if completely and steadfastly maintained, is to reduce the rate of responding to the original level.

It is important not to confuse extinction with punishment. The extinction procedure merely involves the withholding of the reinforcing stimuli that previously sustained the rate of responding. No "aversive" stimuli are presented and no positive reinforcers removed.

In social work practice, one may find some partial analogs to the extinction process in such activities as the withholding of support, reassurance, or "limit-setting. " But not all behavior so labeled is necessarily an extinction procedure. The concept of extinction itself and the principles relating to it are not part of social work's present conceptual framework.

The following case example involves a relatively common problem in institutional contexts and some others as well. It refers to approach behaviors, such as having persons come to see the workers, in which there is no therapeutic gain associated with contact.

Consider the case of Lucille, a patient in the mental
hospital who had been making frequent visits to the
nurses' office for a period of two years.   During the
pretreatment study it was found that she entered the
nurses' office an average of sixteen times a day.
The nurses had resigned themselves to this activity
on the grounds that such efforts as pushing her back
bodily onto the ward had failed in the past and because the patient had been classified as mentally defective and therefore 'too dumb' to understand.

In order to extinguish the problem behavior in
question, the nurses were informed simply that during
the program the patient must not be given any reinforcement (attention) for entering the nurses' office.
It was found that as soon as the extinction schedule
was introduced, there was a gradual and continuing
diminution of entries to the nurses' office.   The
average frequency was down to two entries per day
by the seventh week of extinction, at which time the
program was terminated (20).

The diminution of behavior during extinction will occur
gradually or rapidly, depending on the maintenance schedule.
Besides its downhill slope, the extinction curve typically has
two other features worth noting.   One is that immediately
after the withholding of reinforcement in the extinction procedure, there is often a temporary increase in the rate of
responding.   What appears to be a clinical instance of this
will be seen in the case example below.   The other feature
of the curve is that as the behavior diminishes to a low
level there occurs quite regularly a small but temporary
increase in responding, called a "spontaneous recovery." If
reinforcement continues to be withheld, this small apparent
recovery of the response will again diminish.

Extinction is probably one of the most important means
of reducing or eliminating operant responses and has wide
applicability in social work.   Undesirable motor habits,
verbal behavior such as "psychotic talk, " voluntary crying,
and many forms of misbehavior and difficulties associated
with child management may all be handled effectively through
extinction.

Anyone attempting to make use of extinction in practice
should anticipate the characteristics associated with the extinction curve mentioned earlier.   Furthermore, there may be

minor emotional reactions of a relatively temporary sort
associated with the introduction of an extinction procedure.

The principal difficulty associated with the use of extinction derives from the fact that most of the operant responses
called "problem behavior" have typically been sustained over
long periods of time by intermittent reinforcement.   As such,
these responses are highly resistant to extinction.   Thus the
extinction process must be carefully controlled and monitored.
Given a response history of intermittent reinforcement, it is
especially important that extinction be abrupt and complete
in order to differentiate it from intermittent reinforcement.
The results of research in this area are absolutely clear:
the worker should cease reinforcement completely.   If he
has little control over the reinforcement community, the
chances of utilizing extinction successfully are greatly reduced.

Differential Reinforcement

Differential reinforcement consists of a particular amal-
gamation of positive reinforcement and extinction.   Positive
reinforcement is used to strengthen pro-social behavior while
the extinction technique is used to reduce or eliminate
problem behavior.

There are numerous examples of the use of differential
reinforcement in behavior modification.   Rational speech has
been reinforced while an extinction procedure has been
adopted for a patient's psychotic talk; overactive behavior
has been extinguished for mentally retarded children in a
playroom while also reinforcing more sedentary activities;
operant crying in a nursery school has been extinguished
while the use of words, as incompatible responses to crying,
were simultaneously reinforced; operant vomiting has been
extinguished while at the same time reinforcing alternative
prosocial behaviors.   Indeed, most of the examples labeled
reinforcement in the literature on behavior modification are
really differential reinforcement.

The use of differential reinforcement to alter the verbal
behavior of a 10-year-old girl is illustrated in the following
example.

Mary was a member of a treatment group for delinquent girls and among her problems was that she

talked so rapidly she could not be understood.   The
behavior was apparently maintained by the attention
that this obtained from others.   Thus they would say,
'Mary, what did you say?'   and 'Slow down. '   The
behavior antagonized adults as well as children and
the latter often became so irritated that they attacked
her physically as well as verbally.

In order to have Mary speak more slowly and understandably, the following plan was instituted.   The
other children in the treatment group were encouraged
to ignore rapid talking and not to respond to it.
Furthermore, the children were encouraged to pay
attention to Mary when she spoke slowly and to com-
pliment her for this, and the social worker acted
similarly.

It is interesting that during the course of the first
meeting following the implementation of the plan, Mary
began to speak faster and faster (apparently revealing
here the slight increase in responding, following the
introduction of extinction, of which we spoke before),
but she soon reduced the speed of her talking at the
end of the meeting.   During the second meeting she
occasionally speeded up but usually talked slowly.
Several girls commented that they liked Mary better.
During the third meeting Mary speeded up only once
and then, during the same episode, reduced her speed
again.   In subsequent meetings, her tempo was slowed
so that persons could easily follow her.

Of more than incidental interest is that in the course
of the five-week period Mary was no longer the object
of criticism or physical abuse by the girls.   Furthermore, her complaining disappeared and she seemed
to be better liked, at least by two of the girls in the
group (21).

Because differential reinforcement consists of positive
reinforcement for some behaviors as well as the extinction
of others, the comments made earlier about some of the
practical considerations involving the use of positive considerations involving the use of positive reinforcement as
well as extinction are likewise applicable to differential reinforcement.

Response-Shaping

Schwitzgebel and Kolb have experimented with an unusual means to reach recalcitrant adolescent delinquents. Although there are many features of their change effort, only the efforts pertaining to response-shaping are referred to here:

> Young teen-age delinquent boys were both the clients in the project as well as the subjects of the research. At the outset, these hard-to-reach delinquents were met in neighborhood contexts, largely on street corners, and simply asked if they would like to take a job talking into a tape recorder. Each prospective subject was told that he could talk about anything he wanted to and could quit whenever he wished. He was warned, however, that some of the other employees had changed their opinions about many things, but that this was not really a condition of the job.

> Periodic bonuses were given, both in the form of primary and secondary reinforcers, in addition to paying the subjects for coming for the interviews. If a subject came for an interview he was paid and, depending on the other behaviors he engaged in, given additional bonuses. If the subject did not come for the interview, the researcher would seek the boy out a few days later and try to get him to come, somewhat on his own terms. If a boy came late, he would be welcomed and nothing would be said about his tardiness. Whenever a boy came he would be welcomed, but if he came at a time that was an improvement over his prior tardiness or earliness, he would be given a special bonus. Most of the boys eventually ended up coming precisely on time, over the course of several sessions.

> Furthermore, the boys began to talk about themselves in considerable detail, established strong positive relationships to the professional helpers functioning as researchers, and engaged in a number of prosocial tasks such as preparing for a driver's license test, building simple electronic equipment, or answering correspondence (22).

As part of the general response-shaping procedure, the following points merit elaboration. First, the investigators

began with high probability behaviors.   In effect, they were
"beginning where the client is. " Specifically, the boys were
met in their own neighborhoods, they were placed in the role
of subjects and employees rather than of clients or delinquents,
and they were asked to engage in an activity that for most
of them was relatively easy, namely, talking about themselves or their favorite subjects.   Second, there was a step-
by-step successive approximation of desired terminal behaviors.   Attendance behavior was emphasized at the outset,
then various subjects that the boys talked about received
bonuses, and, still later, the pro-social tasks in which the
boys engaged were not only used to break the monotony but
also to train work-related behaviors.   Third, differential
reinforcement was utilized throughout the procedure.   First
there was reinforcement for coming, then additional bonuses
were given for talking about particular subjects and engaging
in certain activities.

Although many gradual step-by-step procedures are used
in social work practice, there is no concept in social work
that is really synonymous with response-shaping.   Two
principles are involved in the achievement of response-shaping: differential reinforcement of selected responses and the
use of differential reinforcement in a step-by-step procedure
that involves the gradual shifting of the criterion of differential reinforcement for successive approximations of the
desired terminal behavior.

Response-shaping presents a general solution to the apparent dilemma posed by reinforcement theory and by the
practitioner's frequent need to reinforce desired behavior
that has a low probability.   Often the worker may wish to
develop response strength of behaviors not presently in the
client's repertoire--behaviors that are new, complex, or not
easily accessible.   For example, a social worker may wish
to reinforce sensible talk in a psychotic who has been mute
for many years.   A prime requirement of reinforcement,
however, is that the response to be reinforced must first be
emitted.   How then can one reinforce a response that is
most unlikely to appear freely?   Shaping offers a solution to
this dilemma, for it involves the selective use of reinforcement to approximate successively the desired behavior.

The behavioral phenomenon on which response-shaping
builds is called response induction.   In effect, this phenomenon involves the tendency of the strength of a reinforced
response to increase the strength of more closely related re-

sponses than more distantly related responses. Thus, if one is attempting to reinforce audible speech for a person who speaks very softly, the reinforcement of higher levels of volume will tend to increase the probability of emitting responses having higher volume more than responses having lower volume. By means of response induction, the differential reinforcement of only closer and closer approximations of desired terminal behavior progressively strengthens these approximations while it simultaneously weakens more remote responses.

Sidman has suggested some rules relevant to shaping. These are as follows:

1. Behavior must be reinforced immediately; a delay of even a few seconds may result in the inadvertent reinforcement of undesired behavior.

2. The shaper must not give too many reinforcements for approximations of the desired response. Excessive reinforcement at one of the intermediate levels may result in no further movement toward the final objective.

3. The shaper must not give too few reinforcements for approximations of the desired response. Each response level must be securely established before proceeding to the following one, and this can only be done through an adequate reinforcement period. Sidman believes that inadequate reinforcement is a primary reason for failures of shaping.

4. There must be careful specification of the response to be reinforced at each successive level (23).

Punishment

Punishment expresses still another relationship between the rate of responding and consequences in the environment. Tyler and Brown have reported an intriguing demonstration of the use of mild punishment to control the misbehavior of delinquent boys committed by the courts to a training school.

> One of the problems met by the staff was the misbehavior of the boys while playing pool during free time. Misbehavior in this situation consisted of such behaviors as breaking the rules of the game, throwing pool cues, and scuffling. The punishing regimen con-

sisted simply of the matter-of-fact removal of the offending boy, immediately following his offense, to a small time-out room for a period of fifteen minutes. It was found that this simple operation served to suppress the level of infractions without untoward side effects.

The condition of mild punishment was compared with a condition of no punishment in which conventional verbal controls were attempted. 'Now cut that out,' 'I'm warning you,' and 'Don't let that happen again' were among the verbal controls. It was found that punishment was much more effective than these verbal controls, although the effect of punishment, following the removal of time-out regulations, was temporary.

The mild punishment was easy to administer and worked despite its mildness in a situation in which it was alleged that much more harsh punishment was relatively common. Furthermore, the punishment worked when in competition with peer group influences, which often are stronger when placed in competition with staff influences (24).

Punishment is used at various times in social work practice but usually the punishing behavior is cloaked with euphemistic labels. Thus one speaks of the worker's "expression of disapproval," of "withdrawing privileges," of the "use of authority," and of "limit-setting behavior." The writer will use here a more exact conception of punishment consistent with the usage of Azrin and Holz (25). These researchers emphasize punishment as being a consequence of responding that reduces the future rate of that response. There are two operations following an operant response that may have this effect. One is the presentation of a stimulus that is usually "aversive," and the other is the removal of a positive reinforcing condition, such as is illustrated in time out from reinforcement. The reduction of the rate of responding, if it is the essential consequence of these operations, may be temporary, as was illustrated in the case demonstration, or it may be a continuing partial reduction or even complete suppression.

There are many misconceptions about punishment in this society. Likely ones can be illustrated through imaginary criticisms of the demonstration just described. It might be contended, for instance, that the use of punishment of even this mild sort was downright unethical on grounds that it was aversive. It is not the aversiveness alone that is important, for life is rarely devoid of naturally or socially induced adversity. What is important are the effects of aversiveness. Not only were there no side effects in the demonstration described, the research literature indicates that only under highly restricted conditions are there likely to be any of the dire effects sometimes alleged to accompany punishment (26). (A related issue is the general question of ethics, which is touched on briefly on page 286.)

Another possible criticism is that punishment has an ephemeral, short-lived effect. This is really an instance of the general criticism that punishment is ineffective and therefore of no use. This has been amply demonstrated to be false in recent inquiries. Furthermore, the mild punishment used in this study at least had the virtue of controlling misbehavior in a situation in which many conventional verbal controls had been singularly ineffective.

Still another criticism of punishment is that other behavior-reducing procedures are more effective. The research evidence on this matter is not at all unequivocal, although there is some evidence in one comparison of five behavior-reducing procedures that punishment was the most effective by all comparison criteria (27). It remains to be seen whether there are alternative procedures that are as effective as punishment in reducing behavior.

Punishment is clearly a technique to be used for the reduction of behavior, either to weaken it or in some cases to eliminate it. Recent research suggests that in order to increase the efficacy of the punishing operations at least the following should be kept in mind:

1. The punishment should be neither so mild as to be inconsequential nor so strong as to be immobilizing or devastating.

2. The punishment should be tied immediately to the response that one wishes to reduce and should be administered matter-of-factly after the response.

3. Punishment of every response to be reduced should generally be used for obtaining immediate suppressive effects under the conditions during which the punishment is applied.

4.   Alternative pro-social responses incompatible with
the punished response should be allowed and reinforced (28).

Among the side effects that have to be seriously weighed
when considering the possible uses of punishment is that by
using it a professional helper may come to be avoided.
Azrin and Holz have observed that perhaps the most serious
and well-documented side effect of punishment is the possibility that the punishing agent may lose control of the person
punished (29).   This possibility has of course been well
recognized in social work practice.   Another side effect is
the possibility of aggression directed against the punishing
agent.

The general matter of the ethical use of punishment is
a most valid concern.   There are at least four factors that
must be weighed when appraising the ethical suitability of
using punishment.   One is the aversiveness (and social costs
in general) to the client and others of not reducing the
problem behavior; another is the availability of alternative
behavior-reducing techniques that would do the job with less
cost to clients; a third is the probable effectiveness of
punishment in achieving suppression, and it should be effectively reducing, or otherwise its use is irresponsible; and a
fourth is the side effects for the client and helper that would
result from the use of punishment.

Respondent-Related Techniques

Space permits only a brief overview of some of the other
techniques.   Although these are only mentioned, most of them
are just as pertinent to problems of casework as the operant
techniques discussed earlier.

Techniques included here involve problems pertaining
largely to respondent behavior and conditioning procedures
particularly suitable to the alteration of respondent behavior.
Respondent behavior involves so-called reflex behavior, and
it consists of "nonvoluntary responses" implicating mainly
the glands and smooth muscles.   Examples of such non-
voluntary responses are eyeblinks, salivation, sweating,
hunger contractions, and emotional reactions.   Anxiety and
responses of sexual arousal are probably the most common
exemplars of respondent behavior found in casework practice.
The classical conditioning paradigm involves respondent behavior, in which an unconditioned stimulus is paired with a

previously neutral stimulus to produce a conditioned response.
Thus Pavlov's dogs were taught to salivate when a bell
sounded as the sign of food, after the bell and the food had
been paired over a number of trials.   The animal had no
"control" over this behavior of salivation.

The three respondent techniques are classical conditioning (considered both for purposes of establishing cues for
pro-social respondent behavior (30) and for aversive conditioning of problem respondent behavior (31)), systematic desensitization (32), and flooding (33).

Complex Techniques

Techniques are designated as complex because more
than one operant technique may be involved or, more commonly, features of both operant and respondent techniques
are entailed.   Also, these are almost always used in order
to accomplish at least two behavioral objectives.   Behavioral
rehearsal, for example, is often used to reduce problem
responses as well as to increase alternative pro-social responding.

The complex techniques are negative practice (34),
satiation (35), stimulus-shaping ("fading") (36), verbal instructions (37), behavioral rehearsal (one aspect of role-
playing) (38), rule-making (39), model presentation (40), and
position-structuring (41).   There will no doubt be others to
add to the list as theoretical and practical work continues
(42).

Some Mistaken Conceptions

The sociobehavioral approach is only one of several
alternatives with potential utility in practice.   But as a new
viewpoint, it is subject to many of the same ethical issues
customarily raised with the introduction of any powerful
technique or theory.   Ethical issues were raised when psychoanalytic theory first was introduced, and now some critics
of sociobehavioral theory contend that it is unethical (e. g.,
that it is "Machiavellian" or "manipulative").   One can only
reply that the knowledge of the sociobehavioral approach, like
all knowledge, is instrumental, and as such may be used for
good or ill.   Knowledge is itself ethically neutral and values
become engaged only when knowledge is used.   The ethical

issue is generally not applicable if this new knowledge is
used within the context of existing professional ethics.

Another label sometimes applied to this approach is that
the sociobehavioral approach is "mechanistic." Knowledge
is not "mechanistic," unless perhaps it is knowledge about
physical mechanisms or psychodynamic mechanisms. Again,
this allegation applies to its use. The method of change
suggested by the sociobehavioral approach requires for its
implementation a well-trained, ethical, intelligent, and sensitive helper. The qualities in practitioners valued in current
social work practice will not become outmoded by this new
orientation since similar skills are needed for both approaches (43).

Problems of Application

Careful appraisal of the research upon which the techniques discussed here are based will indicate that much more
scientific research buttresses these principles than that which
relates to any other area of direct social work practice.
The fact that more basic research is required and will serve
to extend our knowledge further does not, in this case, serve
as an excuse to fault the principles already established. In
other words, it is thoughtless and even irresponsible for the
critic of behavioral methods to contend that the knowledge of
learning and behavioral modification is too tentative for social
workers to make use of it in practice. If this were true--
which it definitely is not--then the critic would be forced to
apply the criterion of scientific corroboration to the principles
of his own favored approach and, in so doing, would inevitably find such principles wanting because of less extensive
support.

The main problems of the sociobehavioral approach are
presently those associated with how best to apply and use it
in welfare settings. Many such settings are open where
clients are free to come and go at will. Hence there is the
problem of client accessibility. Most welfare agencies provide services that encompass functions, such as the provision of information, of referrals, and of monetary and
sometimes nonmonetary resources, which are in addition to
the modification of problem behavior. The modification and
so-called nonmodification activities of service have to be
integrated compatibly. Open settings present the problem of
countervailing environmental influences that may neutralize

or dominate the interventions of the social worker.   The
challenge is how and under what conditions to try to compete
with such environmental forces.   These are among the
characteristics of welfare service that must be taken into
consideration when applying behavioral methods.   The fact
that all approaches to casework must address essentially
these same challenges does not make them any the less
formidable for the practitioner of the sociobehavioral approach.

At present, the policies, principles and procedures of
an open-setting sociobehavioral approach in social welfare require development, explication and trial through use in
diverse settings.   Assessment procedures that yield reliable
and valid information for routine practice need further work;
the techniques of modification useful in the life situations
clients find themselves in, require developmental research;
ways to achieve and maintain client assessibility need to be
evolved; techniques that stand the best chance of competing
favorably with otherwise countervailing environmental forces
have to be isolated; and principles of learning and behavior
modification require further explication and application for
use by practititioners.

Conclusion

In order to facilitate the continued application and development of sociobehavioral methods suitable in welfare, social
work should give serious attention to the selective and careful use of these techniques.   Because they promise to make
social work practice more effective, they cannot be ignored.
Admittedly they cannot be adopted en masse and uncritically.
They must be tried out and the results appraised.   In this
way, sociobehavioral techniques will get the least of what
they deserve--a fair trial in the court of professional opinion.

Notes

1.   Florence Hollis, Casework: A Psychosocial Therapy
     (New York: Random House, 1964).

2.   For psychotherapy see, for example, Hans J. Eysenck,
     "The Effects of Psychotherapy: An Evaluation, "
     Journal of Consulting Psychology, Vol. 16, No. 5
     (October 1952), pp. 319-323; for a more recent and
     detailed review see Eysenck and Stanley Rachman,

The Causes and Cures of Neurosis (San Diego: Robert R. Knapp, 1965), pp. 242-267; and for reviews of evaluative studies in family services see Scott Briar, "Family Services," in Henry S. Maas, ed., Five Fields of Social Service: Reviews of Research (New York: National Association of Social Workers, 1966), pp. 16-21. An important evaluative study in social work having a control group design is Henry J. Meyer, Edgar F. Borgatta, and Wyatt C. Jones, Girls at Vocational High: An Experiment in Social Work Intervention (New York: Russell Sage Foundation, 1955).

3.   See, for example, Gordon L. Paul, Insight vs. Desensitization: An Experiment in Anxiety Reduction (Stanford University Press, 1966); Peter J. Lang and A. David Lazovik, "Experimental Desensitization of a Phobia," Journal of Abnormal and Social Psychology, Vol. 66, No. 6 (June 1963), pp. 519-525; and Arnold A. Lazarus, "Group Therapy of Phobic Disorders by Systematic Desensitization," Journal of Abnormal and Social Psychology, Vol. 63, No. 3 (November 1961), pp. 504-510.

4.   For relevant reviews, see Eysenck and Rachman, op. cit.; Joseph Wolpe and Arnold A. Lazarus, Behavior Therapy Techniques: A Guide to the Treatment of Neuroses (Oxford, Eng.: Pergamon Press, 1966), pp. 154-165; John M. Grossberg, "Behavior Therapy: A Review," Psychological Bulletin, Vol. 62, No. 2 (August 1964), pp. 73-89; and M. P. Feldman, "Aversion Therapy for Sexual Deviations: A Critical Review," Psychological Bulletin, Vol. 65, No. 2 (February 1966), pp. 65-80.

5.   For a general statement concerning the nature of the sociobehavioral approach, see Edwin J. Thomas, "The Socio-behavioral Approach: Illustrations and Analysis," In Thomas, ed., The Socio-behavioral Approach and Applications to Social Work (New York: Council on Social Work Education, in press). For two relevant statements applicable to interpersonal helping, see Richard B. Stuart, "Applications of Behavior Theory to Social Casework," in ibid.; and Sheldon D. Rose, "A Behavioral Approach to Group Treatment of Children," in ibid.

6.   For some contemporary examples of classifications of
     techniques for behavioral therapy, see Grossberg,
     op. cit.; Eysenck and Rachman, op. cit.; and Arthur
     W. Staats and Carolyn K. Staats, Complex Human
     Behavior: A Systematic Extension of Learning Princi-
     ples (New York: Holt, Rinehart & Winston, 1964),
     pp. 465-512.

7.   The relevance of these observations to remedial action
     should be apparent, but the question sometimes arises
     concerning whether the problems of prevention can be
     handled in this way. The writer believes that they
     can, provided one acknowledges that intervention in
     the present, directed toward such matters as prevent-
     ing the occurrence of a future problem, must necess-
     arily involve some behaviorally active features in the
     present; these present interventions would appear to
     be nothing other than behavioral acquisition, strengthen-
     ing, maintenance, weakening, or elimination.

8.   Although there are other classes of behavior, such as
     the instinctual, the differences between operant and
     respondent behavior are well established and the
     principles for these two realms of behavior are
     different. For a good discussion of these matters,
     see Thom Verhave, "An Introduction to the Experi-
     mental Analysis of Behavior," in Verhave, ed.,
     The Experimental Analysis of Behavior: Selected
     Readings (New York: Appleton-Century, Crofts, 1966),
     pp. 1-47. It is essential to acknowledge that despite
     the importance of the differences between the operant
     and respondent realms of behavior, there would appear
     to be at least some interrelationships. For more de-
     tails see H. D. Kimmel, "Instrumental Conditioning of
     Autonomically Mediated Behavior," Psychological
     Bulletin, Vol. 67, No. 5 (May 1967), pp. 337-346;
     and Robert A. Rescorla and Richard L. Solomon,
     "Two-Process Learning Theory: Relationships between
     Pavlovian Conditioning and Instrumental Learning,"
     Psychological Review, Vol. 74, No. 3 (May 1967),
     pp. 151-183.

9.   For a succinct summary of the principles of operant
     conditioning, see Verhave, op. cit. More detailed
     reviews on specialized subjects in operant behavior
     are to be found in Werner K. Honig, ed., Operant
     Behavior: Areas of Research and Application (New

York: Appleton-Century-Crofts, 1966). Among the
basic secondary sources here are Fred S. Keller and
William N. Schoenfeld, Principles of Psychology: A
Systematic Text in the Science of Behavior (New York:
Appleton-Century-Crofts, 1950); B. F. Skinner,
Science and Human Behavior (New York: Macmillan
Co. , 1953); Honig, op. cit. ; and Staats and Staats,
op. cit. For more elementary statements see, for
example, Fred S. Keller, Learning: Reinforcement
Theory (New York: Random House, 1954), and the
beginning lectures for social workers on this subject
by Edwin J. Thomas in Thomas and Esther Goodman,
eds. , Socio-behavioral Theory and Interpersonal Helping in Social Work: Lectures and Institute Proceedings
(Ann Arbor: Campus Publishers, 1965).

10.   E. L. Thorndike, Fundamentals of Learning (New York:
      Teachers College, Columbia University, 1932).

11.   Gaylord L. Thorne, Roland G. Tharp, and Ralph J.
      Wetzel, "Behavioral Modification Techniques: New
      Tools for Probation Officers, " Federal Probation,
      Vol. 31, No. 2 (June 1967), pp. 21-27.

12.   T. Ayllon and F. Haughton, "Control of the Behavior
      of Schizophrenics by Food, " in Arthur W. Staats, ed. ,
      Human Learning: Studies Extending Conditioning Princi-
      ples to Complex Behavior (New York: Holt, Rinehart
      & Winston, 1962), pp. 458-465.

13.   For a review of these studies, see Leonard Krasner,
      "Studies of the Conditioning of Verbal Behavior, "
      Psychological Bulletin, Vol. 55, No. 3 (May 1958),
      pp. 121-148.

14.   A basic research report on tokens is to be found in
      Teodoro Ayllon and Nathan H. Azrin, "The Measure-
      ment and Reinforcement of Behavior of Psychotics, "
      Journal of the Experimental Analysis of Behavior,
      Vol. 8, No. 6 (November 1965), pp. 357-385.

15.   An introduction to schedules may be found in texts such
      as Staats and Staats, op. cit. , pp. 61-70; more de-
      tailed treatment is found in C. B. Ferster and B. F.
      Skinner, Schedules of Reinforcement (New York:
      Appleton-Century-Crofts, 1957).

16. In this context we shall speak of extinction as a means to eliminate behavior. Although extinction involves one type of reinforcement schedule--namely, the special case of no reinforcement--it is related to positive reinforcement only in this way.

17. See, for example, Ferster and Skinner, op. cit.

18. For a fascinating report, see the description of the study by O. R. Lindsley, B. F. Skinner, and H. C. Solomon, September 1955-November 1956, referred to in Murray Sidman, "Operant Techniques, " in Arthur J. Bachrach, ed. , Experimental Foundations of Clinical Psychology (New York: Basic Books, 1962), pp. 202-203.

19. The writer is referring here to research on reinforcing activities and the so-called Premack Principle.   See David Premack, "Reinforcement Theory, " in David Levine, ed. , Nebraska Symposium on Motivation (Lincoln: University of Nebraska Press, 1965), pp. 123-180.

20. Teodoro Ayllon and Jack Michael, "The Psychiatric Nurse as a Behavioral Engineer, " Journal of the Experimental Analysis of Behavior, Vol. 2, No. 4 (October 1959), pp. 323-334.

21. A case from the Hartwig Project, Neighborhood Service. Organization, Detroit, Mich.   The author is indebted to Sheldon Rose, research director, for permission to cite this case.

22. R. R. Schwitzgebel and D. A. Kolb, "Inducing Behavior Change in Adolescent Delinquents, " Behavior Research and Therapy, Vol. 1, No. 4 (March 1964), pp. 297-304.

23. Sidman, op. cit. , pp. 173-174.

24. Vernon O. Tyler, Jr. , and G. Duane Brown, "The Use of Swift, Brief Isolation as a Group Control Device for Institutionalized Delinquents, " Behaviour Research and Therapy, Vol. 5, No. 1 (February 1967), pp. 1-11.

25. N. H. Azrin and W. C. Holz, "Punishment, " in Honig, op. cit. , p. 381.

26. Ibid. For details, see especially pp. 438-441.

27. W. C. Holz and N. H. Azrin, "A Comparison of Several Procedures for Eliminating Behavior, " Journal of the Experimental Analysis of Behavior, Vol. 6, No. 3 (July 1963), pp. 399-406.

28. Among recent reviews of interest are Azrin and Holz, op. cit. ; Richard L. Solomon, "Punishment, " American Psychologist, Vol. 19, No. 4 (April 1964), pp. 239-254; R. M. Church, "The Varied Effects of Punishment on Behavior, " Psychological Review, Vol. 70, No. 5 (September 1963), pp. 369-402; and Malcolm Kushner and Jack Sandler, "Aversion Therapy and the Concept of Punishment, " Behaviour Research and Therapy, Vol. 4, No. 3 (August 1966), pp. 179-187.

29. Azrin and Holz, op. cit. , pp. 439-440.

30. For examples, see C. Quarti and J. Renaud, "A New Treatment of Constipation by Conditioning: A Preliminary Report, " in Cyril M. Franks, ed. , Conditioning Techniques in Clinical Practice and Research (New York: Springer Publishing Co. , 1964), pp. 219-227.

31. See, for example, Cyril M. Franks, "Alcohol, Alcoholism and Conditioning: A Review of the Literature and Some Theoretical Considerations, " in Hans J. Eysenck, ed. , Behavior Therapy and the Neuroses (New York: Pergamon Press, 1960), pp. 278-302.

32. Joseph Wolpe, Psychotherapy by Reciprocal Inhibition (Stanford: Stanford University Press, 1958); a more recent statement is in Wolpe and Lazarus, op. cit.

33. For relevant empirical reports, see Robert A. Hogan and John H. Kirchner, "Preliminary Report of the Extinction of Learned Fears via Short-Term Implosive Therapy, " Journal of Abnormal Psychology, Vol. 72, No. 2 (April 1967), pp. 106-110; and Stanley Rachman, "Studies in Desensitization--II. Flooding, " Behavior Research and Therapy, Vol. 4, No. 1 pp. 1-7.

34. For example, see G. F. J. Lehner, "Negative Practice as a Therapeutic Technique," in Eysenck, ed., Behavior Therapy and the Neuroses, pp. 194-206.

35. For a practice example see Teodoro Ayllon, "Intensive Treatment of Psychotic Behavior by Stimulus Satiation and Food Reinforcement," in Leonard P. Ullmann and Leonard Krasner, eds., Case Studies in Behavior Modification (New York: Holt, Rinehart & Winston, 1965), pp. 77-84; for a comparative research study on the effectiveness of satiation and other behavior-reductive procedures see Holz and Azrin, op. cit.

36. A recent experimental study is reported by Murray Sidman and Lawrence T. Stoddard, "The Effectiveness of Fading in Programming a Simultaneous Form Dis-crimination for Retarded Children," Journal of the Experimental Analysis of Behavior, Vol. 10, No. 1 (January 1967), pp. 3-17.

37. An example of the explication of selected features of verbal instructions is in J. Stacy Adams and A. Kimball Romney, "A Functional Analysis of Authority," Psychological Review, Vol. 66, No. 4 (July 1959), pp. 234-251; see also Staats and Staats, op. cit., pp. 185-199 and 321-324. For a socio-behavioral procedure that draws heavily on verbal instructions see Richard B. Stuart, "Behavioral Control of Over-eating," Behaviour Research and Therapy, in press.

38. For selected examples and procedures see Raymond Corsini, with the assistance of Samuel Cardone, Roleplaying in Psychotherapy: A Manual (Chicago: Aldine Publishing Co., 1966).

39. For a procedure and rationale useful for parents see Judith M. Smith and Donald E. P. Smith, Child Management: A Program for Parents (Ann Arbor: Ann Arbor Publishers, 1966); for theoretical factors relating to prescriptive phenomena see Edwin J. Thomas and Bruce J. Biddle, "Basic Concepts for Classifying the Phenomena of Role," in Biddle and Thomas, eds., Role Theory: Concepts and Research (New York: John Wiley & Sons, 1966), pp. 26-28. The technique of rule-making, to the writer's know-ledge, has not been identified as a technique in prior writing. This technique along with position structur-

ing, likewise a "new technique, " will be explicated, with the other techniques, in a book on sociobehavioral theory currently in preparation by the author.

40. A recent statement addressed to an explication of aspects of imitation is in Albert Bandura, "Vicarious Processes: A Case of No-Trial Learning, " in Leonard Berkowitz, ed. , Advances in Experimental Social Psychology, Vol. 2 (New York: Academic Press, 1966), pp. 3-48.

41. For an example of position change for the "dingup" see William Crain, "The Chronic 'Mess-Up' and His Changing Character, " Federal Probation, Vol. 28, No. 2 (June 1964), pp. 50-56; for a discussion of role factors that one would have to consider in changing a deviant position see, for example, Edwin J. Thomas, "Role Problems of Offenders and Correctional Workers, " Crime and Delinquency, Vol. 12, No. 4 (October 1966), pp. 354-365; for a discussion of role modification and adjustment see Henry S. Maas, Building Social Work Theory with Social Science Tools: The Concept of Role, Special Report No. 41 (Los Angeles: Welfare Planning Council, Los Angeles Region, 1954).

42. For example, stimulus change, physical force, and deprivation are among other possible candidates.

43. This section was taken, with some modification, from a portion of a lecture by the author, prepared in writing with the assistance of Esther Goodman, in Edwin J. Thomas and Esther Goodman, eds. , Sociobehavioral Theory and Interpersonal Helping in Social Work--Lectures and Institute Proceedings (Ann Arbor: Campus Publishers, 1965), pp. 8-9.

Chapter 8

Application of Small Groups to
Casework Practice and Theory

by Leslie Rosenthal

Five mothers are seated around a table with a caseworker in a child guidance agency. For about the first twenty
minutes of the session four of them have been freely ex-
changing accounts of some of their children's recent experiences and their own maternal reactions. Mrs.
Moore indignantly reports that her daughter was called
'moron' by a teacher and vigorously announces her in-
tention of going to the school to discuss this.

Mrs. Weiss, the fifth member, silent until this
point, then critically expresses her annoyance with
the 'petty' nature of the discussion. The other
group members react sharply, led by Mrs. Shaw
who retorts caustically, 'Any problem raised by anyone but yourself is petty!'

Mrs. Weiss counters with, 'I've passed the stage of talking only about my children here.' Mrs. Moore suggests
tartly, 'Perhaps you're too advanced for this group.'

An uneasy silence descends on the group. The case-
worker-group leader suggests that the members are
in the grip of strong feelings which they are not
expressing. Mrs. Weiss says she knows why she
was so critical before. She proceeds to explain
that Mrs. Moore's protective handling of her daughter
had recalled the crudely aggressive manner in which
her own mother handled such situations, storming
into the classroom and shrieking at the teachers.
Mrs. Weiss adds to Mrs. Moore, 'In a way, I became your daughter and you were like my mother.'

As discussion continues, Mrs. Shaw sits silently
fuming. When the group leader elicits her feelings,

Mrs. Shaw literally bursts out with the accusation
that Mrs. Weiss is continually attacking her, whereas
she had seemed so warm and friendly when she,
Mrs. Shaw, had first entered the group.   When the
group leader observes that Mrs. Shaw seems to feel
betrayed in some way by Mrs. Weiss, she eagerly
confirms this and adds that she feels badly when
Mrs. Weiss acts insensitively toward other group
members as well.

Mrs. Weiss seems surprised by the strength of Mrs.
Shaw's feelings toward her.   Mrs. Moore comments,
'I have a feeling that we're like a family here, like
a bunch of sisters expressing their feelings toward
each other. '   After a short pause, Mrs. Shaw says
thoughtfully, 'I know; she (Weiss) is my mother
here. '

In the concluding minutes the group members respond
to the leader's invitation to evaluate the session.
Mrs. Shaw remarks with satisfaction, 'I know this
was a helpful meeting because for once I expressed
my feelings instead of keeping them inside. '

The preceding digest of a group therapy session illustrates a development which has burgeoned in social work
settings since World War II, namely the wide and varied
use of small groups in clinical casework practice.

A group has been defined as "a plurality of individuals
who are in contact with one another, who take one another
into account, and who are aware of some significant commonality" (1).   As this definition indicates, a basically
distinguishing feature of a group is that its members have
something in common and that this commonality is significant to them.   Common tasks, interests, beliefs, ancestry,
territorial origin and many more features may serve as
bases of meaningful ties among group members.   In some
groups members display intense mutual attachment; in others
members cohere only tenuously.   It is apparent that there
is a broad spectrum along which a large number of groups
can be located depending upon the varied shadings of the
above characteristics and areas of perceived commonality.

The term "group, " then, has been variously classified
on the basis of certain aspects and qualities of the relations
prevailing among group members.   This is reflected in the

well-known dichotomy of "primary" and "secondary" groups. As originally conceived by the American sociologist, Charles H. Cooley (1909), primary group members have warm, intimate, personal ties with one another and share common goals in small group, face-to-face settings. The family, the gang and the friendship group have been cited as foremost examples of the primary group. In secondary groups, relations among members are formalized, contractual and comparatively impersonal. These groups are typically large and intra-group contact is usually intermittent, as in a labor union or statewide professional association.

For the purposes of this chapter, the relevant group is the small group with the classical features of the primary group. Olmstead (2) has stated, "While it is a fruitless task to try to define a small group in terms of numbers, we may suppose that approximately twenty persons represent the upper limit of small group size, with two being the lower limit. " In the group modalities to be described in this chapter, a numerical ceiling of ten is applicable; most therapeutic groups are smaller, as revealed in the survey of American group therapists by Winick, Kadis and Krasner (1961), which indicated a median range of six to eight.

It is axiomatic that the 20th Century has become group-minded. A variety of disciplines--sociology, social psychology--have studied group functioning and produced valuable data. Groups were seen as worth study because they are significant settings for individual behavior and constitute micro-societies where individuals can be observed in social interaction.

The work of Kurt Lewin (1951) in developing ingenious theoretical concepts and experimental models for the study of group functioning ushered in the new field of group dynamics. Lewin advanced as a basic tool for the analysis of group life the perception of the group and its setting as a "social field. " "This means that the social happening is viewed as occurring in, and being the result of, a totality of co-existing social entities such as groups, sub-groups, members, barriers, channels of communication, etc. One of the fundamental characteristics of this field is the relative position of the entities which are parts of the field. This relative position represents the structure of the group and its ecological setting" (3).

The work of the group dynamicists has been character-

ized by the experimental method involving a systematic
manipulation of group variables under controlled conditions.
Such studies necessitated the development of a methodology
for the observation, description and measurement of relevant
dimensions of group structure and functioning. Rating scales
and category systems have emerged as two principal ways
of observing significant group behavior. One of the observational systems most widely known and used is "Interaction Process Analysis" as developed by Bales (1950).
This system involves a standard set of twelve categories
for classifying interaction in any group in respect to emotionally positive responses, emotionally negative responses,
and problem-solving responses. The categories cover the
range of individual behavior from positive praise for others'
contributions to attacking antagonism toward others. The
observer must classify each act (verbal and non-verbal) of
each group member into one of the categories.

A key concept around which a good part of small group
research has centered is that of cohesion, defined as "the
total field of forces which act on members to remain in the
group" (4). Cohesion has been defined and measured in
terms of sociometric friendship choices (Moreno, 1934),
the frequency with which members say "we" as compared to
"I," the degree to which they share norms, and the rate of
absenteeism. Some of the conditions shown empirically to
have enhanced cohesiveness are:

1) Satisfaction of common individual needs for protection, security and affection.

2) Predominance of positive affective ties.

3) Shared ideals and interests.

4) An atmosphere of equality (a democratic as
   distinguished from an authoritarian of laissez-
   faire climate).

5) Group prestige.

6) Symbolic group ceremonials and activities.

7) Common enemies outside the group.

Freud (1922) offered a formulation of group cohesiveness
in the statement that "the essence of a group lies in the

libidinal ties existing in it"--that the members' feelings
toward the leader bind them to him, to each other, and
thus to the group. Freud also offered a theory of instinctively endowed aggression and indicated that intimate
emotional relationships between people are characterized by
the presence of love and hate feelings. Aggression, hostility and ambivalence can then function as group disruptive
elements, just as positive libidinal ties among members can
operate toward cohesion. This polarity of forces which
tend to bring group members together and to rend them
asunder has been described by Spotnitz (1947) who used the
concepts of the "reproductive" and the "inadequacy constellations" in a significant paper on emotional currents in
adolescent girls' interview groups.

Factors endangering group cohesion have been cited by
Schiedlinger (1952):

1) The uninhibited expression of drives (aggressive
or sexual, or both).

2) Marked egocentricity in individual members.

3) Extreme competitiveness and jealousy.

4) Excessive negative transference reactions.

5) Excessive frustration originating from the leader
or the group code.

Any one or a combination of these factors can lead to
disruption in group functioning and to varied symptoms of
group pathology, such as prolonged and intense bickering,
scapegoating, passive resistance, absenteeism and premature
termination. It is obvious that understanding of the factors
involved in cohesiveness-disruption are crucial for the
selection of group members and for the development of that
climate most conducive to the attainment of mutually agreed
upon goals. Awareness of the factors which enhance or
strain group cohesiveness is necessary to the small group
leader in the face of such questions as to whether he should
include highly sadistic and masochistic individuals and the
number of highly aggressive or markedly withdrawn members his group can assimilate.

That groups satisfy basic human needs to belong--what
Slavson termed "social hunger"--is axiomatic. The "gifts

of the group" have been eloquently delineated by Troop:

> Belonging implies acceptance by others, and that
> acceptance is a basic kind of affection from one's
> fellow human beings.   To be in a group also means
> having opportunities for self-expression under circum-
> stances in which others can appreciate it, so that it
> becomes achievement and brings recognition--and
> these are great supporters and strengtheners of that
> precious feeling of self-worth so necessary for men-
> tal health.   Finally, to be in a group means having
> the opportunity to that important communal balance
> of freedom and limitation, which is at the root of
> social responsibility.
>
> The group is not only an alliance through which
> normal needs can be met; it can also be a natural
> healer of hurts, a supporter of strengths and a clari-
> fier of problems.   It may serve as a sounding board
> for expressions of anxiety, hostility or guilt.   It often
> turns out that group members learn that others in the
> group have similar feelings weighing them down in
> their aloneness, that they are not so different or so
> alone--and learning this in live confrontation with
> one's peers is a most powerful change-inducing ex-
> perience (5).

Use of Small Groups in Clinical Settings

The use of the small group in partnership with the casework process was foreseen by Mary Richmond, who said at
the National Conference of Social Work in 1920:

> This brings me to a tendency in modern casework
> which I seem to have noted and noted with great
> pleasure.   It is one which is full of promises, I
> believe, for the future of social treatment.   I refer
> to the new tendency to view our clients from the
> angle of what might be termed small group psychol-
> ogy. . . Halfway between the minute analysis of the
> individual situation with which we are all familiar in
> casework, and the kind of sixth sense of neighbor-
> hood standards and backgrounds which is developed
> in a good settlement, there is a field as yet almost
> unexplored.

Some experimentation in the use of groups appeared quite early in several of the social agency settings that later developed social group work. Konopka (1956) has reported that Hull House brought together a group of youthful drug addicts in 1909 and also experimented with housing groups of the mentally ill.

A salient event in the "developmental history" of the application of small groups to casework practice was the introduction of Activity Group Therapy at the Jewish Board of Guardians in the mid 1930's. This was a response to a number of factors: the continuing impact of psychoanalysis and its dramatic elucidation of the developmental stages of childhood; the use in progressive education of psychoanalytically-derived principles which emphasized the release and satisfaction to be attained in free and spontaneous group activity; the fortuitous encounter between the creative personality of Slavson and an agency climate which encouraged experimentation and inventiveness in therapeutic method (6).

With specific reference to Activity Group Therapy, Slavson notes that an evaluation of treatment needs impressed the agency staff that some form of social treatment was essential (7). A considerable number of children, either because of over-aggressive behavior or because of timidity and fearfulness were unable to adjust to neighborhood play groups or to recreational centers. It was also recognized that there were individual children unable, for a variety of reasons, to establish a treatment relation within the confines of the traditional casework setting and for whom a diluted relation, such as a group supplies, was indicated.

Geared selectively to children in the latency period, Activity Group Therapy utilized a distinctly permissive small group atmosphere (5-8 members) to provide a healing and emotionally corrective group experience for the personally troubled and socially maladjusted. In this setting group members are permitted to discharge pent-up feelings and to express their constructive and destructive impulses. Expressions of anti-social behavior and negative feeling are neither condemned nor condoned but rather are understood as expressive of related emotional stresses.

Activity Group Therapy primarily serves ego reinforcing and ego building ends. It addresses itself particularly to those lags in ego development resulting from devaluated self-image, inadequate and faulty models of identification and blockage of strivings toward self-assertive, independent and spontaneous functioning. The total situation is designed to provide substitute and corrective gratification; to permit release of suppressed aggressiveness and tension and to enhance self-esteem through acceptance and individuation within a second family of "parent" and peers. In child guidance settings it has continued to be a highly effective small group instrument for activating withdrawn and constricted personalities; for providing a nurturing experience in familial acceptance for those defeated in their real families; for offering a road back to childhood for those too-adult youngsters (the worried "little old men") who have been forced prematurely to renounce childhood. For the schizoid child the group is a living spectacle in which, from a relatively safe position on its emotional periphery, he can observe the feeling experiences of others; watchfully test the adult's reactions to his peers and attain vicarious catharsis from the myriad emotional transactions of the group until such time as he is ready to take his own tentative steps toward involvement. For children whose difficulties center around sibling rivalries, there are obvious advantages to a treatment setting featuring the presence of substitute siblings with whom the family drama can be reenacted. Because it utilizes a permissive and unstructured setting, this treatment milieu is counterindicated for those children lacking minimal impulse controls--those who need limits and structure rather than license (8).

In response to the needs of different clients with varied problems, the original structure and technique of Activity Group Therapy were modified. At the Jewish Board of Guardians several types of groups evolved: play groups for pre-school children, activity-interview groups and interview groups for adolescents, therapy groups for mothers and parent guidance groups.

In the play groups, five to six children under six years of age have free access to play materials appropriate for their age and sex. The children play almost wholly on a fantasy level, revealing in their play and interaction their inner tensions, hostilities toward parents and siblings, and misconceptions of life processes. The group leader uses appropriate incidents in the life of the group to interpret the child's behavior to him and to help him toward accepting, understanding and controlling inner impulses. Since children this young need help in the containment of impulses, the expression of aggression in this type of group is limited and conditioned, unlike that in Activity Group Therapy.

Activity-interview groups partly resemble activity groups, but differ in that a direct verbal method involving exploration and interpretation is employed. These groups were initially developed for neurotic children in the latency period (Gabriel, 1939).

The adolescent's conflicts around adult authority and his intense need for the acceptance of his peers led naturally to the development of small group modalities for adolescents in many agencies serving families and youth. In discussing the needs of children and adolescents for group affiliation, Buxbaum (9) has stated: "Whereas the young child finds in the group support for his new-found physical independence from the mother, the adolescent finds reassurance for his moral independence from home. Both child and adolescent feel deserted, ousted from the protective atmosphere upon which they used to rely and not yet sure enough to face the world alone. The group is a highly welcome shelter in the meantime." Interview groups in which members are encouraged to share their feelings with each other are the most commonly encountered small group instrument used with adolescents. When, through the efforts of the group leader, the proper emotional climate is developed, these groups offer highly benevolent settings for their members. Adolescents are understandably concerned with the peer and heterosexual relationships, anxieties around sexual feeling and behavior, emancipation from parents with the attendant rebellion, regression and wavering between childhood and maturity. These areas dominate their group discussions. One of these major themes--conflict with authority--is clearly discernible in the seventh session of a group of 15-17 year old boys and girls who have been meeting weekly in a child guidance setting:

> Hannah began by voicing her unhappiness about a situation at school where her English teacher was insisting on her entering an honor class. Hannah was reluctant because she was already in three other accelerated classes.

> Della asked why Hannah couldn't just tell the teacher that she'd take the courses she herself preferred.

> Phil bragged that he carries six majors. He then reported an incident where he and a friend sat in an

unoccupied car and were reported to the Principal.
He also recounted having had a fight with his mother,
who struck him when he answered her back and
spoke of wanting to get rid of him via one of the
military services.   Phil said he was furious.   When
the therapist asked what he did with his feelings in
the situation, he replied 'I ate them. '

Andy described his mother acting unreasonably and
indicated that when angered, he slams doors.   Hannah
said that when her mother is angry she stays out of
her way.   She also does not talk to her (younger)
sister whom she hates.   Hannah added that in general
she is very quiet in her own home.   Della suggested
that Hannah could retaliate against her parents by
acting like 'Dennis the Menace. '   Hannah continued
that she does not mind not talking too much and
noted that for a long time she couldn't even talk to
her individual worker.   To this Della commented,
'I suspect that you took the easy way out of your
problems. '

Della described that on her recent birthday, her older
sister and future brother-in-law took her out to din-
ner.   However, they insisted on Chinese food rather
than acceding to her wishes and she reacted by sitting
silently in the restaurant and refusing to eat.

Phil returned to describing his mother, stressing her
rigid and dictatorial attitudes which render it impossible for him to discuss anything with her.   Andy
eagerly interjected that he too can never convince
his parents of anything.

Hannah voiced her unhappiness--she has nothing to
look forward to.   Phil said he felt like Hannah because he is so miserable with his mother--he would
give the therapist 'or anybody' a million dollars to
help him get rid of her.   Andy hastily stated that he
wouldn't want to get rid of his mother.

Della suggested that Phil could put a poisonous snake
in his mother's bed.   Andy offered that Phil should
act very nicely to his mother for several weeks and
then put oxygen or leprosy bacteria in her blood 'and
no one will suspect you. '

The session ended as the members continued semi-
humorously to offer further advice to Phil as to how
he could eliminate his mother.

Here, early in the life of this group, mutually shared
defenses of projection, denial and avoidance of examining
their own roles produce a session of complaint, frustration
by and hostility toward insensitive parental (authority)
figures. Each member also describes his own unique way
of expressing his hostility.

In the group's 12th session we see the unfolding of
members' life stories, vividly marked by a theme of aban-
donment and deprivation at early ages. As accompaniment
to the major theme, there is a motif of improper behavior
(stealing, permitting pick-ups). The members seem to be
saying, in effect: "Because we were not taken care of properly
and given enough as little children, we do not behave properly or self-advantageously now. " Excerpts from this 12th
session follow:

> Dan, a new member, was present for his second
> session. He spoke of his wish to become a lawyer,
> explaining that he was interested in anything having
> to do with 'defense. ' Phil showed interest in Dan
> and asked some questions about ambition. Phil then
> said that he felt lost and referred to continuing ten-
> sion with his mother who is constantly critical of him
> and whom he can never please. He did not think it
> had anything to do with his past.

> After a moment Phil recalled that when he was four
> he heard his mother say that when he was a baby,
> he once rolled off the bed and into an open dresser
> drawer so that he was not found for a little while.
> He also recalled hearing a similar story--when he
> was one year old his bed was used for the coats of
> guests at a party and he was completely covered over
> for a while.

> Hannah remembered being sent to kindergarten when
> she was only four years old. Her mother deposited
> her and then rushed home to take care of Hannah's
> baby sister. She recalled that at age three she hit
> her sister over the head with a doll. She continued
> that her hearing disability began in her sixth year.
> She offered another memory from age three and a

half: her father had bought a new car and offered
the whole family a ride but Hannah could not go because of an earache.   She felt very hurt and rejected.

Dan described that when he was four his mother had
to go to a sanitarium and he was placed first with
one aunt and then with another.   His mother has said
that he cried constantly in her absence.   He thinks
he had a recurrent dream at that time of being in a
cave where he was menaced by wolves.   He also reported several other frightening dreams.

Phil suggested that Dan seemed guilty about something.   Dan agreed that he did have a lot of guilt
feeling especially in relation to his father who died
four years previously of cancer.   During the father's
final illness, Dan stole and sold his prized coin col-
lection.   He also stole money from his grandfather
and from the 5 & 10 cent store.

Phil indicated that he too stole, having gone on forays
to stores with a group of boys.   He added wryly,
'As usual, I was the only one who got caught. '

Dan told of spending 'nine-tenths' of his time at
school day-dreaming about sex.   Hannah described
permitting a boy to pick her up on the beach and
then told of having spoken insultingly to a teacher,
thus endangering her chances of passing that course.

Dan (perhaps unconsciously speaking for the whole
group at this point) thoughtfully recalled that his
former individual therapist had once said that Dan is
seeking to destroy himself slowly.

As a group matures and as the members concurrently
develop trust in each other, they reveal and seek help with
their nuclear problems.   The therapeutic process is intensified with the examination of sub-surface motivations for behavior and the unique dynamics of the individual emerges
from the common matrix of the group.

In accordance with the original emphasis on the mother-
child relation in child guidance, groups of mothers were
among the first organized by casework agencies (Durkin,
Glatzer and Hirsch, 1944; Kolodney, 1944; Durkin, 1954).
As agencies began more to welcome fathers in the intake and

treatment processes, group approaches specifically designed
for fathers appeared. In some settings groups involving
both parents were employed. The development of interest
in working with fathers in groups is suggested in the fact
that at the Jewish Board of Guardians in 1955 there were
two fathers' groups as compared to seven in 1961.

The basic approach utilized with fathers, a child-centered and guidance framework, is to involve passive, withdrawn and isolated fathers. The stated aim in a guidance
group is to increase the parental adequacy in everyday relationships with the child by sensitizing parents to the needs,
motivations and developmental norms of children through
discussion of problems and conflicts in the parent-child interaction. The offer of such a group, with its premise that
children are difficult to understand and deal with, and its
code of seeking to understand children's behavior, seems to
support much-needed defenses against paternal feelings of
damage, inadequacy and impotence. For many fathers the
offer or recommendation that they become involved in individual casework treatment seems to be perceived by them
as an accusation and demand for change. In an outstanding
paper on this method Strean (10) notes the positive initial
responses of fathers to the group as reflected in some of
the comments in the group: "If I want to talk, I can talk.
If I want to listen, I listen. " "What a good way to get
away from the wife and kids for the night, smoke a cigar
and relax. " "It's always good to know that other guys have
these troubles too. "

Early sessions of these groups are consistently marked
by projection of responsibility for the children's problems
onto school and television. This dominant early theme is
accompanied by any number of open or thinly disguised
protests against the incessant demandingness of children.
In effect, the group members thus convey to the group leader
their unreadiness for demands from him that they function
more responsibly as fathers. Not infrequently, the group
will present its own needs--its wishes to be given to like
little children--by concentrating on the oral habit disorders
of children. Thus, thumb-sucking and nail-biting are popular topics. When the leader is responsive to this need and
gives information about this particular mode of emotional
expression in children, he is at the same time offering an
emotional demonstration to the fathers of how to respond to
this symptom in their children. As the group leader con-
veys that he is not the child's advocate in court and that he

is accepting of all kinds of feeling toward children, group expression becomes freer and resentment against children, wives, the agency and group leader follows. Members also begin to offer reality checks upon unhealthy paternal behavior in each other. Thus, when one father presented an obviously seductive relationship with a son, another commented: "I think you're carrying palship a little too far." Another father, given to using his own illnesses as emotional blackmail to attain conforming behavior from his children, was told by a fellow member, "Now all you have to do is get cancer and you'll have perfect kids!"

Problems such as bed-wetting, stealing, sibling rivalry, demandingness, masturbation, dawdling and thumb-sucking are major subjects of group discussion and are frequently beneficently affected by wiser parental handling. In an atmosphere blending therapy and education, parents gain awareness of the significant emotional differences between children and adults and are given specific tools and approaches for enhancing familial living (11).

Analytic, or therapy groups, as an interpretive arena with an emphasis on the exploration and expression of feeling and the attainment of self-awareness, constitute a major group treatment tool for addressing the close relation between the behavior of children and their parents' underlying conflicts. This method, illustrated at the beginning of this chapter, has been especially effective with individuals whose character resistances, needs to defeat authority, or inability to assimilate the undiluted intensity of the one-to-one casework relation have contributed to considerable difficulty and frequent treatment impasses. In the child guidance area these groups have been found to be especially indicated for those parents who, unable directly and appropriately to express aggression and negative feeling, unconsciously use their children as instruments of and spokesmen for their own repressed aggressivity.

A basic dynamic of the group treatment structure resides in the opportunities for the establishment of multiple transferences wherein other members are the objects of feeling and attitudes held in earlier life situations toward crucial family members. Those "multi-dimensional" aspects of the group setting are depicted in the opening pages of this chapter as the members of the therapy group re-experience feelings toward their mothers.

A considerable segment of the application of social casework methods in the group setting falls under the heading of "group counseling." In addressing itself to specific adjustment problems of familial living, group counseling uses similarity of situational conflict and similarity of functioning in areas of ego intactness as a basis for selection of members. A generally positive atmosphere, opportunities for members to identify and derive support from each other, and a focus on relationship patterns rather than interpretation of feelings, are some of the major facets of the group counseling method (12). Its basic approach is toward constructive adjustment and adaptation rather than personality reconstruction. Group counseling can be applied to all areas of familial living; groups can be composed of adolescents, parents, wives, husbands, marital couples, the aged, and most recently, whole families.

The dynamics of the analytic therapy groups involve the attainment of insight through the reliving of early traumata and experience via regression within the multiple transference relations within the group. Group guidance and group counseling, the ego (group) therapies, feature release, identification, increased understanding, strengthening of the self-image and identification. These boundaries are by no means immutable or sacrosanct. A therapy group may function for sessions on a guidance level; guidance groups will not infrequently take cognizance of the interactive patterns of its members and hitherto repressed material may at times emerge. Groups have often begun on a declared guidance level and, in time, have plumbed deeper levels as members have attained security and strength in the group setting.

A use of the group setting which should not be overlooked is that of facilitating a psychosocial diagnosis and sound treatment planning. In situations where adequate historical and descriptive material pertaining to behavior patterns is not available, referral to a group offers a valuable arena for the assessment of an individual's basic ego strengths, weighing of adaptive capacities and identification of basic treatment needs. Some agencies have experimented with screening and intake groups which meet for a specified number of sessions and provide diagnostic material upon which treatment plans for all group members can be based (Ginott, 1956).

Some additional uses of the group setting apply to situa-

tions where a period of individual treatment has successfully
dealt with basic problems.   A group experience can then be
used for weaning purposes, for testing the solidity of the
achieved gains and for integration of the acquired adjustive
capacities.

Cutting across differences in the approaches, goals and
methodologies of the wide spectrum of groups employed in
social agency settings are the related and basic elements
common to all of them:

1)   The group is a symbolic family.   In it the individual
group member repeats his familial adaptive pattern, faith-
fully reenacting the role he played or had thrust upon him
by psychological exigency in the very first group of which
he was a member.   Thus, the individual who was physically
or psychologically expelled from his first family will be
difficult to contain in a group because of the need to master
the original trauma of expulsion by repeatedly courting it
again.   As a familial arena the group automatically involves
exposure to the immediate presence of siblings with whom
therapist and time must be shared.   Concurrently, it also
offers a more diluted relation to the therapist-parent figure
than does the one-to-one treatment setting.   For the withdrawn, the guarded, the suspicious and constricted individuals, the presence of others is a boon.   They can be
silent, non-giving and uncommunicative without creating a
therapeutic impasse.   They can sit in relative security and
hear others express with impunity the very feelings they
have had to contain all their lives.   For these members the
benefits of derivative insight and vicarious catharsis are
obvious.   For others with different histories, the group becomes a battleground where their drives toward the exclusion of siblings are enacted and where their egocentricity
and narcissism face the reality impact of social living.   For
the too fearful, for those bereft of even minimal satisfactions
in their original families, the group family may pose dangers
and present realities too harsh for undeveloped ego struc-
tures--it is apparent that the group setting cannot duplicate
the security, protection and control of variables which is
available in the casework dyad.

2)   The "multi-dimensional" aspects, described earlier,
which involve the network of sibling and parental transferences which develop within the group and which strongly
influence the nature and emotional texture of the members'
relationship toward each other.

3) An emphasis on learning through emotional impact
and feeling interaction rather than the step-by-step learning
of individual behavior patterns which frequently is the product
of the one-to-one setting. In the group the fluidity and
multiplicity of emotional forces present can at times make a
kind of emotional awareness arising from the group suddenly
holding up a mirror in which the individual for the first
time sees his patterns reflected.

> In a counseling group session, Mrs. Sanders stresses
> the stimulating intellectual exchanges she has with
> her husband; animatedly describes the books they
> have read and discussed; the opinions on world affairs
> they have shared. In her description she uses such
> words as 'supercilious,' 'extraneous,' 'repercussions,'
> 'empathic.' The other members are silent and an
> atmosphere of gloom pervades the group. The leader
> elicits the reactions of the group. Mrs. Weiss re-
> sponds sadly that for her the session just strengthened
> her feelings of disappointment in her own unachieving
> and non-intellectual husband. Mrs. Marks indicates,
> 'I just feel so inadequate next to Mrs. Sanders--I
> don't even read the newspaper anymore.' Mrs.
> Gordon nods agreement with this. A silence of
> several moments ensues. Mrs. Sanders then thought-
> fully comments, 'Boy, I certainly did a job here to-
> day, didn't I?'

> Mrs. Marks offers supportively, 'You didn't do it; we
> react with our own feelings to what you say.'

> Mrs. Sanders: 'Yes, but there is something I'm
> doing here. Maybe this shows me what effect I have
> on others.' Mrs. Sanders goes on to explain that
> when she enters a group of people whom she con-
> siders intellectually superior, she freezes up. She
> adds that here, however, she can talk.

> Mrs. Marks comments wryly, 'Thank you again--so
> we're a bunch of dummies.' Mrs. Sanders flushes
> deeply and laughs uncomfortably. She then for the
> first time shares with the group her feelings about
> her mother's death when she was a young adolescent
> and her subsequent bitterly competitive relationship
> with her very young step-mother.

4) Identification is a significant and valued process in

treatment. Group therapy tends to stimulate identification;
at the same time, the multiple choice of objects available
with whom to identify provides a safeguard against the client
being limited solely to identifying with the therapist. Healthy
childhood identifications are developed within a framework of
satisfying interaction within a family; the sense of identity is
further developed in the interaction of the individual with
society. The group, as a symbolic family and, as a segment of society, thus provides a benevolent environment for
the attainment of identity.

Resistance in Groups

As it does in all forms of therapeutic endeavor, resistance manifests itself in groups too. A broad definition
of resistance has been Menninger who describes it as "the
trend of forces within the patient which oppose the process
of amelioration change" (13). In a paper on resistance in
the group setting, Spotnitz and Gabriel (1950) directed group
members to give a spontaneous and emotionally significant
account of their life histories, thoughts and ideas and to
help each other to do the same. The "voluntary and in-
voluntary" methods by which the members avoided presenting
this material were considered the resistances. All of the
resistances common to the individual casework setting may
appear in the group situation. Some typical group member
resistances follow.

One member may seem to direct all of his emotional
energies to agreeing with the group leader; to allying himself with him; to supporting his opinions and statements; to
opposing his opposers--in essence, to please the therapist
and to be liked by him. Another member, on the basis of
a different life history, may focus on opposing the therapist
at every turn in pursuit of a need to defeat the authority.
A third member may be observed to subtly incite and insti-
gate fighting and aggression amongst others in the group. A
fourth may dedicate himself to the neutralization and dilution
of aggressive feeling whenever it appears. A fifth may
vividly recount sexual experiences for purposes of excitement
and titillation rather than for understanding for the attainment of proper controls over impulses. Some group members exhibit strong needs to mobilize anger against themselves and to court expulsion from the group. Others,
"help-rejecting complainers," present painful life situations
and then consistently reject every potentially helpful response

offered by their sympathetic fellow members. Some compete to be the sickest and most troubled in the group and thus doggedly resist help. There are those who show strong interest and curiosity in the problems and feelings of others while maintaining a chaste secrecy about themselves. Others may seek to monopolize the group for their own problems exclusively.

Two significant differences in resistance phenomena as they operate in the individual and group settings are discernible:

1) Group members tend to deal with each other's resistances. Bry (1951), in an early paper on resistance in the group setting, stated "The most striking thing in the handling of resistance in groups is that frequently it does not have to be 'handled' at all, at least not by the therapist. The group itself is remarkably effective in dealing with this phenomenon" (14).

2) The individual resistances of group members may unite to form a group resistance--the same form of resistance used by all on a majority of the members of the group at the same time (Redl, 1948; Spotnitz, 1952).

Role of the leader in the group setting

The primary function of the caseworker as group leader is to create that emotional climate in the group which will most enhance the attainment of the group's goals. To this end, even prior to the first group session, the leader has exercised care in the selective process to achieve a workable group balance amongst the diverse personalities who will compose the group.

With the exception of activity group therapy, most groups in casework settings involve the use of language as the basic means of communication. The leader (therapist) then, throughout the life of the group, will address himself to helping group members resolve and overcome all the obstacles to verbal communication. Many group members have never received that special form of love which grants the right to have and to verbally express negative feeling. The group leader often finds that one of his first tasks is to convey to group members the permissibility of having and expressing negative feelings toward each other, the group,

the agency and himself.   Later, barriers to the expression
of affection and positive feeling may receive priority.

The leader also regulates the discharge of emotional
energy in the group.   He prevents the accumulation of anxiety and aggression to a level which might threaten the group
or overload the egos of any of its members.

In the interest of enhancing communication he is alert
to significant non-verbal cues--lateness, restlessness, the
clenched hand, the averted head or the extended silence of
a member which may signal the containment of strong feeling or portend departure from the group.

The ongoing demonstration by the leader of mature and
appropriate behavior in the face of a wide variety of emotional configurations in the group is a critical aspect of
leader role.   His capacities to deal constructively with aggression, his repeated demonstration of respect for the
group and each of its members, and his constant pursuit of
understanding within a context of both feeling and thought--
all these provide a corrective emotional atmosphere and
standards for identification.   In an early session of a
fathers' group, one member belligerently demanded of the
leader, "Do you think we're getting anywhere in this group?"
The leader responded in unruffled and encouraging tones,
"That's a very good question--I wonder what the rest of you
think. "   This constructive response to aggressive challenge
opened the door to a mature expression of group members'
fears, expectations and frustrations, first in the group situation and then within their own family groups.

James Mann has lucidly stressed the significance of the
leader's behavior in the attainment of group goals: "The
group therapist is forever in a position of showing the way
toward more mature relationships so long as he remains
aware of this and makes proper use of it.   It is through
the therapist and the example set by him that each member
can move to more mature relations with other group members.   It is his impartiality and his understanding of inter-
group reactions; his ability to prevent the appearance of a
group scapegoat; his subtle protection of the weak and yet,
his refusal to condemn the strong; his display of strength in
opposing, if necessary, the whole group at the appropriate
time and for the appropriate reason; his capacity for activity
as well as passivity and most of all, his persistent search
for the nature and meaning of the emotional conflicts before

him--all these are necessary demands on the leader in his
role as leader if the group is to move toward more gratifying relationships" (15).

Impact of the Group on the Leader

The traditional casework involves a confrontation between the worker's psychology and that of his client.   In
this encounter the worker is faced with the infinite variety
of one individual's human feeling on conscious and unconscious levels; of unmet needs, lingering frustration and
powerful resistive forces.   These emotional currents, which
can range from sweet compliance through stubborn passivity
to intense defiance, can exert profound emotional pressure
on the worker's psyche.

In the group setting the emotional impingement on the
therapist is amplified and intensified as he is exposed to the
feelings of a number of individuals toward him and simultaneously toward each other.   A caseworker embarking on a
treatment venture with a group faces a series of significant
professional and personal adjustments.   In the shift from
unilateral to multilateral therapeutic relations, he actively
enlists the aid of clients in helping each other; he thus
voluntarily surrenders the therapeutic monopoly he holds in
the individual casework arena.   In the group, his position is
much more exposed; not only is he subject to the scrutiny,
evaluation and judgment of his group members but also to
the powerful impact of feelings which the group members'
own problems, conflicts and resistances, as they blend in
the group matrix, can induce in him.

A number of inherent emotional constellations in the encounter between leader and group inevitably arise which test
his own psychic resources on significant levels and which
are fertile ground for counter-transference:

1) His reactions to hostility, opposition and competition.
When these are thrown directly as his own ego, his
needs to be an admired and loved figure in the group
are sorely frustrated.   When group members are angry,
biting and hostile toward each other, the leader's needs
for a "happy family" are impinged upon.   Opposition and
competition may frustrate leader's needs for power and
control.

2) Identification with certain group members and the problems and group roles--the diffusion of boundaries between leader and group.

3) Group members' resistances, defenses and obduracy as against therapist's needs to achieve results and to feel successful.

4) Reactivation in the group setting of the leader's own unresolved familial conflicts.

Inherent in the group structure are a multiplicity of situations which activate and impinge upon the therapist's own feeling constellations in dynamically crucial areas of authority, aggression, givingness, deprivation, passivity-activity and sexuality. Dormant conflicts and traumata rooted in his own familial tensions are subject to reactivation. It would appear that personality integration of the group leader and self-awareness, necessary for all therapeutic endeavor, are even more vital within a group situation where opportunities for enactment of counter-transference are multiple (16).

Yet, despite some of the emotional pitfalls present, caseworkers who have led groups frequently indicate that the experience has enriched their understanding of individuals and buttressed and sharpened their casework skills. Not a few have observed that their experience with a group has augmented their own selfawareness and insight, thus contributing to their own emotional health (17).

Notes

1. Olmstead, M. S., The Small Group (Random House, New York, 1959), p. 21.

2. Op. cit.

3. Lewin, K., "Frontiers in Group Dynamics," Human Relations (1947) 1:5.)

4. Festinger, L., Shacter, S. and Back, K., Social Pressures in Informal Groups (Harper, New York, 1950).

5. Troop, E., "The Group: in Life and in Social Work,"

Social Casework, (1968) 49:267.

6. Alt, H. , "Forging Tools for Mental Health, " Jewish
   Board of Guardians Monograph #4, 1955.

7. Slavson, S. R. , An Introduction to Group Therapy (Com-
   monwealth Fund, New York, 1943).

8. Rosenthal, L. and Nagelberg, L. , "Limitations of
   Activity Group Therapy, " Internat. J. Group Psychother. ,
   (1956) 6:128.

9. Buxbaum, E. , "Transference and Group Formation in
   Children and Adolescents, " Psychoanal. Study of the
   Child, Vol I (Internat. Univ. Press, New York, 1945).

10. Strean, H. , "A Means of Involving Fathers in Family
    Treatment: Guidance Groups For Fathers, " Amer. J.
    Orthopsychiat. , (1962) 32:719.

11. Slavson, S. R. , Child-Centered Group Guidance of
    Parents (Internat. Univ. Press, New York, 1958).

12. Grunwald, H. , "Group Counseling in a Casework Agency, "
    Internat. J. Group Psychother. , (1954) 4:183.

13. Menninger, K. , Theory of Psychoanalytic Technique
    (Harper and Row, New York, 1958), p. 55.

14. Bry, T. , "Varieties of Resistance in Group Psycho-
    therapy, " Inter. J. Group Psychother. , (1951) 1:107.

15. Mann, J. , "Some Theoretic Concepts of the Group
    Process, " Internat. J. Group Psychother. , (1955) 5:235,
    p. 239.

16. Rosenthal, L. , "Counter-transference in Activity Group
    Therapy, " Internat. J. Group Psychother. , (1953) 3:431.

17. Grotjahn, M. , "The Process of Maturation in Group
    Psychotherapy and in the Group Therapist, " Psychiatry,
    (1950) 13:65.

Bibliography

1. Bales, R. F. , Interaction Process Analysis: A Method

For the Study of Small Groups. (Cambridge, Addison-Wesley, 1950).

2. Cooley, C. H. , Social Organization. (New York, Chas. Scribner, 1909).

3. Durkin, H. , Glatzer, H. and Hirsch, J. , "Group Therapy with Mothers," Am. J. Orthopsychiat. , (1944) 14:1.

4. Durkin, H. , Group Therapy for Mothers of Disturbed Children. (Springfield, Ill. , Chas. Thomas, 1954).

5. Gabriel, B. , "An Experiment in Group Treatment," Am. J. Orthopsychiat. , (1939) 9:146.

6. Gabriel, B. and Halpert, A. , "Group Therapy for Mothers and its Effect on Their Children," Internat. J. Group Psychother. , (1952) 2:143).

7. Ginnot, H. , "Group Screening of Parents in a Child Guidance Clinic," Internat. J. Group Psychother. , (1956) 6:405.

8. Kolodney, E. , "Treatment of Mothers in Groups as a Supplement," Mental Hygiene, July, 1944.

9. Konopka, G. , "The Generic and the Specific in Group Work Practice in the Psychiatric Setting," in H. B. Trecker, ed. Group Work in the Psychiatric Setting (New York, Morrow & Co. , 1956).

10. Lewin, L. , Field Theory in Social Science (New York, Harper, 1951).

11. Lyon, V. , "The Caseworker as Group Therapist. " Internat. J. Group Psychother. , (1953) 3:198.

12. Moreno, J. L. , Who Shall Survive ? (Nervous and Mental Disease Publishing Co. , Wash. D. C. , 1934).

13. Redl, F. , "Resistance in Therapy Groups, " Hum. Rel. , (1948) 1:307.

14. Rosenthal, L. , "Group Therapy in Child Guidance" in S. R. Slavson, ed. The Fields of Group Psychotherapy (New York, Internat. Univ. Press, 1956).

15. Rosenthal, L. and Nagelberg, L., "Limitations of
    Activity Group Therapy," Internat. J. Group Psycho-
    ther., (1956) 6:166.

16. Schiedlinger, S., Psychoanalysis and Group Behavior
    (New York, Norton, 1952).

17. Slavson, S. R., An Introduction to Group Therapy.
    (New York, Commonwealth Fund, 1943).

18. Spotnitz, H., "Observations of Emotional Currents in
    Interview Group Therapy with Adolescent Girls."
    J. Nerv. Ment. Dis., (1947) 106:565.

19. Spotnitz, H. and Gabriel, B., "Resistance in Analytic
    Group Therapy: A Study of the Group Therapeutic
    Process in Children and Mothers," Quart. J. Child
    Beh., (1950) 2:71.

20. Spotnitz, H., "A Psychoanalytic View of Resistance in
    Groups," Internat. J. Group Psychother., (1952) 1:3.

21. Taggart, A. and Schiedlinger, S., "Group Therapy in a
    Family Service Program," Soc. Casework, (1953)
    34:378.

22. Troop, E., "The Group in Life and Work," Soc. Case-
    work, (1968) 39:267.

23. Winick, C., Kadis, A. and Krasner, J., "The Training
    and Practice of American Group Psychotherapists,"
    Internat. J. Group Psychother., (1961) 11:419.

Author Index

Ackerman, N. , 35, 197,
210, 222
Adams, J. S. , 287, 295
Alexander, F. , 55, 64, 92,
112
Allport, F. H. , 123, 191
Allport, G. , 139, 141, 142,
143, 163, 191
Alt, H. , 303, 319
American College Dictionary,
36
Angrist, S. , 204, 223
Aronson, H. , 203, 207,
208, 222, 225
Asch, S. , 199, 222
Austin, L. , 20, 36, 232,
243
Ayllon, T. , 276, 278, 287, 292,
293, 295
Azrin, N. , 276, 284, 285,
286, 287, 292, 294,
295

Babcock, C. , 233, 243
Back, K. , 300, 318
Bales, R. F. , 300
Bandler, B. , 76, 112
Bandura, A. , 287, 295, 296
Baratz, J. , 259, 266
Bartlett, H. , 7, 24, 28, 36
Bateson, G. , 33, 42
Beatman, F. , 12, 36
Bell, N. , 139, 175, 191,
193, 195
Benedict, R. , 222
Berelson, B. , 248, 249,
252, 264
Bernstein, A. , 203, 213,
214, 215, 222

Bernstein, S. , 36
Berrien, E. K. , 86, 112
Bertalanffy, L. von, 123,
125, 126, 128, 129,
130, 133, 134, 135,
139, 140, 142, 144,
155, 163, 165, 166,
167, 184, 185, 188,
191, 192
Biddle, B. J. , 198, 201,
202, 203, 204, 205,
206, 222, 287, 295
Billingsley, A. , 228, 229,
237, 238, 242, 244
Blau, P. , 228, 229, 239,
242, 244
Boehm, W. , 17, 22, 24,
31, 32, 36, 77, 90,
95, 98, 112, 209, 210,
211, 212, 222
Borgatta, E. F. , 267, 290
Boulding, K. , 126, 192
Bowers, S. , 11, 12, 16,
25, 37
Bowlby, J. , 58, 112
Bradford, L. , 251, 265
Braithwaite, R. , 6, 37
Brenner, C. , 47, 73, 112
Briar, S. , 267, 290
Brown, G. D. , 283, 293
Brown, W. , 257, 266
Bruck, M. , 48, 112
Bry, T. , 315, 319
Buckley, W. , 128, 129, 131,
133, 134, 135, 136,
143, 144, 163, 164,
165, 181, 188, 191,
192, 194
Building Social Work Knowl-

323

328   Social Casework

Schwitzgebel, R. R. , 202,
226, 281, 293
Scott, W. , 228, 229, 239,
242, 244
Sears, R. , 63, 106, 120
Seeley, J. , 68, 120
Selan, K. , 200, 201, 213,
220, 223
Selltiz, C. , 6, 43
Selye, H. , 133, 147, 187,
194
Selznick, P. , 144, 240, 244
Shacter, S. , 300, 318
Shafer, C. M. , 147, 151,
155, 162, 163, 189,
195
Sherman, M. , 213, 214,
215, 218, 219, 220,
225
Shour, E. , 233, 243
Shulman, L. , 146, 153, 162,
188, 195
Shutz, W. , 251, 265
Shyne, A. , 209, 226
Sidman, M. , 277, 283, 287,
293, 295
Siporin, M. , 66, 120
Sister Mary Paul Janchill,
134, 138, 148, 149,
150, 151, 160, 162,
163, 195
Skinner, B. F. , 273, 276,
277, 292, 293
Slavson, S. R. , 301, 303,
310, 319, 321
Smith, D. E. P. , 287, 295
Smith, J. M. , 287, 295
Solomon, H. C. , 277, 293
Solomon, R. L. , 273, 286,
291, 294
Spiegel, J. , 200, 201, 208,
213, 226
Spitz, R. , 58, 120
Spotnitz, H. , 83, 120, 301,
314, 315, 321
Staats, A. , 272, 273, 276,
287, 291, 292, 295

Staats, C. , 272, 273, 276,
287, 291, 292, 295
Stamm, I. , 43, 77, 78,
79, 110, 120, 121
Stark, F. , 43, 226, 249,
265
Sternbach, O. , 205, 215,
226
Stiles, E. , 232, 243
Stoddard, L. T. , 287, 295
Strean, H. , 70, 102, 111,
121, 147, 195, 199,
202, 206, 208, 213,
214, 215, 216, 218,
219, 220, 225, 226,
249, 250, 265, 309,
319
Strode, R. , 14
Stuart, R. B. , 270, 287, 290
295
Studt, E. , 153, 188
Sullivan, H. , 227
Sutherland, R. , 227

Taggart, A. , 321
Tharp, R. G. , 274, 275
Thomas, E. , 8, 9, 22, 35,
41, 43, 48, 121, 198,
201, 202, 203, 204,
205, 206, 222, 270,
273, 287, 288, 290,
292, 295, 296
Thompson, J. , 234, 244
Thorndike, E. L. , 273, 292
Thorne, G. L. , 274, 275,
292
Towle, C. , 71, 76, 81, 99,
100, 109, 121
Troop, E. , 302, 318, 321
Tyler, R. , 26, 43
Tyler, V. O. , 293

Varley, B. , 215, 227
Verhave, T. , 273, 291
Vickers, G. , 128, 137
Vinter, R. , 232, 233, 235,
236, 239, 241, 243,

Subject Index